ANTIQUE & VINTAGE

Fashions

1745 TO 1979

a Collector's Guide

Barbara Johnson, Ph.D.

cb

COLLECTOR BOOKS

A Division of Schroeder Publishing Co., Inc.

On the Cover:

Front cover
Top left: Cleopatra style headdress, circa 1917 (p. 148). **Center:** Psychedelic floral print mini dress, circa 1972 – 1974 (p. 282). **Bottom, left to right:** Plaid silk dress, circa 1856 – 1858 (p. 42); Black and green gown, circa 1933 (p. 185); Black and cream striped dress, circa 1872 (pp. 62 – 63); Salmon, chartreuse, and olive colored satin evening gown, circa 1954 – 1955 (p. 241).

Back cover
Top left: Light blue satin dress, circa 1906 (pp. 128 – 129). **Top right:** Mustard and turquoise silk gown with embroidery and ruffled train, circa 1877 (p. 66). **Bottom left:** Silk satin bodice with painted pansies and butterflies, circa 1883 (p. 81).

Cover design by Beth Summers
Book design by Lisa Henderson

Collector Books
P.O. Box 3009
Paducah, Kentucky 42002 – 3009

www.collectorbooks.com

The current values in this book should be used only as a guide. They are not intended to set prices, which vary from one section of the country to another. Auction prices as well as dealer prices vary greatly and are affected by condition as well as demand. Neither the author nor the publisher assumes responsibility for any losses that might be incurred as a result of consulting this guide.

Searching for a Publisher?

We are always looking for people knowledgeable within their fields. If you feel that there is a real need for a book on your collectible subject and have a large comprehensive collection, contact Collector Books.

Proudly printed and bound in the United States of America

Contents

Dedication..4

Introduction 4

Chapter 1, 1745 – 1799 6

Chapter 2, 1800 – 1839 14

Chapter 3, 1840 – 1849 28

Chapter 4, 1850 – 1859 36

Chapter 5, 1860 – 1869 46

Chapter 6, 1870 – 1879 60

Chapter 7, 1880 – 1889 70

Chapter 8, 1890 – 1899 94

Chapter 9, 1900 – 1909 118

Chapter 10, 1910 – 1919......................134

Chapter 11, 1920 – 1929......................156

Chapter 12, 1930 – 1939 176

Chapter 13, 1940 – 1949 204

Chapter 14, 1950 – 1959 230

Chapter 15, 1960 – 1969 260

Chapter 16, 1970 – 1979 276

Glossary 296

Bibliography 298

Index 302

Dedication

This work is dedicated to my mother Diane whose organizational skills and infinite patience over the many years this project developed made this work possible. She was always supportive from the creation of the book through the completion of the manuscript and all the many years of photography in between. Diane's artistic talents made many of the antiques look stunning for the camera. My heartfelt thanks extend to her for her tireless efforts. She enabled this work to be the beautiful testament to antique and vintage fashions that you are about to see. I wish also to dedicate the book to my sister Michelle who traveled to the ends of the earth for many years to help me find some of the best examples of clothing and accessories within these pages. Michelle's fine eye for fashions enabled me to find many choice items for this project. I am grateful to her for her keen eye for beauty, her constant and enthusiastic support for the project and her uncanny ability to always find the best treasures. I would also like to dedicate this work to Mike who helped me hunt out some of the wonderful items depicted inside. Our shared love for nineteenth and twentieth century history made hunting for antiques together a memorable experience.

Introduction

Why do we collect or wear antique or vintage fashions? Perhaps of all antiques and collectibles, fashion has the strongest ability to link us to the past. As we wear or display our treasures, we empathize with the original wearers about their times and their skilled craftsmanship with a needle. Whether the garment is of the finest silk, chiffon, velvet or rayon, it entices us to imagine what life was really like in that brief sliver of time, which is our common history. We conjure up clearer, more definable visions of people dressed in familiar garb from old photographs and books which we keep locked safely away in our memories of times past. We collect, admire and wear fashions because it is the most personal way we can connect to our ancestors. Collectors respect historical artifacts and enjoy the nostalgic connection we feel to our past. This book extols the common individual in a state of finery as well as ordinary dress.

The purpose of this work is to be an accurate guide for dating and pricing antique and vintage clothing and accessories for collectors. It is an ambitious project to attempt to date and identify fashions over two hundred years beginning with the eighteenth and spanning through the twentieth centuries. I intended that this book give the collector, curator or enthusiast a chance to accurately examine and portray garments that are easily found in the private sector rather than in museums. Most items depicted can be commonly acquired at estate and tag sales, through online dealers, retail dealers, at live auctions and at Internet auction sites. My work provides the collector with photographs of real clothing and accessories in unaltered conditions so that they can identify artifacts in their collections using the pictures. Any garments the collector might possess that are not similar to the photographs can be identified and valued more readily through the use of the fashion trend lists that cover each year chronologically for almost two hundred years.

An exhaustive study of thousands of fashion periodicals, catalogs, patterns, fashion plates and illustrations over a two hundred year period provided the historical reference materials used to create the fashion trends lists. The fashion trends lists run every year from 1798 to 1979 inclusive and sporadically between 1745 and 1787. Each year's lists have illustrative and non-illustrative trends. Captions of photographs should be used to identify and value other similar items of the times as well as the ones depicted. All photographed fashions were dated accurately using fashion periodicals and were placed with that year's fashion trend list. For the sake of space, their design features are not oftentimes duplicated in the text lists but are mentioned in the captions. Fashion plates oftentimes indicated the fashion trends that were about to be seen the next month after publication. Remember fashion plates showed idealized versions of fashion. Versions of the latest Parisian or American modes were always copied by everyone seeking to look trendy rather than out of style.

I have grouped all garments and accessories by year in a timeline fashion. I have provided a conservative date range if certain trends appeared to be fashionable for one or more years. Fashionable trends could begin in a particular year but continue to be worn by individuals years afterwards. Use of the term circa is applied to mean "around" that date. Fashions depicted in the work range from the everyday to the best clothing worn by average and not so average individuals.

Prices were determined by examining the realized and asking prices of one hundred and ten Internet antique and vintage fashion retailers. Sometimes Internet auction prices can be wildly high or very low for a rare or common garment. They can not be considered accurate representations of prices for antique and vintage clothing compared to the current retail market. Price ranges reflect the values from poor to excellent condition for a piece. High prices can be commanded if the garment is in pristine condition, is rare, has a famous labels, excessive ornament or unusual stylistic features.

Buying vintage and antique clothing is a wonderful experience when you can score a wonderful find and own a new treasure. One can purchase low at an auction and buy high with a dealer or at a trade show. Internet auction sites are wonderful places to buy and sell items. They are great places to buy bargains that are well below market value. One can bid on a dress at an auction where nobody shows keen interest or a small antique store and steal away with a find. One might expect to pay much more for a dress at a trade show, online or at a store where there is more exposure of the item to collectors. Great deals and finds are available for buying and selling favorably at antique and vintage clothing stores, internet web, antique mall and auction sites, estate and tag sales, thrift shops, textile shows and flea markets. No matter where you find your antique and vintage fashions, it is rewarding to know that a collector can accurately date and price their treasures.

The eighteenth century evokes images of abject luxury in dress. Brocaded silks and ruffles bedecked men and women's costume with relish. The Age of Enlightenment ushered in an age of opulence in personal dress. Men and women displayed the finery of their form through splendid attire richly embroidered with ornament and spangles. Men's costume was equally as elaborate as women's garb. Elaborately high hairstyles complimented large ladies hats. The minor sampling of trends shown in no way attempts to reproduce every nuance of fashion in the eighteenth century. The book's greatest value is to be used as a guide to identify some common fashion trends observable in period fashion plate illustrations that accent several of the pieces listed here.

Collectors can still find early costume pieces available for purchase online, from collectors, and from museum collections. All pieces are hand sewn. Sequins are made of metal and can show signs of oxidation or a darkening of the metal. Colonial era shoes worn by the elite were fashioned from silks richly embroidered or plain. They would be worn with shoe buckles identifiable by their teeth clasp at the center of the buckle. Floral motifs in embroidery can be identified and compared by studying drawings and designs for early silk textiles and botanical prints. Men's waistcoats were oftentimes embroidered in the front and had plain silk backing in the rear. Pocket and button details on early textiles are gorgeous testaments to their skill with the needle. Much appreciated are the eighteenth century woven silks in botanical patterns made in Spitafields, England. Millinery fashions like the eighteenth century calash bonnet protected a lady's high hairstyle from wind and weather while traveling out of doors. Calashes were fashioned in linen gauze or silk fabrics with green being a common color. The skillful craftsmanship of such a millinery concoction involved rows of cane with silk sewn accordion style around the frame so that the bonnet would collapse. Decorative textiles like the lady's dress aprons displayed skillfully embroidered flowers fashioned from tiny chenille threads embellishing the silk. Colonial era shoes are sometimes still found. Whether embroidered, plain, or bedecked in metallic ornament and spangles, their unique character makes them a rare treasure to discover.

Fashion Trends for the Year 1745
(Illustrated and Non-Illustrated)

- Sleeves widen at the wrist
- Straight sleeves
- Tight tops
- Very wide A-line skirts [1]

Ladies' olive-green silk embroidered apron features eighteenth century floral chenille thread embroidery, circa 1745 – 1760s. $1,400.00 – 2,100.00.

Details of chenille embroidered flowers on the apron front and around the two side pockets, circa 1745 – 1760s.

1. William Holland, *Taste a la Mode*, 1745

Flame stitch or Irish stitch pocketbook with purple silk satin on the inside revealing two pocket compartments, satin stitched embroidered flowers, monogram and the embroidered word, "Souvenir," circa 1740s – 1790s.
$1,200.00 – 3,800.00.

Spitafields silk ladies' letter or pocket case, silk design is circa 1760 and pocketbook is circa middle to late eighteenth-century.
$570.00 – 1,950.00.

Details of woven Spitafields silk dress fabric featuring a flower and bud, circa 1750s – 1760s.
$450.00.

Details of an eighteenth century man's embroidered disassembled waistcoat featuring hand-embroidered leaf vines and blue cornflowers, circa 1760 – 1785.
$875.00 – 1,600.00.

Provenance places these silk embroidered ladies' shoes at 1764.
$2,000.00 – 4,000.00.

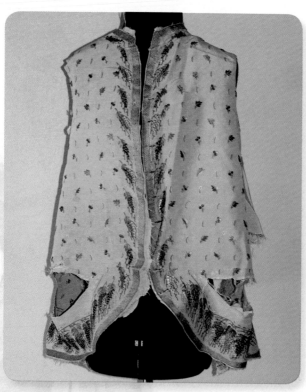

Disassembled eighteenth century man's embroidered waistcoat featuring hand-embroidered silk of purple and green in the shape of grapevines, leaves, and grape bunches, circa 1760s – 1780s. $875.00 – 1,600.00.

Details of embroidered grape vines.

Details of embroidered leaves and grapes.

Details of an eighteenth century man's embroidered waistcoat featuring hand-embroidered rosebuds, leaves, and silver metallic sequins, circa 1760s – 1780s. $875.00 – 1,600.00.

Eighteenth century green silk ladies' calash bonnet with caned supports, back and side views, circa 1770 – 1800. $650.00 – 800.00.

Rare eighteenth century gray and cream striped silk ladies' calash bonnet with cane supports, circa 1770 – 1800. $650.00 – 800.00.

Fashion Trends for the Year 1771

(Non-Illustrated)

- Fichus
- High hairstyles
- Tight bodices
- Vertical ruffles [1]

Ivory silk embroidered ladies' shoes, circa 1772 – 1785.
$2,000.00 – 4,000.00.

Fashion Trends for the Year 1775

(Illustrated and Non-Illustrated)

- Drooped shoulders
- Fichus
- Flat topped, brimmed hats
- Overskirts with ruffled ornament
- Tall bonnets [2]

Shoe buckles with engraving and raised designs, circa 1775 – 1790.
$250.00 – 550.00.

Fashion Trends for the Year 1787

(Non-Illustrated)

- Flat topped hats with large plumes
- High wide brim hats with ruffles
- Huge hats
- Large ruffled fichus [1]

Fashion Trends for the Year 1790

(Illustrated and Non-Illustrated)

- Elbow ruffles
- Fichus
- High crown bonnets
- Tight sleeves
- V shaped bodices
- Wide skirts [2]

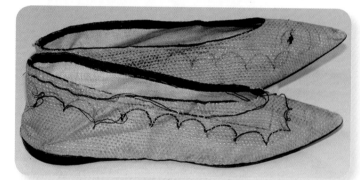

Green silk shoes with raised glossy spots, gold embroidery, circa 1790s.
$1,650.00 – 4,000.00.

Fashion Trends for the Year 1793

(Non-Illustrated)

- Bustles
- Fichus
- Full skirts
- Huge hats
- Large mop caps [3]

Fashion Trends for the Year 1794

(Non-Illustrated)

- Dresses have full sweep trains
- Long pelerines
- White muslin dresses [4]

1. *Lady's Magazine,* No. XXV, May 1771
2. *Lady's Magazine,* April, September 1775

1. *Journal der Luxus und der Moden,* T 10, 16. 1787
2. William Holland, *Taste a la Mode,* February 1, 1790
3. *Journal der Luxus und der Moden,* 2nd annJe, 1793
4. *Lady's Monthly Museum,* December 1798

Fashion Trends for the Year 1799
(Non-Illustrated)

- Empire waists
- Muslin
- Sleeves gathered and cuffed above the elbow
- Slight sweeping trains
- Spencer jackets [1]

Black silk gown, empire waistline, long sleeves to be pushed up and gathered, gathered waistline, ruffled collar, circa 1795 – 1800.
$1,600.00 – 2,400.00.

The early nineteenth century ushered in important changes in fashion. The early years after the French Revolution brought about a return to simplicity and classicism. Empire waists and muslin gowns evoke images from the early novels of Jane Austen. The world opened up further to eastern influences including Turkish designs. This was an age of Napoleon's new Empire, a return to that which was pure in the classical sense yet showing imperial opulence. Early clothing collections might sport an early Spencer jacket, an early nineteenth century invention named after the Earl of Spencer. Empire waistlines would gradually position themselves lower to a natural waistline by the 1830s.

The 1820s –1830s showed a steady trend towards a fullness of skirt yielding to greater embroideries and design applications on the skirt and bodice. The Romantic era of fashion in the 1830s brought about the largest of the puff sleeves and full skirts in the early part of the nineteenth century rivaling the sleeves of the 1890s. Jagged design features on sleeves and exaggerated Apollo knot hairstyles called for larger bonnets. Slouching shoulders and Gigot sleeves marked important silhouette lines of the 1830s. Collectors can marvel at the beautiful brocaded silks, the delicate netting, roller printed cottons, and elaborated shirred bonnets as familiar aspects of period clothing for this decade.

Fashion Trends for the Year 1800

(Non-Illustrated)

- Empire waistlines
- Gold bracelets
- Muslin dresses
- Spencer jackets with back panels
- Tight or slightly puffed upper sleeves
- Turkish influence on robe styles of dress [1]

Fashion Trends for the Year 1801

(Non-Illustrated)

- Close, flat bonnets
- Empire waists
- Peplums
- Slight trains
- V shaped bodice decoration [2]

Fashion Trends for the Year 1802

(Non-Illustrated)

- Empire dresses
- Long coats of contrasting colors
- Long trains
- White muslin [1]

Fashion Trends for the Year 1803

(Illustrated and Non-Illustrated)

- Draped overskirts
- Dresses with overdresses
- Empire waists
- Low décolletage
- Slippers with crisscross ribbon
- Trains
- Turbans
- White muslin [2]

Brown silk satin Spencer, round low neckline, high empire waist, floral embroidery, and ruffled neckline decoration, circa 1803 – 1805. $1,650.00 – 1,975.00.

1. *Journal des Dames et des Modes*, Frankfurt, 1800, Plate 18; *Lady's Magazine*, November 1800
2. *Journal des Dames et des Modes*, Frankfurt, 1801, Plate 37

1. *Journal des Dames et des Modes*, Frankfurt, 1802, Plate 366
2. *Journal des Dames et des Modes*, Frankfurt, 1803, Plates 13, 18, 19, 23, Supplement #26, 27, 32

Fashion Trends for the Year 1804

(Non-Illustrated)

- Empire waists
- Lace necklines
- Muslin dresses
- Ribbon ties
- Small puffed sleeves
- Very low necklines [1]

Fashion Trends for the Year 1805

(Illustrated and Non-Illustrated)

- Draped dresses
- Embroidery in floral colors
- Empire bodice
- Gauze materials
- Grecian crown headdresses
- Muslin dresses
- White
- Wool shawls [2]

Straw bonnet with light green silk ribbon tied into rosettes, circa 1805 – 1807.
$600.00 – 1,375.00.

Fashion Trends for the Year 1806

(Non-Illustrated)

- Embroidery
- Empire waists
- Extremely low necklines
- Flowing trains
- Grecian headgear
- High ruffled collars
- Low necklines
- Mantua court gowns
- Muslin gowns
- Spencer jackets in colors
- Trained evening gowns
- Turbans
- White muslin[1]

Fashion Trends for the Year 1807

(Non-Illustrated)

- Bonnets
- Colored trims
- Crepe
- Dress underskirts
- Ermine trim
- Flowers on muslin dresses
- Small puffed sleeves
- Tooth shaped overskirts
- Turbans
- Very low bust line [2]

Fashion Trends for the Year 1808

(Non-Illustrated)

- Angular overdresses
- Empire gowns
- Ermine trimmed robes
- Mantua court gowns
- Skirts with smaller trains
- Straight lines
- Straight or trimmed overdresses
- Tiny puffed sleeves
- White muslin dresses [3]

1. Vernor Hood, May 1804; *Lady's Magazine,* July & October, 1804; *Journal des Dames et des Modes,* Frankfurt, 1804, Plate 3
2. *Lady's Magazine,* Undated Plates, 1805

1. Vernor Hood Sharp & Poultry, May 1806; *Journal des Dames et des Modes,* Paris, 1806, Plate 725; *Bell's Court,* March 1, 1806; *La Belle Assemblée,* July 1, 1806
2. *Lady's Magazine,* April 1807; *Bell's Weekly Messanger,* January, June, September 1807; *Lady's Magazine,* 1807; *Journal des Dames et des Modes,* Paris, 1807, Plates 780, 791
3. Vernor Hood, Feb. & June 1808; *La Belle Assemblée,* January, March, April, May, August, 1808

Fashion Trends for the Year 1809

(Non-Illustrated)

- Colorful mantles
- Draped capes
- Embroidered colors on white muslin
- Full sleeves
- Jewel colors mixed with white muslin
- Jockey style caps [1]

Fashion Trends for the Year 1810

(Non-Illustrated)

- High turn down collars
- More natural waistlines appear [2]

Fashion Trends for the Year 1811

(Illustrated and Non-Illustrated)

- Empire waistlines
- Frogging
- Huge ruffled collars
- Polish design influences
- Princess lines [3]

Fashion Trends for the Year 1812

(Non-Illustrated)

- Empire waistlines
- Military influences on trims
- Muslin dresses
- Open overskirts
- Overblouses [1]

Fashion Trends for the Year 1813

(Illustrated and Non-Illustrated)

- Deep colored coats
- Giant muffs
- Lace caps
- No trains on dresses
- Overdresses that are more open
- Stand-up ruffled collars [2]

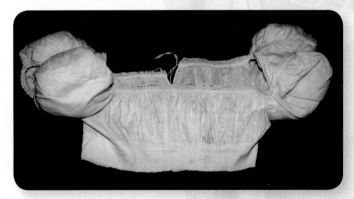

Muslin infant's bodice with empire waist, circa 1813. $325.00.

Roller printed toddler dress, gathered neckline, drawstring waistline, abstract print bands, circa 1811 – 1813. $650.00.

1. *Journal des Dames et des Modes*, Paris, 1809, Plate 609; Ackermann's *Repository*, January, July, 1809, Fabric Swatch Plates January 1809, May and June 1809; *La Belle Assemblée*, March, April, May, November, 1809
2. *La Belle Assemblée*, January 1810
3. *La Belle Assemblée*, March, August, 1811; Ackermann's *Repository*, December, 1811, Fabric Swatch Plates March, April, August, November 1811; *Journal des Dames et des Modes*, Paris, Plate 1138

1. Ackermann's *Repository*, January 1812, Fabric Swatches March, July, April 1812; *The Proprietors*, October 1812
2. Ackermann's *Repository*, February, April, Fabric Swatches March, June 1813; *La Belle Assemblée*, July & December 1813

Fashion Trends for the Year 1814

(Non-Illustrated)

- Empire dresses
- High top hats
- Stand up lace collars [1]

Fashion Trends for the Year 1815

(Non-Illustrated)

- Ankle length A-line dresses
- Empire waists
- High ruffled caps
- Military styles
- Romantic ruffled bonnets
- Ruffled underskirt bottoms [2]

Fashion Trends for the Year 1816

(Non-Illustrated)

- High ruffled collars
- Saw tooth designs
- Underskirts with dresses [3]

Fashion Trends for the Year 1817

(Non-Illustrated)

- Empire waists
- Fringe
- Ruffles on skirt bottom
- Slightly puff sleeve [4]

Fashion Trends for the Year 1818

(Illustrated and Non-Illustrated)

- A-line silhouettes
- Empire waists
- Lace used profusely
- Large and full bonnets
- Overmantles
- Ruffled skirts [5]

Straw bonnet of the Romantic era with high wide brim and tall crown to accommodate the top knot fashionable hairstyles of the day including the Apollo knot, circa 1818. $370.00 – 450.00.

Fashion Trends for the Year 1819

(Illustrated and Non-Illustrated)

- Empire waists
- Ruffles on sleeves
- Ruffles on hem flounces
- Ruffles on bonnets [1]

Early nineteenth-century linen purse with blue beadwork, leaf shaped metal sequins, and silk fringe, circa 1810s – 1850s. $760.00 – 1,200.00.

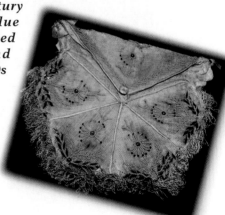

1. *Journal des Dames et des Modes,* Paris, 1814, Plate 1385; Ackermann's *Repository,* Plate 26 Vol. 7
2. *Journal des Dames et des Modes,* Paris, 1815, Plate 1468; *Lady's Magazine,* June 1815; *La Belle Assemblée,* December 1815
3. *Journal des Dames et des Modes,* Paris, 1816, Plate 1597; *La Belle Assemblée,* March 1816
4. *La Belle Assemblée,* May, June, August 1817
5. *La Belle Assemblée,* April 1818; *Journal des Dames et des Modes,* Paris, 1818, Plate 1778

1. *Journal des Dames et des Modes,* Frankfurt, 1819, Plate 24; *Journal des Dames et des Modes,* Paris, 1819, Plate 1801; *La Belle Assemblée,* May, August, September 1819

This white dotted muslin gown has an empire waist and deep hem. The puff sleeves are gathered to produce a bubble effect. The bodice is slightly shirred and the dress's fabric is embroidered with six-petal flowers, circa 1819 – 1820. $1,600.00 – 2,300.00.

Fashion Trends for the Year 1821

(Non-Illustrated)

- Double puff upper sleeves
- Ermine trim
- Frogging
- Horseshoe ruffles
- Lower hem ornamentation
- Printed silks
- Rows of lace
- Scalloped ruffles
- Tight lower sleeves [1]

Fashion Trends for the Year 1822

(Illustrated and Non-Illustrated)

- Gathered horizontal curved bodices
- Lower hem trim
- Puffs
- Scalloped swirls on the hem
- Zigzag hem trim [2]

Straw bonnet, deep neck, wider brim, olive green silk trim, brocaded silk ribbon bow, inner lining of olive green silk, circa 1822 – 1823. $600.00 – 1,375.00.

Fashion Trends for the Year 1820

(Non-Illustrated)

- Crisscross ribbon tied pointy shoes
- Halfway down the calf dress lengths
- High ruffled bonnets
- Rose trim on sleeves
- Shorter skirts
- Small puffed upper sleeves
- Sweetheart necklines
- Waists are lower [1]

Black silk lace mourning bonnet veil, circa 1820s. $115.00.

1. *Journal des Dames et des Modes,* Paris, 1820, Plates 1879, 1886, 1909, 1945, 1946

1. *Journal des Dames et des Modes,* Paris, 1821, Plates 1967, 1972, 1990, 2002; Ackermann's *Repository,* October 1821; *Journal des Dames et des Modes,* Paris, 1821, Plates 1967, 1972, 1990, 2002; Ackermann's *Repository,* October 1821
2. *La Belle Assemblée,* July, October, December 1822; *Petit Courrier des Dames,* 1822; *Journal des Dames et des Modes,* Paris, 1822 Plate 2037, 2107; *Journal des Dames et des Modes,* Frankfurt, 1822, Plate 45; *Lady's Magazine,* July 1822

Fashion Trends for the Year 1823

(Illustrated and Non-Illustrated)

- Horizontal ruffles
- Lower one third of the hem is ornamented
- Scalloped hems
- Turbans with high plumes [1]

White muslin gown with short sleeves, shirred bodice and waistline slightly lower than the empire waistline of a decade before. The skirt has an inserted band of netting, circa 1823 – 1824.
$865.00 – 3,000.00.

Fashion Trends for the Year 1824

(Illustrated and Non-Illustrated)

- Asymmetrical decoration
- Less than the lower third of hem ornamented with ruffles
- More rows of ruffles on the skirt
- More ruffles and puffs on the top of dresses
- Multi-ruffled sleeves
- Overskirts
- Sleeves have rosettes fashioned from fabric [1]

Child's bodice of ecru muslin with embroidered polka dots, wide puffed sleeves that end in a ruffle of lace, bodice insert embroidered with polka dots, circa 1824.
$575.00.

Fashion Trends for the Year 1825

(Illustrated and Non-Illustrated)

- Bodices have a V shape
- Deep pelerines
- Lower hem ornamentation
- Square open necklines
- Top hats with high crowns
- Wide open necklines [2]

1. *Journal des Dames et des Modes*, Paris 1823 Plates 2186, 2189, 2203; *Journal des Dames et des Modes*, Frankfurt, 1823, Plates 2, 6, 14, 16, 22, 24, 25, 26, 32, 36, 37, 39; *Lady's Magazine*, No. 7 & 12, 1823; Ackermann's *Repository*, October 1823; *The Ladies Little Messanger*, #162, 1823

1. *Lady's Magazine*, No 2, August, October, November, 1824; *Petit Courrier des Dames*, 1824, Plate 257; *Journal des Dames et des Modes*, Frankfurt, 1824, Plates 1, 2, 3, 6, 9, 14, 17, 19, 20, 23, 25, 26, 29, 33, 34, 42, 47; *Journal des Dames et des Modes*, Paris, 1824, Plate 2255; Ackermann's *Repository*, July 1, 1824; *La Belle Assemblée*, March & April 1824; *Corriere delle Dame, Moda di Francia*, 1824, Plate no. 53
2. *La Belle Assemblée*, January, February, June, August, September, October 1825; *Lady's Magazine* No., 10, 1825; Ackermann's *Repository*, 1825; *Journal des Dames et des Modes*, Paris, 1825, Plates 2331, 2336, 2360, 2369, 2370; *Journal des Dames et des Modes*, Frankfurt, 1825, Plate 25; *Petit Courrier des Dames*, 1825, Plates 351, 356, 377; *Weiner Moden*, May & August 1825

Fashion Trends for the Year 1827

(Illustrated and Non-Illustrated)

- Frilly skirts
- More ornamentation with lace
- Ornamentation goes up the skirt
- Ruffles
- Wider skirts [1]

Watered silk bodice with tape tie closure and front boning, circa 1825.
$575.00.

Ivory silk lace bonnet veil circa 1825.
$125.00.

Fashion Trends for the Year 1826

(Non-Illustrated)

- Leg o'mutton sleeves
- Wide hem dresses
- Wide hem ruffles
- Wide horizontal collars [1]

These silk ladies' slippers were worn with ribbons crisscrossed around a lady's ankle. These "straights" were made without a left and a right foot and are sometimes labeled with the French words "gauche" for left and "droit" for right. Shoe manufacturers often included printed company labels inside these shoes. These shoes were worn circa 1827 – 1840s.
$350.00 – 950.00 per pair.

1. *Journal des Dames et des Modes*, Paris, 1826, Plates 2381, 2382, 2379, 2387, 2389; *Journal des Dames et des Modes*, Frankfurt, 1826, Plate 16; *Lady's Magazine*, No. 9 No, 4, 1826; *La Belle Assemblée*, February, June, October, November 1826; *Ackermann's Repository*, April, July – December 1826; *Townsend's Monthly*, Plates 82, 83, 1826

1. *Petit Courrier des Dames*, 664, 666 1827; *Journal des Dames et des Modes*, Frankfurt, 1827, Plates 1, 5, 17, 19; *Journal des Dames et des Modes*, Paris 1827, Plates 2474, 2482, 2496, 2552, 2502; *La Belle Assemblée*, No 28, April 1, 1827, No 29 May 1, 1827; *Lady's Magazine*, 8, 1827; Unknown Fashion Plate December 1827

Toddler leather straight shoes (without a left or a right), embroidery on the front, shirred ruffling and silk ribbon bows, circa 1827 – 1840s.
$350.00 – 950.00.

High muslin day cap to accommodate the popular towering high top knot hairstyle known as the Apollo knot, circa 1830 – 1833.
$370.00 – 450.00.

Fashion Trends for the Year 1828

(Non-Illustrated)

- Graduated puff sleeves — large to small
- Higher skirt lengths
- Sleeve graduates to smaller second puff
- Upper sleeve puffs [1]

Fashion Trends for the Year 1829

(Non-Illustrated)

- Double puffed sleeves
- Full skirt above the ankle
- Leg o'mutton sleeves
- Ornament is wide on the lower hem
- Puffed off the shoulder sleeves
- Shirring of the bodice
- Three rows on the skirt
- Wide puffed sleeves [2]

Fashion Trends for the Year 1830

(Illustrated and Non-Illustrated)

- Full puffed sleeves
- High puffed sleeves
- Ornament is two thirds of the way down the skirt
- Tight undersleeves
- V pointed bodices [3]

Fashion Trends for the Year 1831

(Illustrated and Non-Illustrated)

- Additional ruffled lace at the elbow
- Large puffed sleeves on the upper arms
- Mock fichu collars
- Ornament is two third of the way down the skirts
- Skirts are above the ankle
- V points over undersleeves [1]

Rare silk chiffon bodice in canary yellow, scalloped shell lace, stiff whalebone down the bodice front, shirred fabric, dropped sleeves widen at the wrist in a zigzag pointed tooth shape lined by folded satin ribbon trim, circa 1831.
$575.00.

1. *Petit Courrier des Dames*, #546, #567, July 1828; *Journal des Dames et des Modes*, Frankfurt, Plates 27, 28, 40, 48, 52; Ackermann's *Repository*, January & May 1828; *La Belle Assemblée*, No 41 New series, May 1 & September 1828; *Townsend's Monthly Selection*, March 1828, plates 220, 221; Newest Fashions for January & July 1828
2. James Robins & Co., January 1829; Ackermann's *Repository*, February & March 1829; *Weiner Modenzeitung*, XXXV, 1829; *La Belle Assemblée*, February 1, & June 1 1829; *Journal des Dames et des Modes*, Paris, 1829 Plates 2689, 2714, 2727, 2720, 2721, 2722, 2725, 2726, 2737; *Townsend's Monthly Selection*, 1829, Plate 282
3. Unknown fashion plate June 1830; *Le Mercure des Salone, Modes de Paris 1830 No. 3*, 1830 No 17; *La Belle Assemblée*, March & May 1st, 1830; *Journal des Dames et des Modes*, Frankfurt, 1830, Plates 22. 37, 39, 40 – 46, 48; *Journal des Dames et des Modes*, Paris 1830, Plates 2783, 2784, 2790, 2792, 2793, 2813, 2817, 2820, 2822, 2828, 2836, 2837, 2842, 2844, 2846; *Ladies Pocket Magazine*, 1830

1. *Journal des Dames et des Modes*, Frankfurt, 1831, Plates 1, 2, 5, 8, 9, 10, 14, 15, 17, 19, 23, 24, 26, 28, 31, 32, 34, 35, 37, 39, 40, 41, 43, 44, 45, 50, 52; *La Belle Assemblée*, March & November 1831; *Petit Courrier des Dames*, 1831, Plates 816, 824, 828, 849, 841; Newest Fashions, August 1831, Plate 1832

Fashion Trends for the Year 1832

(Non-Illustrated)

- Bodice ornaments
- Bodice pleating
- High bonnets
- Large leg o'mutton sleeves
- Lower puffed sleeves
- Overdresses [1]

Fashion Trends for the Year 1833

(Illustrated and Non-Illustrated)

- Above the ankle skirts
- High crown bonnets
- Pelerines
- Puffed upper sleeves
- Ruffled low neckline
- Straight collars [2]

- Huge puffed sleeves
- Low, shirred and puffed sleeves
- Ruffles at the elbow
- Skirts above the ankle
- Sleeves taper to the cuff
- Three rows of lace over puffed sleeves
- Wide collars [1]

This dark brown glazed cotton gown with large gigot sleeves is specially propped outward by elbow pads stuffed with straw. The waistline is approaching normal position and the skirt and bodice are tightly shirred, circa 1834 – 1835.
$800.00 – 3,000.00.

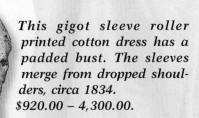

Although in poor condition, this bonnet is a good study example. Tan silk caned and shirred silk bonnet, brocaded silk ribbon, circa 1833.
$370.00 – 450.00.

This gigot sleeve roller printed cotton dress has a padded bust. The sleeves merge from dropped shoulders, circa 1834.
$920.00 – 4,300.00.

Fashion Trends for the Year 1834

(Illustrated and Non-Illustrated)

- Apollo knot hairstyle
- Cavalier hats with plumes
- Drop shoulders
- Huge brim bonnets

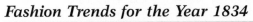

1. *Weiner Modenzeitung*, XXIV, 1832; *The Beau Monde*, January, March, December 1832; *Petit Courrier des Dames*, 132, Plates 856, 869, 874, 879, 900, 933; *La Belle Assemblée*, May 1832; *Journal des Dames et des Modes*, Frankfurt, 1832, Plates 2, 3, 5, 7, 8, 10 – 18, 21, 34, 35, 36, 38, 39, 40, 42, 44, 45, 46, 47, 51
2. *Journal des Dames et des Modes*, Frankfurt, 1833, Plates 4, 5, 6, 9, 10, 21, 23, 24, 26, 27, 28, 29, 32, 38, 39, 40, 41, 43, 44; *La Mode*, Plate July 20, 1833; *Petit Courrier des Dames*, 1833, Plates 980, 997., 951; *Le Follet Courrier des Salons*, 1833, Plates 289, 269, 281; *Bell's Court*, 1833, April and July 1833; *The World of Fashion and Continental Fueilletons*, May 1833; *Lady's Cabinet*, 1833; *The World of Fashion and Continental Fueilletons*, 1830s Plates 433, 484, 458, 546

1. *Mirror of the World*, February 1834; *Journal des Dames et des Modes*, Costume Parisien 1834; *The Beau Monde*, November 1834; *Petit Courrier des Dames*, October 1834; *Le Follet, Courrier (Lady's Magazine) du Salons* 1834, Nos. 6, 17, 16, 113, 353

Fashion Trends for the Year 1835

(Non-Illustrated)

- Bonnets have lower upturned brims
- Fan bodices
- Flat shirred sleeves half way up the upper arm
- Off the shoulder looks
- One ruffle on the hem
- Rows of lace flounces
- Very large puffed sleeves [1]

Fashion Trends for the Year 1836

(Illustrated and Non-Illustrated)

- Bows on skirts
- Four ruffled layered sleeves
- Off the shoulder fan bodices
- Romantic large bonnets
- Rounded bodices
- Turbans
- Two ruffles on hem
- V off the shoulder collars [2]

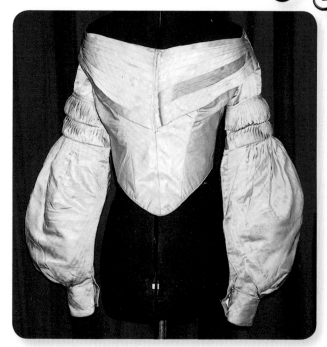

Silk bodice with pleated portrait neckline, sleeve tops narrowly pleated, full sleeves enlarge below the elbow to blouse at the cuff, circa 1836. $850.00 – 1,000.00.

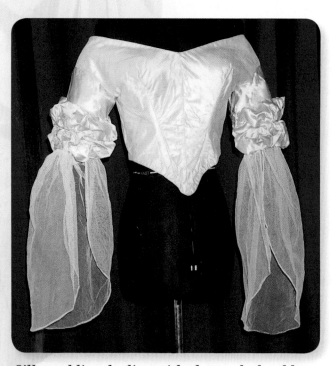

Silk wedding bodice with dropped shoulders, double puffs at each elbow, and netted petal shaped lower sleeves, circa 1836. $850.00 – 1,000.00.

Fashion Trends for the Year 1837

(Illustrated and Non-Illustrated)

- Dropped shoulders
- Floral appliques
- Large bonnets
- Low necklines
- Overdresses
- Puffs at the elbows
- Sleeves puff to the wrist
- Sleeves taper
- Three rows of ruffles on sleeves
- Underskirts
- V pointed bodices
- Wide brim ruffles [1]

1. *The Beau Monde*, August 1835, Plates 2 & 3; *Petit Courrier des Dames*, October 1835; *Journal des Dames et des Modes*, Frankfurt, 1835, Plate 17; *Weiner Modenzeitung*, January 1835; *Le Follet, Courrier des Salons*, 1835; *Fuller's Fashion Magazine* February & May 1835; *Petit Courrier des Dames*, November – December 1835
2. *Last and Newest Fashions*, 1836; *Le Miroir des Dames*, 1836 No, 89; *Petit Courrier des Dames*, circa 1836

1. *Godey's Lady's Book*, January and March 1837; *Le Follet, Court Magazine*, May 1837; *Costume Parisien, Journal des Dames, et des Modes*, 1837, Plates 3438, 3453, 3475

Watered ivory taffeta dress with split open skirt meant to reveal a decorative underskirt, off the shoulder bodice, upper puffed sleeves, looser lower sleeves, circa 1837.
$1,700.00 – 2,000.00.

Off the shoulder dress of geometric printed silk, shirred bodice, two rows of ruffles above the elbow, sleeves widening beneath the ruffles then narrowing at the cuff, circa 1837.
$575.00 – 2,000.00.

Fashion Trends for the Year 1838

(Illustrated and Non-Illustrated)

- Drooped capes
- Lower puffed sleeves
- Many small ruffles of lace
- Overskirt
- Shirred upper sleeves
- Stripes, solids and prints
- Three rows of ornament on the skirt [1]

Ivory silk bodice, pleated sloping V neckline, shirred with heavy pleats of silk satin, deep pointed bodice bottom, small puff sleeves, circa 1838 – 1839.
$850.00 – 1,000.00.

1. *Godey's Lady's Book*, February, May – August, November, December 1838; *Modes de Paris Petit Courrier des Dames*, March 31st, 1838; *La Belle Assemblée* August 1838; *Latest Fashions* 1838

Fashion Trends for the Year 1839
(Illustrated and Non-Illustrated)

- Floral appliques
- Off the shoulder bodices with lace necklines
- Ruffled hems
- Ruffled overskirts
- Shirred bonnets
- Smaller and rounded bonnets [1]

Ivory silk wedding gown with shirred and V shaped portrait neckline, tight sleeves ending in rows of ruffles and tulle flounce, silk fabric ribbed with stripes and embroidered with petal flowers, circa 1839.
$1,700.00 – 2,000.00.

Early micro-beaded reticule or drawstring purse, floral motif, olive green top, circa 1800s – 1830s.
$500.00 – 1,000.00.

1. *Weiner* Moden Zeitung, 1839 Nos. 30, 40; *La Belle Assemblée,* January – December 1839

Queen Victoria's ascent to the throne in 1837 marked a new era in fashion. The new queen would usher in an age of different tastes and opinions compared to the old ways of the Regency era. Fashion took a more austere turn during this decade. The 1840s was also an age of great poverty and strife for many. We think of the literary characters penned by Bronte or Dickens that show strength against social adversity and hardships. Fashion in the 1840s provided women with slender fitting garbs, fan front bodices, dropped sleeves, tight bodices that hung wistfully off the shoulder. Women wore smaller bonnets than the frivolous confections of Romantic era milliners. The restraint and sensibility of Victorian fashion would gradually transform itself again and again as decades passed.

For now the early Victorian woman of the times was a feminine delicate creature with ring curls drooping down the sides of her face tucked under her bonnet. She dressed in pastels or earth-toned silks ornamented with tight fan pleats. Fabrics were opulent in their craftsmanship. Silks were of thin brocades patterned in abstracts or flowers. Bonnet ribbons could also possess the minutest details such as delicate flowers or stripes woven into them. Drooping necklines and sloped shoulders made women appear delicately frail, as if they were china dolls. Bonnet shapes and sizes diminished but could sometimes be elongated along the face. Bonnets in this decade made fascinating use of woven straw to create abstract or floral type designs.

Pink crinoline bonnet with white silk flowers on the inside framing the face ornamented with silk organza patterned ribbon, circa 1840. $785.00 – 830.00.

Fashion Trends for the Year 1840

(Illustrated and Non-Illustrated)

- Drooped shoulders
- Full skirts
- Neckline of ruffles
- Off the shoulder bodices
- Ornamental buttons
- Tight bodices
- Tight sleeves
- V necklines on bodice [1]

Fancy plaited woven straw bonnet, long front sides to cover ladies' sausage curls, circa 1840. $245.00 – 830.00.

1. *Godey's Lady's Book,* January – December 1840; *La Belle Assemblée,* March 1840; *Latest Fashions* 1840

Brown roller printed polka dot cotton bodice, drooping appearance, off the shoulder neckline, small puff sleeves, circa 1841 – 1842.
$200.00 – 1,500.00.

Fancy woven straw bonnet in two-tone colors of black and taupe straw, long front sides would be tied with a ribbon under the chin to cover ladies' sausage curls, circa 1840.
$245.00 – 830.00.

Fashion Trends for the Year 1841

(Illustrated and Non-Illustrated)

- Deep V bodices
- Full skirt
- Off the shoulder bodices
- Plain shirred bodices
- Shirred bonnets
- Tight sleeves
- Waistline is V shaped or straight [1]

Close-up view of brown roller printed polka dot cotton bodice.

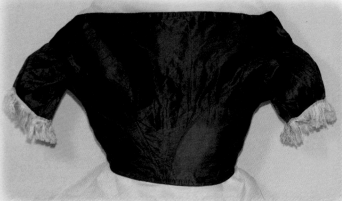

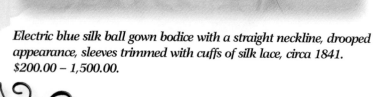

Electric blue silk ball gown bodice with a straight neckline, drooped appearance, sleeves trimmed with cuffs of silk lace, circa 1841.
$200.00 – 1,500.00.

1. *Godey's Lady's Book,* January – June, September 1841; *Latest Fashions,* 1841; *Graham's Magazine,* April, October 1841; *La Belle Assemblée,* January, March – October 1841

Fashion Trends for the Year 1842
(Illustrated and Non-Illustrated)

- Drop drooped shoulders
- Full skirts
- Off the shoulder bodices
- Overskirts
- Rounded waists
- Ruffled sleeves
- V pleated bodices
- Voluminous sleeves at elbow [1]

Ivory silk shirred and caned bonnet, circa 1842.
$785.00 – 830.00.

Woven straw bonnet, circa 1842.
$785.00 – 830.00.

Rare brown silk quilted winter hood with long deep points framing the face, matching silk chin ties, circa 1842.
$200.00 – 600.00.

1. *Graham's Magazine,* January – December 1842; *Godey,* March, May 1842; *Latest Fashions* 1842

Fashion Trends for the Year 1843

(Illustrated and Non-Illustrated)

- Narrow bonnets
- Three rows of deep skirting
- Tight bodices
- Tight upper sleeves
- V necks [1]

Silk brocade dress with V neck, bodice shirred, smocking below the bust, sleeves with a tightened lower section starting at the elbow, circa 1843.
$400.00 – 3,000.00.

Fashion Trends for the Year 1844

(Illustrated and Non-Illustrated)

- Bodices with lace
- Full skirts
- Lace at the elbow and cuff
- Off the shoulder dresses
- Overskirts
- Portrait necklines
- Short, straight, or two tiered sleeves
- Straight lace necklines
- V pointed bodices [1]

Brown silk dress bodice, fan front and bodice pleats, circa 1844.
$200.00 – 1,500.00.

1. *Godey's Lady's Book,* January – December 1843; *Journal des Demoiselles* June & August 1843; *La Belle Assemblée* November 1843

1. *Weiner Modenzeitung,* 1844, No 16 January to May 1844; *Godey,* January, March 1844; *Lady's Cabinet,* 1844 January – December 1844; *Latest Fashions* 1844; *Petit Courrier des Dames,* February 1844; *Columbian Magazine* February, March, May – June, August, October, December, 1844

Black silk mourning dress with shirred fan front, bodice pleats, circa 1844.
$400.00 – 3,000.00.

Tartan plaid silk dress, boat neck, off the shoulder, sleeves ending in two ruffles, shirred bodice, smocked V point, circa 1844 – 1847.
$400.00 – 3,000.00.

Silk and woolen blended day dress with detail of fan front bodice, loose fitting sleeves and a double capped over sleeve trimmed in matching fringe, circa 1844 – 1848.
$400.00 – 3,000.00.

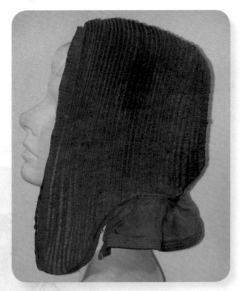

Taupe cotton drawn bonnet with neck curtain, caned supports, deep low front to cover ladies' long sausage curls, circa 1844.
$250.00 – 800.00.

Fashion Trends for the Year 1845

(Illustrated and Non-Illustrated)

- Drooping appearance at the hips
- Full circular skirts
- Narrow tight bodices
- Shirred bodices
- Short pagoda sleeves
- Undersleeves under pagoda sleeves
- V openings
- V shirring on bodice [1]

Black mourning straw bonnet with patterned silk ribbon curtain and ornamentation, circa 1845.
$785.00 – 830.00.

Light blue grosgrain taffeta with plain sleeve, rickrack, ornamental buttons, and chemical lace pelerine collar, circa 1845.
$400.00 – 3,000.00.

Fashion Trends for the Year 1846

(Non-Illustrated)

- Frogging
- High necks
- Military influences
- No buttons
- Slight pagoda shaped sleeves
- Tight bodices [1]

Fashion Trends for the Year 1847

(Illustrated and Non-Illustrated)

- Full skirts
- Drooping shoulders
- Narrow sleeves[2]

1. *Lady's Gazette of Fashion,* June 1845 – December 1845

1. *Townsend's Monthly Selections,* 1846; *Graham's Magazine,* January 1846 – December 1846; *Lady's Gazette of Fashions,* January – June 1846
2. *Graham's Magazine,* January 1847

"Faux feather" Jenny Lind brisé fan made of leaves that are printed and molded fabric pieces made to resemble feathers. Each feather is embellished with silver metallic sequins and wooden carved sticks with delicately pierced ornamentation and tassel, circa 1847 – 1852.
$20.00 – 75.00.

Jenny Lind brisé fan, faux silk feathers, silver stars, and teardrop spangles, pierced ivory sticks, circa 1847 – 1852.
$20.00 – 75.00.

Jenny Lind brisé fan, pierced and gilded Indonesian buffalo hide fan, circa 1840s to the twentieth century.
$20.00 – 75.00.

Jenny Lind brisé fan, faux fabric feathers, metal star spangles, carved and pierced wood sticks, brown silk tassel, circa 1847 – 1852.
$20.00 – 75.00.

Fashion Trends for the Year 1848

(Non-Illustrated)

- Close, shirred bonnets
- Collarettes
- Full skirts
- Plaids
- Plain bodices
- Printed silks
- Ruffled or plain skirts
- Sleeves end in a cuff
- Straight sleeves
- Tight bodices [1]

Fashion Trends for the Year 1849

(Illustrated and Non-Illustrated)

- Coal scuttle bonnets
- Gathered full skirts
- Large lace Chantilly ruffles
- Low V bodices
- Off the shoulder necklines
- Straight bodices [2]

Coal scuttle bonnets were worn from 1849 – 1855. This striped brown silk coal scuttle bonnet dates to circa 1849.
$785.00 – 830.00.

1. *Mode di Parigi*, April, June, November 1848; *Lady's Gazette of Fashion*, January – July 1848
2. *Graham's American Monthly Magazine*, XXXIV January – December 1849; *Lady's Gazette of Fashion*, January – October 1849; *Godey's Lady's Book*, January – December 1849; *La Belle Assemblée*, January, March, May, June, July , December 1849

Dramatic changes took place in the 1850s regarding women's fashion designs and silhouettes. The 1850s ushered in a decade of larger skirts, more elaborate sleeves and fancy plaid silks. Women wore gigantic bell skirts supported with large cage crinolines. Their dresses were made of vibrant colors in bold plaids accented by elaborately trimmed bonnets. Fabrics could also be of the most intricate silk brocade. Silk or cotton fringe embellished wide pagoda sleeves. The taste for opulence was expressed in the beautiful ball gowns of silk brocade.

The feminine form became encased in the wide skirts and wide pagoda sleeves as seen in contemporary illustrations. Bonnets were elaborate compliments to the exaggerated costume of the decade. Plaid silks had been worn in the previous decade. Richer colored plaid dresses were the result of new dyes being invented and introduced to satisfy women's taste for bolder looks. These inventive plaid silks with delicate fringes were eagerly worn by fashionable society. Specialty silk taffetas would have an iridescent sheen in sharp contrast to the previous decade's earth tone plain fabrics and pastel colored silks.

Fashion Trends for the Year 1850

(Non-Illustrated)

- Coal scuttle bonnets of shirred silk
- Drooping shoulders
- Insert lace
- Narrow sleeves open at bottom
- Ruffled bottom cuffs
- Slight peplums
- Tartan plaid silks
- Three tier ruffle skirts
- V openings on bodices [1]

1850s – 1870s black lacquer, gilded, and painted paper scenic fan depicting men and women at leisure in a pastoral setting.
$50.00 – 250.00.

1850s – 1870s ivory fan with pierced sticks and printed scene on paper, gilded decoration, mirror on the stick used to see behind the viewer, sticks ornamented with gold and silver foil, pastoral scene with people dancing.
$50.00 – 250.00.

1850s – 1870s ivory fan with pierced sticks and printed scene on paper, gilded, mirror on the stick used to see behind the viewer, sticks ornamented with gold and silver foil and metal studs, classical scene with women bathing in a lake with swans — possibly "Leda and the Swan."
$50.00 – 250.00.

1850s – 1870s black lacquer, gilded, and painted paper scenic fan depicting men and women in eighteenth century garb in an outdoor country setting.
$50.00 – 250.00.

1850s – 1870s ivory fan, pierced sticks, gilded mirror on the guard used to see behind the viewer, sticks ornamented with gold and silver foil and metal studs, printed paper agricultural scene depicting men and women in country eighteenth century clothing.
$50.00 – 250.00.

Fashion Trends for the Year 1851

(Non-Illustrated)

- Capes and jackets falling over hips
- Coal scuttle bonnets
- Full skirts
- Three tier lacey skirts
- Wide pagoda sleeves [1]

Fashion Trends for the Year 1852

(Illustrated and Non-Illustrated)

- Coal scuttle bonnets
- Deep V collars
- Full skirts
- Lace trims
- Wide fan sleeves [1]

Silk brocade mint green and black brocaded flowers, black Chantilly lace, and trim fringe, circa 1852 – 1855.
$2,000.00 – 4,000.00.

Details of mint green and black brocade silk, bow trim, and black Chantilly lace, circa 1852 – 1855.

1. *La Belle Assemblée,* January – June 1851; *Lady's Book,* January – December 1851; *Les Modes Parisiennes,* 1851 (Peterson's); *Graham's Magazine,* 1851

1. *Godey's Lady's Book,* January – June 1852; *Graham's Magazine,* 1852; *Godey,* March & April 1852

Fashion Trends for the Year 1853

(Illustrated and Non-Illustrated)

- Circular skirts
- Full skirts
- Large ruffled bands at hips
- V opening bodices
- V pointed bodices [1]

Fashion Trends for the Year 1854

(Illustrated and Non-Illustrated)

- Checkered silks
- Close fit shirred bonnets
- Floral silks
- Full skirts
- Lower sleeve opening to reveal undersleeves
- Narrow upper sleeves
- Three-quarter sleeves
- Tight bodices
- Vertical bodice decoration [1]

Black satin bodice, deep point, and pink horizontal strips of fringe in a V shape, circa 1853. $250.00 – 450.00.

Brown floral silk chiffon gown with narrow bell sleeves and a single short sleeve oversleeve. The pink and brown floral print is gossamer silk chiffon. The faux buttons are crafted from silk corded knots, circa 1854. $400.00 – 3,000.00.

Cream brocade silk wedding gown, wide V neck collar, loosely draped bodice, smocking, wide pagoda sleeve, fringe at elbow and cuff, silk brocade fabric, circa 1853. $850.00 – 1,400.00.

1. *Graham's Magazine,* January – December 1853; *Godey's Lady's Book,* January, May 1853

1. *Godey's Lady's Book,* January – December 1854; *Le Bon Ton,* May 1854

Child's check-ered brown silk dress with rust and cream ribbon trim and wide pagoda sleeves, circa 1854. $450.00 – 500.00.

Pink and black checkered child's silk bodice, shirred top, drop sleeve with puckering at the top, red and black fringe trim, circa 1854. $70.00 – 225.00.

Taupe silk child's dress with rust colored gimp trim, circa 1854. $575.00 – 1,265.00.

Brown iridescent silk gown, two piece, faux fabric buttons, skirt with rosettes of black Chantilly lace behind them, short sleeves effect dropping to a fuller but tighter pagoda sleeve, wide bow at the back of the gown, circa 1854. $500.00 – 850.00.

Ribbed cotton sheer blouse, flower print, pagoda sleeves edged in cream fringe, circa 1854 – 1855. $150.00 – 250.00.

This taffeta day bodice has double ruffled cuffs, cinched waist, and covered buttons. It was the style to have two bodices, one for day and one for evening that accompanied the same skirt and made it easy for ladies to make a transformation. Two rows of finely pleated organza run vertical on the bodice, circa 1854. $150.00 – 250.00.

Turkish inspired metallic embroidered shoes with side lace closures, circa 1854 – 1856. $450.00.

Evening gown bodice to match the daywear bodice, a clever duo for a Victorian transformation dress between day and eveningwear accompanied by the same skirt. Off the shoulder portrait neckline in taupe colored silk, covered buttons, and a single row of knife pleated ruffles on the portrait neckline, circa 1854. $150.00 – 250.00.

Fashion Trends for the Year 1855

(Illustrated and Non-Illustrated)

- Applique flowers
- Bows on bodices
- Coal scuttle bonnets
- Embroidery
- Large overskirts of Chantilly ruffles
- Low rounded necklines
- Open dresses
- Rounded bodices
- Ruffled upper sleeves
- Small puff sleeves
- Two tiered skirts
- V banding on bodices [1]

Child's iridescent brown and black striped taffeta bodice with curved ruffles trimming, circa 1856. $70.00 – 225.00.

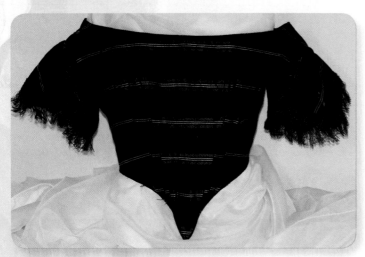

Black silk off the shoulder green and gold striped bodice with short angular sleeves trimmed in emerald green fringe, deep pointed waistline, circa 1855 – 1856. $150.00 – 250.00.

Fashion Trends for the Year 1856

(Illustrated and Non-Illustrated)

- Double ruffle sleeves
- Double tier skirts
- Large peplums on bodices
- Multi-tiered skirts
- Off the shoulder bodices
- Overskirts
- Plaid silk bows
- Profuse embroidery
- Round bodice necklines
- Rows of lace
- Triple three tiered skirts [2]

Gold, brown, gray, and black plaid silk dress, velvet covered black buttons, narrow pagoda sleeves with crisscross velvet ribbon on the sleeves, velvet edging, lace undersleeves, circa 1856 – 1858. $800.00 – 1,500.00.

Details of crisscross velvet ornament on the dress.

1. *Godey's Lady's Book,* 1855
2. *Peterson's* Magazine, December 1856; *Godey's Lady's Book,* January, March, June, July – December 1856

Black, gray, and purple striped dress with fringed yoke collar and matching peplum, circa 1856.
$400.00 – 1,400.00.

Fashion Trends for the Year 1857
(Illustrated and Non-Illustrated)

- Fringe
- Low back capes
- Military style bodices
- Small brimmed bonnets
- Wide skirts [1]

Brown and green checked linen dress, double pagoda sleeves that narrow at the cuff, double sleeve at the upper arm, circa 1857 – 1859.
$450.00 – 850.00.

Olive green and electric blue brocaded dress, shawl front collar, electric blue fringe, and narrow bell sleeves trimmed in bands of matching blue velvet, circa 1856.
$400.00 – 3,000.00.

Cotton abstract striped day dress with double layered pagoda sleeves, banding decorating the edges on the bodice and the sleeve hems, circa 1857 – 1858.
$750.00 – 1,400.00.

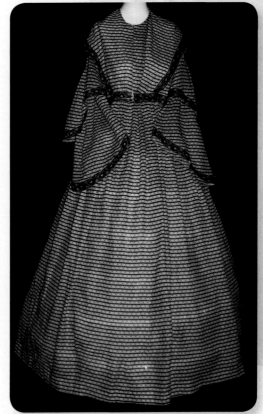

1. *Godey's Lady's Book,* July – December 1857; *Les Modes Parisiennes,* February 1857

Chapter 4, 1850 – 1859

Fashion Trends for the Year 1858

(Illustrated and Non-Illustrated)

- Fully shirred bonnets
- Huge under sleeves
- Large pagoda sleeves
- Very full skirts
- Wide back capes
- Wide curtains at neck [1]

Apple green plaid silk dress, wide pagoda double sleeves, full skirt, tight apple green fringe trimmed with embroidered ribbon, circa 1859.
$750.00 – 1,400.00.

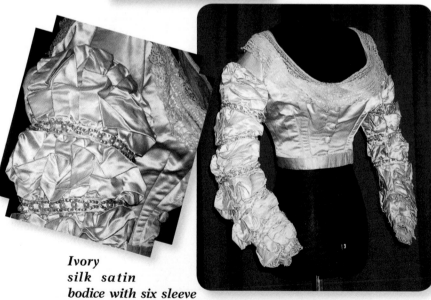

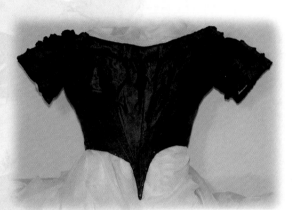

Purple silk evening bodice, neck and sleeve ruffles edged in black silk ribbon, deep pointed bodice, circa 1858.
$150.00 – 250.00.

Details of green fringe and rose embroidered ribbon trim.

Fashion Trends for the Year 1859

(Illustrated and Non-Illustrated)

- Fringe
- Huge pagoda sleeves
- Huge skirts
- Lace undersleeves
- Large flat straw hats
- Shirred and ruffled sleeves
- Skirts with large overskirts
- Stripes [2]

Details of spun glass pearls dividing the puffed sections of the sleeve.

Ivory silk satin bodice with six sleeve puffs gathered by bands of spun glass pearl beads, neckline bordered in bobbin lace, circa 1859.
$450.00 – 700.00.

1. *Home Magazine,* January – February 1858
2. *Godey's Lady's Book,* January – June 1859; *Musees des Familles,* September, 1859

Pumpkin colored roller print cotton dress, wide pagoda sleeves, and square neckline, circa 1859.
$850.00 – 1,400.00.

Roller printed pink cotton bonnet with long neck curtain and shirring, circa early to the middle of the nineteenth century.
$200.00 – 375.00.

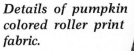

Details of pumpkin colored roller print fabric.

Black Chantilly lace pagoda under-sleeve, circa 1850s – 1860s.
$50.00 – 100.00.

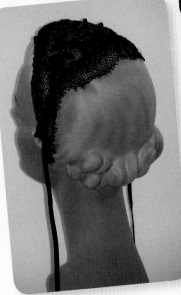

Black net and red chenille headdress embellished with thermoplastic black beads, circa 1850s – 1860s.
$50.00 – 75.00.

Quilted powder blue silk bonnet with tiny silk bows running down the top, circa early to the middle of the nineteenth century.
$200.00 – 375.00.

Chapter 5
1860 – 1869

As America entered the decade of her Civil War, the 1860s showed important design changes and features in fashion from the previous decade. Women still wore large crinoline skirts but they were smaller than the 1850s versions. Most dresses gradually developed a train. Dresses took on a military appearance during the Civil War. Peg or bishop's sleeves had replaced the wider, more frivolous pagoda examples of the antebellum 1850s and early 1860s period. Colorful silk plaids were still popular. Dresses had an uncanny characteristic row of buttons and a V yoke of fringe or ruffles on the bodice that gave the dresses a military feel. Sleeves were narrow and tight fitting. Spoon or fanchon bonnets were some of the latest changes in millinery fashions. Parasols were stylishly covered in black Chantilly lace. Zoave jackets were popularly worn during the war years. Formal wear hung very low on the shoulders. Skirts started out large at the start of the decade only to narrow into slight trains over the next ten years.

Fashion Trends in the Year 1860

(Illustrated and Non-Illustrated)

- Long wide coats
- Many ruffled layered skirts
- Pagoda sleeves three-quarters in length
- Sleeves edged in ruffles with tiers
- Two tiered skirts three-quarters down the skirt
- Very deep full pagoda sleeves
- Wide skirts [1]

Velvet satin brocade men's waistcoat with single-breasted lapels, circa 1860s.
$200.00.

Fashion Trends in the Year 1861

(Illustrated and Non-Illustrated)

- Ball gowns with low necklines
- Ball gowns with shirring
- Button ornaments
- Drooped shoulders
- Large full skirts
- Pagoda sleeves
- Rows of lace and ruffles
- Shirred bodices
- Straight waists
- Upper sleeve double ruffles
- V-shaped bodices
- Very wide plain skirts
- Voluminous sleeves
- White undersleeves
- Wide pagoda sleeves [1]

Netting and ribbon wired headdress, circa 1860s.
$165.00 – 200.00.

---

1. *Musée des Familles*, January 1860; *Peterson's Magazine*, December 1860; *Godey's Lady's Book*, January – December, 1860

1. *Musée des Familles*, September 1861; *Peterson's Magazine*, February 1861; *Godey's Lady's Book*, February, May – August, December 1861

Ivory silk wedding shoes with cut steel buckles and ruffled ornamentation, circa late 1861. $400.00 – 450.00.

Green linen and silk blend pagoda sleeve gown with white silk trim and faux bodice buttons, circa 1862. $400.00 – 850.00.

Fashion Trends in the Year 1862

((Illustrated and Non-Illustrated)

- Bands of black satin
- Belts with back streamers
- Full skirts
- Full sleeves loose to the wrist
- Full three-quarter puffed sleeves
- Jeweled taffeta colors
- Less voluminous skirts
- Military style
- Pointed pagoda sleeves
- Rows on the bottoms of skirts
- Square bodices
- V pointed bodices
- Wide pagoda oversleeves [1]

Micro-beaded reticule or drawstring purse with image of an architectural scene and band of intertwined floral decoration, circa 1830s – 1890. $200.00 – 500.00.

Brown, green, and white striped iridescent dress, pagoda sleeves that widen at the wrist and end with ruffles, circa 1862. $400.00 – 850.00.

1. *Musée des Familles*, No. 9, 1862; *Peterson's Magazine*, March, June, October, December 1862; *Godey's Lady's Book*, February – August, October – December, 1862

Fashion Trends in the Year 1863

(Illustrated and Non-Illustrated)

- Full skirts
- Gathered skirts
- Off the shoulder evening bodices
- Open overskirts
- Puffed white undersleeves
- Ruffled puff sleeves
- Slight flare on trains
- Slight pagoda sleeves
- Slight trains
- Soutache braided trim
- Square necklines
- Swiss waists
- Very wide pagoda sleeves
- Very wide skirts
- Wide back bows
- Wide flared sleeves
- Zoave jackets [1]

- Chantilly white or "blonde" lace
- Flared trains
- Fringe
- Loose open sleeves
- Military looks
- Straight sleeves
- Swiss waist belts
- Zoave jackets [1]

Rare and unusually hot pink silk gown with large puffs on the rear hip sides, circa late 1864.
$800.00 – 1,500.00.

Child's peach wool dress trimmed in soutache braiding, circa 1863 – 1868.
$575.00 – 600.00.

Fashion Trends in the Year 1864

(Illustrated and Non-Illustrated)

- Bodices with two points on waist
- Chantilly black lace

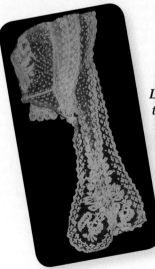

Lace cap with lappets, circa the first half of the nineteenth century.
$165.00 – 200.00.

1. *Peterson's Magazine,* January – December 1863; *Godey's Lady's Book,* May, June, December 1863; *Musée des Familles,* September 1863, Plate No. 12

1. *Godey's Lady's Book,* March, June, July, August, September, October 1864; *Peterson's Magazine,* June, August 1864

Lace headpiece with side lappets, circa the first half of the nineteenth century. $165.00 – 200.00.

Fashion Trends in the Year 1865

(Illustrated and Non-Illustrated)

- Flared trains
- Full forward hats
- Full floor length skirts
- Military looks
- Military style bodices
- Narrower straighter skirts
- Plain dresses
- Pleated yokes
- Shirred bodices
- Slim sleeves
- Spoon bonnets [1]

Gray shirred silk spoon bonnet, floral and feathered trim, circa 1865. $250.00 – 600.00.

Rear view of spoon bonnet, circa 1865.

Rust and cobalt blue iridescent silk checked dress, crystal buttons, dropped puff sleeves with white eyelet embroidered cuffs, circa 1865. $800.00 – 1,500.00.

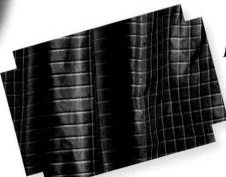

Details of rust and cobalt silk.

1. *Godey's Lady's Book*, January, March, July, August, September, 1865; *Musée des Familles*, September 1865; *Peterson's Magazine*, January – December 1865; *Englishwoman's Domestic Monthly*, August, September, October & December, 1865

Very rare child's spoon bonnet, shirred light gray silk wired for support, original silk flower trims, circa 1865.
$250.00 – 600.00.

Black silk taffeta dress, lace cuffs, peg sleeves, and velvet striped banding, fabric covered buttons, circa 1865.
$800.00 – 1,500.00.

Rust silk dress with raised brocaded black stripes and lighter rust dots, lower skirt ruffle, embroidered ribbon work on the cuff, circa 1865.
$800.00 – 1,500.00.

Aquamarine taffeta girl's dress, flat front bodice, peacock blue buttons, single ruffle yoke and cuffs, gathered hem with raised sides, circa 1865.
$400.00 – 800.00.

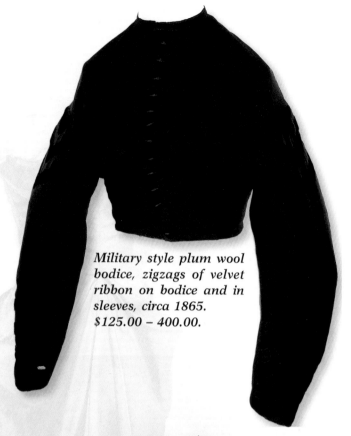

Military style plum wool bodice, zigzags of velvet ribbon on bodice and in sleeves, circa 1865. $125.00 – 400.00.

Linen dress with green rickrack, ribbon trim, and green buttons, belt with back bow reportedly worn in April 1865 when President Abraham Lincoln's funeral train passed by the wearer's city. $800.00 – 1,500.00.

Green cotton bodice with dark green velvet stripes on the sleeves and a V shape decoration on the bodice, circa 1865. $125.00 – 400.00.

Linen dress with matching shoulder cape.

Rust silk plaid wrapper or housedress, circa 1865.
$1,600.00.

Back view of linen dress with cape, as seen on the previous page.

Back view of linen dress without cape showing the belt's bow, as seen on the previous page.

Slate gray iridescent silk taffeta dress, yoke trimmed with three rows of satin ribbons, fabric covered buttons, circa 1865.
$800.00 – 1,250.00.

53

Fashion Trends in the Year 1866
(Illustrated and Non-Illustrated)

- Crisscross ribbon designs on dresses
- Cuffs
- Curved straw hats
- Edging in lace or ribbon
- Fanchon bonnets
- Full slight trains
- Low squared jackets
- Military bodices
- Overskirts
- Plain sleeves
- Square low bodices [1]

Black silk taffeta jacket, jet trimming, wide open front and peg sleeves, circa 1866 – 1867.
$125.00 – 400.00.

Green and black silk striped gown with fuchsia fabric covered buttons and shirred sleeves, circa 1866.
$800.00 – 1,500.00.

Green taffeta dress with sweeping train, white taffeta bands covered in black lace on the neck yoke and triangular shapes at the cuffs, circa 1866.
$800.00 – 1,500.00.

1. *La Mode Illustrée*, 1866, Nos. 28, 44; *Peterson's Magazine*, January – December 1866; *Godey's Lady's Book*, February, March, June, July – December, 1866; *Magasin des Demoiselles, Journal Mensuel*, October & November, 1866; *Peterson's Magazine*, January & February 1866; *Englishwoman's Domestic Monthly*, February, July, October, November 1866; *Musée des Familles*, June 1866

Details of the green taffeta gown's sweeping train, as seen on the previous page.

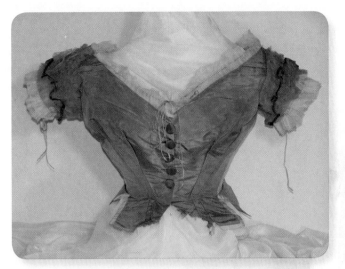

Off the shoulder bodice of blue taffeta with matching buttons, white trim at the neckline shirred and tied with thin ties, circa 1866. $450.00 – 750.00.

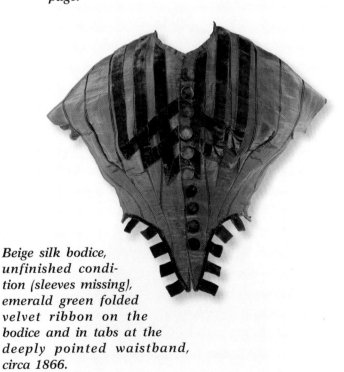

Beige silk bodice, unfinished condition (sleeves missing), emerald green folded velvet ribbon on the bodice and in tabs at the deeply pointed waistband, circa 1866. $125.00 – 400.00.

Electric blue silk fanchon bonnet with black Chantilly lace and white chiffon trims, circa 1866 – 1868. $165.00 – 600.00.

Rust silk fanchon bonnet with lace, silk ribbons, bows, and jet beaded sprays projected upward using coiled wire springs, circa 1866 – 1868.
$165.00 – 600.00.

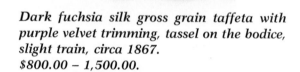

Dark fuchsia silk gross grain taffeta with purple velvet trimming, tassel on the bodice, slight train, circa 1867.
$800.00 – 1,500.00.

Fashion Trends in the Year 1867

(Illustrated and Non-Illustrated)

- Bands of lace on sleeves
- Fanchon bonnets
- Flat straw hats
- Fringe
- Less frills on the skirt
- Low waist bodices
- Lower skirts
- Military looks in dresses
- Military styled plain bodices
- Multiple rows on puff sleeves
- Ornamental buttons on the rear
- Oversleeves
- Ruffles of lace
- Slight flare in back of dresses
- Slight trains
- Square jackets
- Thin sleeves
- V shirred bodices
- Very deep off the shoulder looks
- Zoave jackets [1]

1. *Peterson's Magazine,* February, July, August, October, November, December 1867; *Godey's Lady's Book,* January, April, June, July, August, September, 1867; *Magasin des Demoiselles, Journal Mensuel,* February, March, August, September & October, 1867; *Englishwoman's Domestic Monthly,* April & June 1867; *Musée des Familles,* October & November 1867

Silk taffeta dress, red plaid with fabric buttons and purple fringe on the bodice, shoulders, and cuffs, circa 1867.
$800.00 – 1,500.00.

Flat topped black hat with small purple flowers and remnants of original feathers, circa 1867. $200.00 – 600.00.

Ivory linen dress, chevron design on the skirt, slight peplum, military style, large faux buttons on the bodice, peg sleeves, circa 1867. $765.00 – 1,500.00.

Flat topped black Chantilly lace hat with small purple flowers, circa 1867. $200.00 – 600.00.

Flat topped lace cap with black Chantilly lace, circa 1867. $200.00 – 600.00.

- Bodice belts
- Crisscross bodices
- Fanchon bonnets
- Fringe ornamentation
- Military styles
- Ornamental bands in contrasting color
- Overskirts with fringe
- Overskirts
- Pointed trains
- Pronounced trains
- Ruffled skirt on bottoms
- Skirts are narrower
- Split sleeves
- Striped outfits with lace and ornament
- Trains swoop to the back of the skirt
- Two tone button ornament
- Undersleeves
- Underskirts [1]

Back view of pinstripe gray taffeta girl's dress, dipped front and back bodice, two rows of pleats on the skirt, circa 1867.
$600.00 – 800.00.

Three cutwork and embroidered collars, circa middle of the nineteenth century.
$20.00 – 45.00 each.

Plaited straw hat with Greek key straw top piece, circa 1867.
$200.00 – 600.00.

Fashion Trends in the Year 1869

(Illustrated and Non-Illustrated)

- Aprons
- Bodices covering the hips
- Bow ornamentation
- Fanchon bonnets
- Lace on dresses
- Lace on trains
- Lace ornamentation

Fashion Trends in the Year 1868

(Non-Illustrated)

- Back ties

1. *Peterson's Magazine,* May – July, September, November 1868; *Musée des Familles,* January & March 1868; *Magasin des Demoiselles, Journal Mensuel Musée des Familles,* January, March, June, August, September, 1868; *Englishwoman's Domestic Magazine,* April & July 1868; *Godey's Lady's Book,* January, March, May, August, November 1868; *Harper's Bazar,* Supplement December 1868

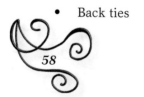

- Petal overskirts
- Pleats
- Puffs
- Puffs on the bustles
- Rows of ruffles
- Ruffles
- Straight trains
- V panels over skirts
- Wide circular buttons
- Wide shirred overskirts [1]

Ivory chiffon fanchon bonnet with satin cording, bows, and attached ivory Chantilly lace ribbon worn as a "necklace" around the neck, circa 1869 – early 1870. $165.00 – 600.00.

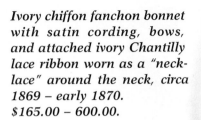

Cigar brown and rust silk taffeta gown, three tiered ruffled skirt, wide pagoda oversleeves, narrow undersleeves, peplum, belt, bib design on bodice, ruffles and bows, circa 1869. $800.00 – 1,500.00.

Pink bustle overskirt with zigzag applique trim, circa 1869. $250.00 – 600.00.

Young girl's silk dress fashioned with tiny black and beige checks, blue silk neck ruffle and plain waistband, silk trimming on the multi-ruffled skirt, circa 1869. $575.00 – 600.00.

British carved ivory parasol, blonde or ivory lace covering, finger loop, hinged handle, silver ornament, silk lining, circa 1830s – 1870s $1,650.00.

1. *Peterson's Magazine,* January – December, 1869; *Godey's Lady's Book,* April, May, July, October-December, 1869

Fashion in the 1870s brought forth the end of the cage crinoline and the emergence of the bustle. Early 1870s dresses kept some of the 1860s stylistic features. New innovations in style included lower sweeping trains, bows and design elements on the back of the dresses that made them appear to drag down into a lower swag bustle skirt. Eventually the 1870s gown transformed itself into the princess line silhouette by the end of the decade. Princess line dresses would be one piece, straight in line and had a long train. Women projected a slim, sleek appearance in such garments.

The 1870s decade was also the era of the first bustle. Filled with ruffles, bustles and plenty of puffs, ladies sported this new silhouette with pride after the post-war period. After the war was over, there was a feminine yearning for frivolity in dress. The prosperous would wear fashions that had many rows of puffs, ruffles and frills often trimmed with contrasting color or black lace. The intricate pleating, tucks and ruffles on these garments were astounding. Some ensembles had an apron effect in the front. The most elaborate garments had asymmetrical features to their designs in contrasting colors of silk, embroidered ribbon and ornamental buttons. Hats perched high atop the head became the finishing touch to the new look. Parasols for carriages remained small but longer and sturdier than the previous decade's delicate examples. Popular designs had rows of shirred and gathered ornamental ruffled trim spiraling outward from the center. Hats sloped forward. Renaissance-inspired fashions included new square necklines.

Fashion Trends in the Year 1871

(Illustrated and Non-Illustrated)

- Chantilly lace
- Fan pleats
- Necklines have V ruffles
- Puffs
- Rows of knife pleats on skirts
- Skirts narrow
- Stripes
- Trains increase in length
- Vertical rows of ruffles [1]

Ivory and pink silk flower hat with ribbon streamers, circa 1871.
$275.00 – 320.00.

Fashion Trends in the Year 1870

(Non-Illustrated)

- Banding
- Contrasting colors
- Fanchon bonnets
- Knife pleats
- No bustles
- Open panels
- Overskirts
- Pleats
- Rows of ruffles
- Rows of saw tooth ornament
- Ruffled trim on hems
- Ruffled trim on overskirts
- Ruffled trim on sleeves
- Tight ruffle edges [1]

Apple green taffeta bodice with deep V neckline is trimmed with cream gauze ruffles. The deep green color contrasts with apple green pockets. The gauze neck and cuffs are trimmed with green cording and ribbons. The pockets and bodice are covered with fabric covered buttons, circa 1871.
$625.00 – 1225.00.

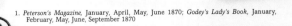

1. *Peterson's Magazine*, January, April, May, June 1870; *Godey's Lady's Book*, January, February, May, June, September 1870

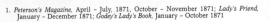

1. *Peterson's Magazine*, April – July, 1871, October – November 1871; *Lady's Friend*, January – December 1871; *Godey's Lady's Book*, January – October 1871

Blue gray taffeta trimmed with scalloped black Chantilly lace, apron effects, deeper peplum bodices, widening sleeves, geometric effects, bands of lace, ruffles, and taffeta bows, circa 1872. $975.00 – 2,800.00.

Slate blue straw hat with original blue velvet ribbon and flora trim, circa 1871. $275.00 – 320.00.

Fashion Trends in the Year 1872
(Illustrated and Non-Illustrated)

- Apron fronts
- Bands of Chantilly lace
- Bustle apron overskirts
- Floral trims
- Front gown ruffles
- Knife pleats
- Low basque waists
- Plain skirts
- Saw tooth overskirts
- Square necklines
- Trailing gowns
- V necklines [1]

Black and cream striped dress of ribbed cotton, circa 1872. $1,900.00 – 2,800.00.

1. *Peterson's Magazine,* February, May-July, December 1872; *Godey's Lady's Book,* March – December 1872

Side view of black and cream striped dress, circa 1872, as seen on the previous page.

Fashion Trends in the Year 1873

(Non-Illustrated)

- Apron effects
- Black Chantilly lace trim
- Bodices look lower
- Bustles
- Fancy dresses and skirts
- Fringe
- Lower overskirts
- Military looks
- Points
- Trains
- V pointed big oversleeves [1]

Fashion Trends in the Year 1874

(Non-Illustrated)

- Bustle puffs
- Chantilly lace
- Front cascading ruffles
- Huge rear bustles
- Lower skirt ornament
- Musketeer cuffs

- Polonaise jackets
- Puffed bustles
- Puffed bustle with overskirts
- Puffy sleeves
- Ruffled skirts
- V bodices [1]

Fashion Trends in the Year 1875

(Illustrated and Non-Illustrated)

- Angular cut overskirts
- Bustles with draped cascades
- Deep high bustles
- Deep tails to the bodice
- Front aprons
- Gathers of contrasting colors
- Long sweeping trains
- Off the shoulder bodices
- Open square bodices
- Pleats and puffs
- Round bodices
- Rounded low waist bodices
- Velvet and taffeta
- Very low formal bodices [2]

Girl's dress of linen and silk blended fabric, blue silk edging, slight ruffled peplum and cuff trim, bows, buttons down the back, angular collar style decoration, circa 1875 – early 1880s.
$425.00 – 975.00.

1. *Peterson's Magazine,* January, March, August 1873; *Godey's Lady's Book,* January – March, May – July 1873

1. *Peterson's Magazine,* January, April, August, October 1874; *Godey's Lady's Book,* January, April – October, December 1874
2. *Peterson's Magazine,* February – April, June-July, September – October 1875; *Godey's Lady's Book,* January – August, October – December, 1875

Fashion Trends in the Year 1876

(Illustrated and Non-Illustrated)

- Aprons
- Drooped rear bustles
- Low pointed bodices
- Low ruffle trains
- Many ruffles
- Princess line fronts [1]

Plaid cotton centennial dress, red, white, and blue patriotic trim on the bodice, skirt, pockets, collar, and cuffs, circa 1876. $575.00 – 750.00.

Brown silk brocade child's dress trimmed with salmon pink satin piping and silk insert, buttons down the back, slightly flared peplum, circa 1875 – early 1880s. $575.00 – 750.00.

Black Chantilly lace and ivory silk parasol, carved ivory handle with monogram, circa 1875. $1,650.00.

Side view of 1876 centennial dress.

Details of carved ivory handle with twisted rope design and monogram, circa 1875.

1. *Peterson's Magazine,* February, May, August, October, December 1876; *Demorest's Monthly Magazine,* June & July 1876

Fashion Trends in the Year 1877
(Illustrated and Non-Illustrated)

- Bodices are tight at the hips
- Bodices tighten at the waist
- Contrasting panels
- Knife pleats
- Low falling bodices
- Lower skirts
- Narrow slit necklines
- Overlapping lace
- Points over hips
- Princess lines
- Princess lines flare to the skirt bottoms
- Rows of overlapping sashes and ruffles
- Ruffles
- Satin ruffles
- Shirring
- Sweeping trains [1]

Light brown boy's wool jacket with hook closure and soutache embroidery on the lapels, cuffs, and jacket edges, circa 1875 – 1885.
$125.00 – 250.00.

Brown and tan velvet and silk bonnet, circa 1877.
$275.00 – 325.00.

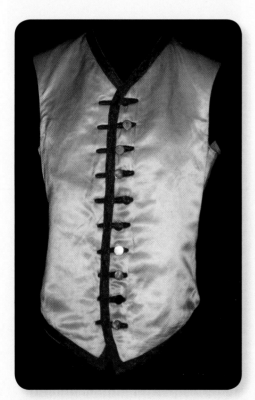

Middle to late nineteenth century prairie or sunbonnet fashioned from woven straw and black cotton.
$185.00 – 275.00.

Men's centennial vest made of ivory satin and trimmed in gold braiding with gold buttons, circa 1876.
$200.00 – 575.00.

1. *Peterson's Magazine*, April, November, December 1877; *Demorest's Monthly Magazine*, December 1877; *Godey's Lady's Book*, February – April, June – August, 1877

Mustard and turquoise silk princess-line gown with train, profusely edged with turquoise blue embroidered flowers, taffeta ruffles and bows, asymmetrical design, circa 1877.
$1,900.00 – 2,800.00.

Details of the train.

Detailed view of dress skirt ornamentation.

Fashion Trends in the Year 1878

(Illustrated and Non-Illustrated)

- Bands of fabric
- Fabric panels open to reveal underskirts
- Knife pleats on hem ruffles
- Low bodices
- Necklines
- Open wraps
- Pleats
- Princess lines
- Ruffle at elbows
- Ruffles
- Skirt of contrasting colors
- Slight sweep trains
- V shaped basque waists [1]

Detail of the pearly gray and cream striped silk taffeta dress's side and train.

Pearly gray and cream striped silk taffeta gown with train in the princess style, circa 1878.
$1,900.00 – 2,800.00.

1. *Peterson's Magazine*, January, February, July, August, November December 1878; *Demorest's Monthly Magazine*, February & June 1878; *Myra's Journal of Dress and Fashion*, October 1878

Princess-line navy velvet and cream silk shirred gown with train, blonde Chantilly lace edging, circa 1878.
$1,900.00 – 2,800.00.

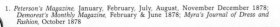

Detailed view of the navy velvet and cream dress's train and bustle bow, as seen on the previous page.

Black and white pinstripe taffeta bustle dress, basque waist, circa 1878 – 1883. $975.00 – 1,895.00.

Fashion Trends in the Year 1879

(Illustrated and Non-Illustrated)

- Close skirts
- Knife pleats
- Plain sleeves
- Princess lines
- Ruffled and banded cuffs
- Ruffled trains
- Two aprons over hips
- V shaped shirred lace necklines
- Very low bodices [1]

Princess-line gown with train, taffeta ruffles, fabric covered buttons, V shaped neckline, lace on the neck-line and cuffs and two bows on the bodice and waist, circa 1878.
$1,900.00 – 2,800.00.

1. *Peterson's Magazine*, January, August, September 1879; *Myra's Mid-Monthly Journal*, December 15, 1879

Red silk apron with hand-painted daisies and
wheat sheaves, circa late 1870s – early 1880s.
$350.00 – 500.00.

Polonaise cotton bodice, brocaded
fabric, pointed hip coverings, pearl
buttons, circa 1879.
$325.00 – 450.00.

Black silk apron with embroidered daisies on
the apron, waistband, and back bow streamers,
circa late 1870s – early 1880s.
$275.00 – 450.00.

Black apron with embroidered flowers and
leaves trimmed in black bobbin lace, circa
1870s – 1880s.
$275.00 – 450.00.

The 1880s heralded a climate of prosperity and a taste for elegance among society's upper and middle classes. Reaping the benefits of development from decades of the Industrial Revolution, women looked to ornament themselves in a new kind of finery. Dress of this period changed almost year to year with different ornamentation and bustle characteristics. The second bustle period arrived in 1883. Victorians would come to see many evolutions of the bustle and skirt designs through this decade.

The bustle dresses in the 1880s had very stoic and simplistic daytime bodices. Dress ensembles resembled suits. Bodices were very plain although fabrics could be of elegant silk, or wool, trimmed with glass or metallic ornamental buttons in a single row to close the bodice. The 1880s bustle gowns were not dragging and drooping. Skirt lengths reached the floor. The new bustle was quite pronounced. More formal garments had long trains in addition to the bustle. The interesting design features and changes included how many ways one could drape or extend the fabric around the bustle as it came from the bodice. Bodice tails could be long flat strips down the back. Skirts could have side puffs or drapery, fold over the hip or appear to lie halfway down the skirt. All together the clothing of this decade reminds us of the austere yet elegant forms Victorian dress can communicate.

Navy blue checkered silk taffeta bustle dress, contrasting fabric and striped ornament at the bustle and cuffs, circa 1880.
$600.00 – 950.00.

Fashion Trends for the Year 1880

(Illustrated and Non-Illustrated)

- Curved hats
- Narrow skirts
- Princess lines
- Side hip panels [1]

Straw hat, protruding front, high telescopic crown that narrows as it ascends, woven bands of straw ornamenting the brim, circa 1880.
$80.00 – 230.00.

Side view of bustle on the navy blue checkered dress.

1. *Peterson's Magazine,* February – August, October, 1880; *Young Ladies Journal,* June 1880; *Myra's Journal of Dress & Fashion,* February 1, 1880; *Journal des Demoiselles,* October 1880

Black grosgrain silk shirred taffeta bonnet, circa 1880. $78.00 – 245.00.

This saffron yellow silk taffeta gown is partially constructed with silver and gold threaded metallic brocade on the detach-able collar, dress front, and hip drapery. The skirt is trimmed with rows of ruffles. The hip buckle is ornamented with bronze colored beads, circa 1881. $975.00 – 1,800.00.

Black woven tulle with hat exposing the wire supports, decorative straw trimming, ribbon ties, and small cylindrical shaped crown, circa 1880. $80.00 – 230.00.

Fashion Trends for the Year 1881

(Illustrated and Non-Illustrated)

- Drop waists
- Side hip drapery
- Side hip ruffles [1]

Close-up view of hip pleating done in silver cloth with gold and silver embroidery.

1. *Peterson's Magazine,* May & October 1881; *Godey's Lady's Book,* March 1881

Woven plaid bodice with ruffled cuffs, circa 1881.
$250.00 – 600.00.

Light brown silk brocaded bustle dress with garnet velvet and taffeta accents, asymmetrical pleated jabot, and ruffled hem, circa 1882.
$800.00 – 1,250.00.

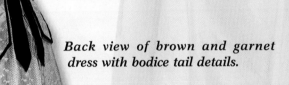

Back view of brown and garnet dress with bodice tail details.

Fashion Trends for the Year 1882

(Illustrated and Non-Illustrated)

- Basque waists
- Double puffs
- Full skirts
- Hats of velvet with close feathers
- Narrow skirts
- Side hip puffs [1]

1. *Peterson's Lady's Magazine,* January – March, June – September, 1882; *Journal des Demoiselles,* May 1882; *Myra's Mid-Monthly Journal,* March 15, 1882

Light silk and linen blend dress accented by dark brown silk taffeta, overlapping skirt at the hips, and knife pleated skirt hem edge, circa 1882.
$475.00 – 800.00.

Brown and electric blue silk plaid princess dress, military style cuffs, hip tied apron effect in electric blue, circa 1882.
$700.00 – 1,250.00.

Black velvet bodice with profuse jet trim on the triangular neckline, large five petal jet flower ornamental buttons running down the bodice front, white silk covered with black lace sleeves, circa 1882.
$475.00 – 800.00.

Dark blue taffeta and velvet gown, velvet cuffs, hip puffs, back bustle of taffeta and velvet rectangular panels, circa 1882 – 1883.
$475.00 – 800.00.

Light and dark brown silk and linen blended dress, brown taffeta accents, deep pointed over-skirt, knife pleats on the skirt and cuffs, and basque waist, circa 1883.
$475.00 – 800.00.

Fashion Trends for the Year 1883

(Illustrated and Non-Illustrated)

- Curved bustles
- Front aprons
- Off the shoulder bodices [1]

Olive green plush hat with watered silk ribbon in autumn colors, black satin band, and black feather plume, circa 1883.
$85.00 – 250.00.

1. *Delineator,* April No. 4, 1883

Back view of the silk and linen dress showing the unique bustle.

Salmon pink ribbed silk taffeta silk dress with tight fitted bodice, deep neckline trimmed in silk ruffles, sharp point at the waist, asymmetrical sash on the front and the sides embellished with two rows of taffeta puffed panels, circa 1883. $950.00 – 1,800.00.

Black cotton bodice, black jet and glass beads sewn throughout the entire garment, circa 1883. $95.00 – 200.00.

Detail of the brocaded salmon silk fabric.

Apricot colored velvet and ivory satin bustle gown, pleated satin apron, skirt
embellished with spun glass and pearl beads, sleeves and neckline embellished
with ball fringe, circa 1883.
$1,300.00 – 1,800.00.

Girl's patterned taffeta brocade with tiny embroidered scallops and flowers on the bodice and skirt hem, leg o'mutton sleeves covered with dotted tulle, skirt insert embellished with silk thread embroidered fine lace, circa 1883.
$300.00 – 500.00.

Details of the pearl and spun glass beading on the front of the skirt, as seen on the previous page.

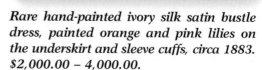

Rust colored voided velvet and silk taffeta bodice, ornamental buttons depicting a helmeted knight, circa 1883.
$250.00 – 400.00.

Rare hand-painted ivory silk satin bustle dress, painted orange and pink lilies on the underskirt and sleeve cuffs, circa 1883.
$2,000.00 – 4,000.00.

Side view of the painted dress's bustle, as seen on the previous page.

Front view: silk workbag or reticule with embroidered birds and blossoms, Asian influenced design circa 1883.
$75.00 – 125.00.

Detailed view of the painted bustle dress's skirt detail, as seen on the previous page.

Back view.

Taupe and black pinstripe silk bustle dress, satin banding, and fabric covered buttons, circa 1883. $475.00 – 950.00.

Slate blue gray silk taffeta dress with apron front and bustle in the rear, high collar, bobbin lace, ruffled underskirt, circa 1883. $950.00 – 1,300.00.

Ivory silk taffeta fancy skirt with a row of taffeta ruffles on the skirt edge and a facing of metal gold cord embroidering the skirt throughout with scrolls and floral ornamentation, circa 1883 – 1884. $425.00 – 900.00.

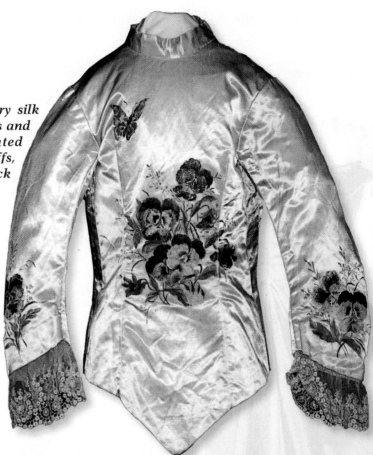

Rare painted bodice, ivory silk front painted with pansies and butterflies, sleeves painted with pansies at the cuffs, plain button down back closure, circa 1883. $1,000.00 – 2,000.00.

Details of painted bodice.

Blue wool bodice, white daisy embroidered appliques on the bodice front and hips, circa 1883.
$600.00 – 900.00.

Black silk and white floral embroidered apron with Asian inspired design, circa 1883.
$50.00 – 100.00.

Details of embroidered floral bodice applique.

Asian influenced paper fan, bamboo sticks, cording, circa 1883.
$50.00 – 125.00.

Fashion Trends for the Year 1884
(Illustrated and Non–Illustrated)

• Draped and puffed skirts [1]

Blue damask silk bustle gown, plain bodice ornamented with embroidery, openwork on apron and cuffs, original crystal centered buttons, circa 1884.
$1,250.00 – 1,800.00.

1. *Peterson's Magazine,* March & October 1884; *Illustirte Frauenzeitung,* 1884

Plum silk taffeta gown with low apron, deep plum velvet bodice, side panels, tightly buttoned bodice, notched collar, circa 1884 – 1885. $475.00 – 975.00.

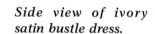

Side view of ivory satin bustle dress.

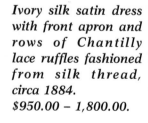

Ivory silk satin dress with front apron and rows of Chantilly lace ruffles fashioned from silk thread, circa 1884. $950.00 – 1,800.00.

Fashion Trends for the Year 1885

(Illustrated and Non–Illustrated)

- Apron effects on skirt fronts
- Flower trims
- Rows of skirt ruffles [1]

Peacock and turkey feather fan, carved sandalwood sticks, circa 1885.
$50.00 – 100.00.

Burgundy silk taffeta and voided velvet gown, circa 1885.
$800.00 – 1,200.00.

Silk embroidered hand fan depicting the American eagle, U.S. flags, and U.S. shield (motifs in the U.S. Great Seal), butterfly embroidered edging, painted "E. Pluribus Unum" motto, black lacquered handle with gilded decoration and tassels, circa nineteenth century.
$50.00 – 125.00.

Blue satin and wine velvet hat with jet trim and ruffled ornamentation, circa 1885.
$75.00 – 125.00.

1. *Peterson's Magazine,* January – August 1885

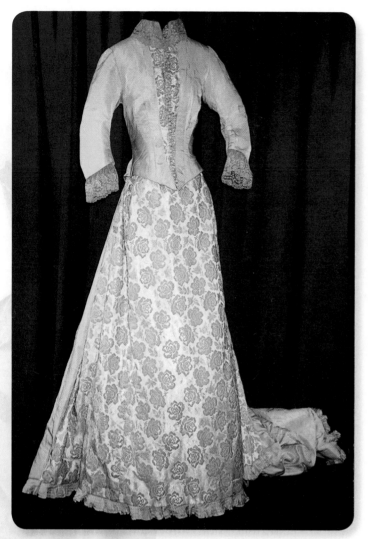

Side view of silk bustle dress with sweeping train.

Ivory silk taffeta and voided velvet gown, point de gaze lace collar and cuffs, long ruffled silk taffeta train, circa 1885.
$1,300.00 – 1,800.00.

Tyrolean style hat of black straw, circa 1885.
$400.00 – 800.00.

- Collars with plain fronts
- Fronts of skirts have gathered apron effects
- High collar bodices
- Plain bodices
- Straight skirt fronts
- Straight sleeves
- V pointed bodices
- Velvet and silk
- Waists are high and plain [1]

Voided velvet black bustle coat with rabbit cuffs and collar trim, circa 1886.
$795.00 – 1,200.00.

Voided velvet polonaise style bodice with chenille fringe, circa 1885.
$235.00 – 400.00.

Detailed view of chenille fringe.

Side view of voided velvet black bustle coat, circa 1886.

Fashion Trends for the Year 1886

(Illustrated and Non–Illustrated)

- Apron effects draped at the bustle
- Bodices fan outward in ruffles or pleats

1. *Delineator*, May 1886; *Peterson's*, April – August, November – December 1886; *Godey's Lady's Book*, January – June 1886

Honey colored straw hat, pinched up brim and two feather pompoms, circa 1886.
$125.00 – 390.00.

Brown parasol with corded brown floral lace, incised wooden stick, ball handle, plain finial, circa 1886.
$50.00 – 125.00.

This yellow 1880s bustle dress was converted to a post 1910 gown. This gown has an underskirt and bodice insert of yellow triangular velvet tuffs, bodice closure in lace–up corset fashion, and half sleeves, circa 1886.
$975.00 – 1,200.00.

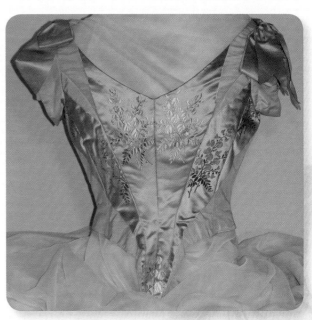

Middy bloomer and short sleeve bathing costume (missing belt), circa 1886. $200.00.

Laced and brocaded yellow silk bodice with white embroidered flowers and fern leaves, bow epaulettes, deep waist point, circa 1887. $650.00 – 900.00.

Details of silk brocaded pattern on the bodice.

Fashion Trends for the Year 1887

(Illustrated and Non–Illustrated)

- Aprons overlapping fabric panels
- Asymmetrical closures
- Bustles
- Draped skirt fronts
- Full bustles and trains
- High collars
- Larger posteriors
- Ruffles
- Straight sleeves
- Tight bodices
- V point bodices [1]

1. *The Young Ladies Journal,* Supplement, Christmas 1887; *Peterson's Magazine,* July, October – December 1887; *Harper's Bazar,* September & October 1887; *Journal des Demoiselles,* May 1887

Fashion Trends for the Year 1888
(Illustrated and Non–Illustrated)

- Apron drapery
- Bodices with back tabs
- Crowns of hats upturned
- Draped fronts of skirts
- Evening bodices are tight fitting with small straps
- Front lace panels over skirts
- Full skirts
- High necks
- High vertical feather hats
- Higher hats
- Lace over fabric in parts of dress
- Open V–necks
- Plain tops
- Round protruding bustles
- Slight bustles
- Tight fitting bodices
- Vertical direction in hats
- Voided velvet [1]

Black taffeta gown, satin panels beaded with rust, chartreuse, and black glass beads accenting a floral brocade design, asymmetrical lace swag, lace cuffs, beaded collar, circa 1887.
$700.00 – 1,800.00.

Grosgrain taffeta gown, tight bodice, V-necks and waists, lace chiffon with embroidered edging along the collars and lower dress cuffs, ornamental strands of glass pearls at the neckline, dress hem of a contrasting wide band of delicate crochet lace, circa 1888.
$700.00 – 1,200.00.

Detailed view of the beadwork and embroidery on the dress cuffs.

1. *Peterson's Magazine,* January, May, June, August November, December 1888; *Der Bazar,* February, March, July, September, October 1888

Fashion Trends for the Year 1889

(Non–Illustrated)

- Blue
- Crisscross or military jacket bodices
- Drapery on skirts
- Floral prints
- Full skirts
- Higher hats with feathers
- Printed silks
- Printed stripes
- Rust color
- Shirred and pleated soft bodices
- Slight rear bustle
- Slight round pointed waists
- Thin ruffles
- Wide sleeves [1]

Formal gown fashioned from Lyons silk of bold yellow-orange damask on ivory ground, black embroidered lace netting on the bodice and collar, open V front, circa 1888.
$1,300.00 – 1,800.00.

Dark salmon brushed cotton parasol with ecru lace trim, twenty-eight inches long, curved handle, circa 1880s.
$125.00 – 185.00.

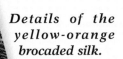

Details of the yellow-orange brocaded silk.

1. *Der Bazar*, February – June, September – October 1889; *Peterson's Magazine*, January, April – September 1889

Woven and plaited golden straw and mustard velvet child's bonnet, velvet on the brim underside, circa late 1880s to early 1890s. $75.00 – 125.00.

Red silk and velvet bonnet, circa late nineteenth century. $85.00 – 185.00.

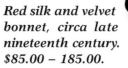

Ruffled silk muffler scarf, circa 1880s – 1890s. $50.00 – 150.00.

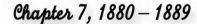

Cockade fan, floral design on waxy printed paper with leather sticks, circa 1880s to the turn of the twentieth century.
$50.00 – 125.00.

Asian influenced hand-painted fan that depicts birds on a snowy ground alongside plain red satin, circa 1880s.
$50.00 – 125.00.

Half-mourning (black and white) cotton tulle day cap with shirred lace and ribbon bows, circa 1880s.
$75.00 – 125.00.

The 1890s ushered in a decade of beauty and magnificent fashion creations. Opulently dressed women would proudly wear each year's finery as they filled the estates and ballrooms of society's best families. Great men reaped the benefits of building industrial fortunes from steel, coal and oil. America's wealthy class had made their fortunes through ingenuity, luck and historical circumstance. They spent their wealth seeking to mimic European taste and refinement. The affluent perpetuated a grand and bold style rich in opulence that would be called the second Bustle Era.

Clothing in this decade was rich and exciting. Ladies silhouettes are descried as the "hour glass shape." The shoulder silhouette enlarged and evolved into huge puff sleeves. Skirts were very full and voluminous. Many different types of ruffed and lace collars appear over the bulbous puff sleeves. Each year the puff sleeve took on a unique character. Silk fabrics of those times remained some of the finest examples in the century. As the decade ended and the nineteenth century drew to a close, dresses made an exciting exit by exhibiting the most exquisite silhouettes. Shape and execution in the costume was both unique and flattering. Most connotations of Victorian clothing bring to mind either the bustle or the large puff sleeves seen in this decade. Hats and parasols were also unique in their features and embellishments of lace, beading and silk flowers. As women left the nineteenth century, they turned their eyes towards the new and exciting developments in dress the twentieth century would bring.

Fashion Trends in the Year 1890

(Illustrated and Non–Illustrated)

- Cuffs
- Day dresses with no trains
- Decorated hems
- Draped front skirts
- Droopy shirring on skirts
- Evening dresses with trains
- Floor length skirts
- Full sleeves
- No bustles
- Pointed V waists
- Ruffled jabots
- Sleeves are close fitting
- Sleeves narrow
- Slight puff on sleeve

- Slight rear bustles
- Slightly puffed on upper sleeves
- Tight bodices
- Upper sleeves are slightly high
- Waist has slight peplum over bustle [1]

Ball gown, sleeveless bodice covered in sheer netting embroidered with strips of thin ribbon, plain silk taffeta skirt and train, draped netting, circa 1890.
$650.00 – 1,250.00.

1. *The Domestic Monthly, An Illustrated Magazine of Fashion,* May 1890; *Der Bazar,* February, April – July, August, October – December, 1890; *Peterson's,* July, September, 1890; *Harper's Bazar,* January 18, 1890

Pink girl's formal bodice with black velvet collar, pompom bow in the rear, banding at the waist and sleeve ornament, circa 1890 – 1891.
$240.00 – 480.00.

Purple velvet bonnet with lilac and white silk and velvet flowers and purple velvet ribbon, circa 1890.
$425.00 – 875.00.

This girl's gray and taupe wool striped dress has dark purple velvet panels, sleeve tops, and triangular points on the hem. The girl who wore the dress left playing cards and coffee beans in the pocket, remnants of an enjoyable time of playing games in Victorian child-hood, circa 1890.
$480.00 – 780.00.

Ivory silk grand parasol with rows of embroidered lace insertion on the top in a scalloped design hanging over the side, ribbon bow trim over the handle, circa 1890s.
$500.00 – 1,000.00.

Fashion Trends for the Year 1891

(Illustrated and Non-Illustrated)

- Asymmetrical puffed upper sleeves
- Deep V bodices
- Droopy appearance
- Floral and print dresses
- High standing shoulders
- No bustles
- Princess waistlines
- Sleeves with tight puffs on top
- Slim tight skirts
- Straight sleeves
- Tight bodices
- Vertical design aspects to the sleeves [1]

Rust velvet shirred bonnet with embroidered decoration, shirring and matching tie, circa 1891.
$75.00 – 185.00.

Top: cut steel Victorian chain link belt with loop for a chatelaine, circa 1890s.
$500.00 – 975.00.

Bottom: cut steel and velvet choker, circa late nineteenth century.
$50.00 – 150.00.

Left: cut steel shoe buckles, circa 1920s.
$5.00 – 50.00 each.

1. *Delineator*, August 1891; *Der Bazar*, January, May, July – September, November–December, 1891; *Peterson's Magazine*, January 1891; *Demorest's Family Magazine*, June 1891

Black chipped straw bonnet, violet and white silk flowers, curled black feathers, circa 1891.
$75.00 – 185.00.

Chipped straw bonnet with red and white silk flowers, shirring, and tan straw lacing, circa 1891.
$75.00 – 185.00.

Fashion Trends for the Year 1892

(Illustrated and Non-Illustrated)

- Double puffed upper sleeves
- Draped fabric on bodices
- High collars
- No bustles
- Open V-neck
- Rows of puffed sleeves
- Slight flare to the back
- Slight trains
- Straight skirts
- Tight lower sleeves
- Two full upper sleeves
- V and double pointed bodices
- V pointed bodices
- Wide waistbands [1]

Ivory silk gown with raised dots, fitted bodice with ruffled closure, wide drooped sleeves and wide ruffle of embroidered tulle three-quarter undersleeves, circa 1892 – 1893.
$1,200.00 – 3,750.00.

1. *Journal des Demoiselles,* July, September, November 1892; *Der Bazar,* January, March, June, August 1892

Fashion Trends for the Year 1893
(Illustrated and Non-Illustrated)

- A-line plain skirts
- Bodices with peplums
- Horizontal skirt ruffles
- Leg o'mutton sleeves
- Narrow lower sleeves
- Pointed bodices
- Pointed leg o'mutton sleeves
- Ruffled point oversleeves
- Slight flare in rear of skirt
- Top bulbous sleeves taper to elbows [1]

Orange-yellow silk brocade gown, brown chiffon epaulettes, gold metallic cording, three-dimensional floral beaded decoration of pink, green, and bronze glass beaded flowers, bronze glass beaded fringe, circa 1892.
$1,200.00 – 3,750.00.

Coffee colored silk taffeta gown with leg o'mutton sleeves and embroidered net lace collar, circa 1893.
$475.00 – 875.00.

Details of beaded decoration on the shoulders and back.

1. *Le Bon Ton and Le Moniteur de la Mode Monthly Report,* Fall 1893, October 1893; *L'Art de la Mode,* October – December 1893

Black satin bodice and skirt, leg o'mutton sleeves, wide metal buckle at the waistline, high collar, circa 1893. $190.00 – 360.00.

Very rare Christmas revels or fancy dress ball costume, perhaps with the theme of "Spring," bunches of forget-me-knots alongside dangling silk ribbons embroidered with metallic sequins and bells, circa 1893. $1,200.00 – 3,750.00.

Black silk faille taffeta capelet with embroidered and corded lace at the sleeves, circa 1893 – 1894. $150.00 – 500.00.

Details of a dress sleeve with dangling ribbons and bells, as seen on the previous page.

Wine silk satin dress, ivory brocade silk fichu collar and half sleeve cuffs, floral tape lace on the collar, spun glass beaded trim, circa 1893 – 1894. $875.00 – 1,100.00.

Rust silk taffeta gown with contrasting rust velvet sleeves and bodice front, leg o'mutton sleeves, circa 1893. $1,200.00 – 3,750.00.

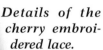

Details of the cherry embroidered lace.

Black satin dress with mustard brocade bodice insert, carnival glass iridescent beads in a leaf pattern and strands dangling at the waistline for a peplum effect, circa 1893.
$875.00 – 1,200.00.

Fashion Trends for the Year 1894

(Illustrated and Non-Illustrated)

- Double puffed elbow sleeves
- Double puffs on sleeves and sleeve caps
- Full skirts
- Fully shirred bodices

Black satin evening bodice, short sleeves, cherry and leaf embroidered lace, circa 1893 – 1894.
$600.00 – 1,875.00.

Gold and white silk brocade gown with ivory satin, wide collar, gigantic leg o'mutton sleeves, silver and glass pearl trim, overskirt effect, circa 1894.
$1,200.00 – 3,750.00.

- Gathered long trains with square or rounded corners
- Leg o'mutton sleeves covered with ruffled fabric
- Medium size leg o'mutton sleeves
- Sleeves are not tight at the elbow
- Tight lower sleeves
- Waists are slightly pointed [1]

Side view of gown with bows.

Silk taffeta dress, very large leg o'mutton sleeves, upper sleeve epaulets of ivory lace, ribbon streamers on skirt, elbows, shoulder, and waist, circa 1894. $1,200.00 – 3,750.00.

1. *Delineator*, September 1894; *Le Bon Ton et le Moniteur de la Mode United*, August 1894; *Young Ladies Journal*, March 1894

Rare ivory net dress with floral embroidery over a pink under-dress, rows of metallic tinsel trim on the collar, dress, and sleeves, circa 1894.
$1,200.00 – 3,750.00.

Details of tinsel gown sleeve.

*Ivory silk taffeta leg o'mutton sleeve dress,
shirred lace along the collar and bodice
front, lace ruffle and taupe bow epaulets,
matching cuff lace, taupe ribbon satin
belt, slight flared train, circa 1894.
$1,200.00 – 3,750.00.*

*Ivory silk satin wed-
ding gown, large leg
o'mutton sleeves, tight
fitting bodice, long train,
circa 1894.
$1,200.00 – 3,750.00.*

Victorian black straw hat with purple silk ruffles, olive green and purple striped ribbon backed with black velvet and twisted into large loops, black sequins, green feathers, circa 1894.
$125.00 – 285.00.

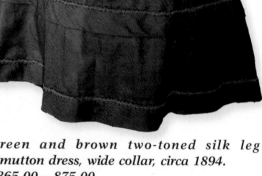

Purple silk dress with olive green ribbon sleeve and bodice trim, flatter leg o'mutton sleeves, circa 1894.
$475.00 – 850.00.

Green and brown two-toned silk leg o'mutton dress, wide collar, circa 1894.
$365.00 – 875.00.

Ivory silk gown, two tiered ruffled upper sleeves, tight lower sleeve, satin loops of ribbon on the bodice, mauve, pink, plum, and white crepe paper flowers on the skirt hem and epaulettes, circa 1894. $1,200.00 – 3,750.00.

Yellow satin ball gown with puffed sleeves, slight train, bow at waist, circa 1894. $1,200.00 – 3,750.00.

Details of crepe paper flowers on the skirt hem.

Ivory silk faille taffeta gown with wide chemical lace and netting collar, ribbon embroidery, double puffed upper sleeves, ruffled train, large satin bow at the waistline, circa 1894.
$1,200.00 – 3,750.00.

Back view of the sweeping train.

Ivory silk chiffon and satin ball gown with puffed sleeves, off the shoulder neckline, satin floral brocade fabric, fine skirt panel of sheer fabric with satin stripes, neckline of chiffon trimmed in lace and ruffled hemline, circa 1894.
$1,200.00 – 3,750.00.

Fashion Trends for the Year 1895

(Illustrated and Non-Illustrated)

- Full length skirts
- Large lace and velvet collars over the sleeves
- Leg o'mutton wide sleeves
- Narrow waists
- Peplums
- Sleeves are slightly bloused and tapered
- Tight lower sleeves
- Upper full sleeves gathered at elbow then tight at the cuff
- V or straight waistbands [1]

- Flat hats
- Full skirts with slight trains
- Huge puffed upper sleeves
- Huge sleeves that widen at the elbow
- Lace shirred over the sleeves
- Leg o'mutton tight lower sleeves
- Natural waists
- Small hats with high vertical trims
- Straight or elbow ruffle
- Tight sleeves
- Undersleeves
- Voluminously puffed leg o'mutton sleeves
- Wide V yokes
- Yoke collars [1]

Light brown silk taffeta gown with huge leg o'mutton sleeves, circa 1895. $365.00 – 875.00.

Fashion Trends for the Year 1896

(Illustrated and Non-Illustrated)

- A-line skirts
- Basque bodices
- Basque fitting coats
- Circular upper puffs

Plaid woolen leg o'mutton jacket, velvet upper collar and cuffs, circa 1896. $190.00 – 360.00.

Wedding or ball gown bodice of ivory silk satin, voluminously puffed sleeves, satin bow at the waist, circa 1896. $200.00 – 400.00.

1. *Standard Delineator,* September October 1895; *Le Bon Ton et Le Moniteur de la Mode,* November 1895

1. *Delineator,* February, March, June, December, 1896; *Standard Delineator,* January – May, July, August, 1896; *Toilettes Publishing Co.,* August, September, November 1896; *Young Ladies Journal,* January 1896

Huge leg o'mutton sleeved ivory silk wedding gown, high collar, wrap around waist, plain full train, bow on the side of the bodice, lace epaulettes over the large puffed sleeves, circa 1896.
$1,200.00 – 3,750.00.

Fashion Trends for the Year 1897

(Illustrated and Non-Illustrated)

- Boaters with vertical plumes and feathers
- Bulbous topped sleeves
- Crisscross lace
- Flat straw hats with feathers
- Gathered backs
- Jackets with low deep peplums
- Jackets with ruffles at the shoulder
- Jackets with tight sleeves
- Lower basque waists
- Narrow leg o'mutton sleeves
- Open jackets
- Peplum bodices
- Plain full skirts
- Princess waists
- Puffs narrow towards the wrist
- Puffy formal dresses
- Skirts edged with trim
- Skirts have trains
- Sleeves are smaller on top
- Sleeves have bows
- Slightly flared skirts
- Small leg o'mutton sleeves
- Straight waistbands
- Tapering full skirts
- Triangular points
- Vertical designs on hats
- Wings as hat decorations [1]

Black velvet short capelet with jet passementerie and dangles, circa 1897 – 1898.
$150.00 – 500.00.

Fine white batiste cotton dress, high collar, swag of white tulle with lace edging across the bodice, double ruffle of lace on the cuffs, circa 1897.
$365.00 – 745.00.

Ivory gauze fabric dress with black polka dots and red ribbon bodice embellishment, circa 1897.
$365.00 – 650.00.

1. *Standard Designer,* July, October, November 1897; *Young Ladies Journal,* February 1897; *Delineator,* January, April, June, October, November 1897

Beige and pink abstract print silk bodice, shirring, violet velvet ribbon striping, back neck bow, and ruffled cuffs, circa 1897. $450.00 – 600.00.

Powder blue silk floral brocade gown, ruffled sleeve tops, high collar, peplum, large hip bows, metallic trim and ribbon rosettes, cut steel and mother of pearl buttons, circa 1897. $875.00 – 1,200.00.

Side view of hip bows with metallic trim and ribbon rosettes.

Fashion Trends for the Year 1898

(Illustrated and Non-Illustrated)

- Ball gown overskirts
- Bows on collar backs
- Flaring sleeves
- Full skirts
- High collars
- High necklines
- High standup collars
- Overlapping ruffles on bodices
- Overlapping ruffles on skirts
- Peplums
- Ribbons on hats
- Shirred tight bodices
- Skirts with mermaid lower flare
- Sleeves taper from elbow to wrist
- Slightly puffed sleeves
- Slight trains
- V point bodices
- V waistlines
- Vertical feathers on hats
- Yokes [1]

Late nineteenth century ivory silk satin child's bonnet with stand-up ruffle and ribbon bows on the side.
$125.00 – 285.00.

Black velvet bows atop this toque hat trimmed with peach velvet, rhinestone embellishment, and ivory lace, circa 1898 – 1899.
$125.00 – 285.00.

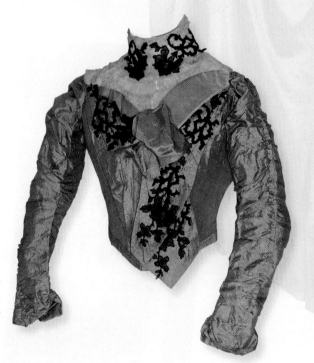

Textured light blue and yellow shirred change-able taffeta blouse, shirred cream chiffon, yellow velvet decoration, black floral lace appliques, and shirred sleeves, circa 1898.
$250.00 – 450.00.

1. *Delineator,* March, May, August, November 1898; *Standard Designer,* June 1898

*Rust velvet hat with high front tapering lower to the back, curly trimmed ribbons, sweeping ostrich feathers, circa 1898.
$125.00 – 285.00.*

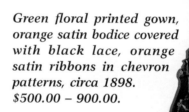

*Green floral printed gown, orange satin bodice covered with black lace, orange satin ribbons in chevron patterns, circa 1898.
$500.00 – 900.00.*

*Ivory Battenburg lace bodice, pigeon pouter waist, high collar, circa 1898 – 1899.
$250.00 – 365.00.*

Ivory point de gaze lace fan, mother of pearl gilded sticks, circa last half of the nineteenth century.
$50.00 – 250.00.

Girl's black cotton bodice, slightly puffed upper sleeves, red cotton yoke finely pleated, black braiding, circa 1898.
$50.00 – 100.00.

Fashion Trends for the Year 1899
(Illustrated and Non-Illustrated)

- Bodices with high collars
- Cinched waists
- Circular yokes with lace collars
- Circular yokes with ruffles
- Full skirts
- High neck stiffened collars
- Hourglass silhouettes
- Jacket waists cinched
- Jacket-like bodices
- Jackets with belted waists
- Jackets with embroidery
- Jackets with velvet lapels
- Large, high toque hats
- Narrow upper and lower sleeves
- No puffs on sleeves
- Peplum bodices
- Peplums curve down the back
- Shirred velvet hats with feathers
- Skirts flare at the bottom
- Small hats embellished with wire ribbon
- Tight straight sleeves
- Vertical lines
- Waists with yokes [1]

Boy's cap of woven straw and a blue ribbon band with bow, remnants of a blue pompom or bow on top, circa 1886 – 1900.
$75.00 – 265.00.

1. *La Mode du Petit Journal,* January, April, November 1899; *Delineator,* January, January – February, April – August, November – December 1899; *McCall's* Vol. XXVI No 4, December 1899; *Designer,* July – September, December 1899; *Journal des Demoiselles,* February 1899

Details of ivory satin wedding gown bodice with orange blossom clusters, circa 1899.

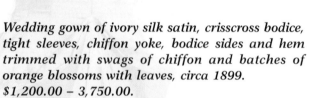

Wedding gown of ivory silk satin, crisscross bodice, tight sleeves, chiffon yoke, bodice sides and hem trimmed with swags of chiffon and batches of orange blossoms with leaves, circa 1899. $1,200.00 – 3,750.00.

Dove gray silk velvet gown, ivory chiffon bodice insert, cut work embroidered with silver metal sequins, asymmetrical wrap-around skirt closure, ruffled chiffon underskirt, embellished train, and Paris label, circa 1899. $1,200.00 – 3,750.00.

Fuchsia pink cotton bodice with shirred black netting overlay, ivory lace yoke, fuchsia pink ribbon embellishments, circa 1899. $200.00 – 400.00.

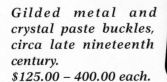

Black Chantilly lace fan embellished with silver metallic sequins, black ebony sticks, silver metal sequins inlaid into the sticks, circa 1890s – 1900s. $50.00 – 250.00.

Gilded metal and crystal paste buckles, circa late nineteenth century. $125.00 – 400.00 each.

The "Gibson Girl" was a popular icon in our culture. She represented a woman who radiated the beauty of a flower with her draped and puffed garments encasing and enveloping her in luxury. The decade before woman's suffrage was achieved, we indeed saw women placed on a pedestal to be idealized for their feminine charms and adored for their fine taste. The look was feminine and frilly. The coiffures incorporated massive upsweeps of hair topped with large hats dripping with feathers and flowers. Many types of lace and elaborate netting usually trimmed the high collars. Silks of all kind from bold patterns to delicate brocades made up the gowns of the day. Chiffon was a popular new fabric. Ruffles offered a new way to describe femininity. This was the era of the elaborate syncopation of ragtime alongside the beautiful fashions when women resembled delicate flowers.

Fashion Trends for the Year 1900

(Illustrated and Non-Illustrated)

- Banding
- Bodice V points
- High necks
- Hourglass looks
- Natural sleeves
- Princess line formals
- Sleeves at the three-quarter length tighten
- Small double puffs
- Stiff collars
- Upper sleeves
- V openings at bodices
- Waists tucked into waistband with belt [1]

Ivory satin wedding gown, deep chiffon ruffled collar edged in satin ribbon, ivory satin undersleeves, elbow ruffle, and chiffon ruffle at the bottom of the skirt, circa 1900.
$495.00 – 650.00.

Silk fan, hand painted, floral scene, metal sequins, circa 1900 – 1910.
$50.00 – 85.00.

Navy wool bathing suit with white stripes, two piece, circa 1900.
$150.00 – 180.00.

1. *Designer,* April, November, December 1900; *La Mode du Petit Journal,* September – December 1900; *Delineator,* March, May, July, August, November 1900

Fashion Trends for the Year 1901

(Illustrated and Non-Illustrated)

- Falling forward hats
- Hats made of twists of stiffened taffeta with flowers
- High neck collars
- Inserted lace strips
- Low evening necklines
- Narrow pleats on bodice and necklines
- Pigeon breasts
- Side bodice bows
- Sleeves full and narrow at the wrist cuffs
- Slightly curved back silhouette [1]

Black lace hat with silk feathers and horsehair sprays, circa 1901 – 1902. $150.00 – 200.00.

Light blue and cream abstract print silk satin dress with black ribbon and ivory lace inserts, yoke, and high collar, circa 1901. $495.00 – 750.00.

Brown wool dress with scrollwork revealing dark brown velvet underneath, cream under-sleeves, circa 1901. $495.00 – 750.00.

1. *La Mode du Petit Journal,* June 1901; *Edward Grossman & Co., Fall and Winter,* 1901 – 1902; *L'Art de la Mode et le Charm United,* November 1901; *Designer,* January, April, May, June, August, November, December, 1901

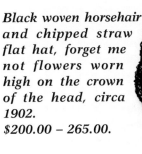

Black woven horsehair and chipped straw flat hat, forget me not flowers worn high on the crown of the head, circa 1902. $200.00 – 265.00.

Pink cotton printed dress, three tiered ruffled skirt, elbow and yoke ruffles, high collar, circa 1901. $245.00 – 575.00.

Fashion Trends for the Year 1903

(Illustrated and Non-Illustrated)

- Bird wings on hats
- Blouses fuller at the cuff
- Bodices droop
- Bodices with vertical pleats
- Eton jackets
- Flat and forward hats
- Flowers
- High collars
- Large hats
- Long sleeves
- Pigeon breasts
- Rear end of dresses protrude
- Rows of lace
- Ruffled sleeves
- Satin
- Shirred waists
- Skirts slinky and flared
- V neck yokes
- Velvet bows [1]

Fashion Trends for the Year 1902

(Illustrated and Non-Illustrated)

- Bishops sleeves
- Circular flounces
- Clinging gowns
- Form fitting skirts
- Louis XV coat bodices
- One or two graduated circular hem flounces
- Rippled and graduated skirts
- Serpentine skirts
- Shawl collars
- Short double–breasted jackets [1]

Huge Gibson Girl style hat, small crown, elliptically shaped brim protruding forward, shirred silk top and underside, circa 1903. $375.00 – 425.00.

1. *Delineator,* January 1902; *Designer,* October 1902; *Edward Grossman & Co., Fall and Winter* 1901 – 1902

1. *Designer,* January February, October, November, December 1903

Ivory silk taffeta gown with train, embroidered bodice, lace appliques, light blue ribbon loops and streamers, slightly drooped sleeves tighten at the elbow then puff and tighten at the cuff, pigeon breast, V shape neckline, satin banding ornamentation, circa late 1903.
$495.00 – 750.00.

White cotton batiste dress with painted flowers and ruffles of Valenciennes lace, circa 1903.
$290.00 – 635.00.

Details of floral painted decoration on the hem.

Green cotton dress, drooped cuffs, triangular caps on the shoulders, jacket bodice with high lace collar, Venice lace appliques on the skirt and bodice front, circa 1903. $325.00 – 795.00.

Fashion Trends for the Year 1904

(Illustrated and Non-Illustrated)

- Bodices with small pointed V's
- Cavalier hats
- Drop shoulder dress
- Fuller upper sleeves
- Hanging lace yokes
- Hats full and going forward
- Leg o'mutton sleeves
- Narrow bands of pleats on skirts
- Natural lower arms
- Receding pigeon breasts
- Rows of lace ruffled sleeves
- Rows of ruffled lace evening necklines
- Shirred and pleated waists
- Side feathers on hats
- Skirts with rows of layers
- Sleeves are similar to 1903
- Sleeves puff at the elbow
- Smaller hats with wide appearance
- Surplice waist
- Wide wrist lace flounces [1]

Silk brocade ivory dress with train, pigeon breasted bodice, sleeves that blouse above a high tight cuff, floral lace appliques of embroidered chiffon, circa 1903.
$675.00 – 785.00.

Linen duster with wide Venice lace collar, circa 1904.
$145.00 – 175.00.

1. *La Mode du Petit Journal*, February, March, August – December 1904; *Designer*, February – April, June, September, December 1904

Rust silk gown with high lace collar, rust silk ruffled trim, lace yoke, receding pigeon breast, circa 1904 – 1905.
$635.00 – 850.00.

Black velvet wide brim hat, Cavalier style with large ostrich plume, circa 1904.
$375.00 – 425.00.

Peacock blue bodice with black velvet straps and white lace ruffle, circa 1904 – 1906.
$145.00 – 290.00.

Fashion Trends for the Year 1905

(Illustrated and Non-Illustrated)

- Batiste
- Bird wings on hats
- Box jackets
- Dot embroidery
- Eton jackets
- Flowering prints
- Girdles

Black velvet toque hat, ostrich feather and jet orna-mentation, circa 1904.
$235.00 – 285.00.

- Hats with flowers underneath
- Hats with tilts on the side
- High necks
- Lace yokes
- Long sleeves
- Messaline
- Organdy frocks
- Pleated skirts
- Redingotes with and without peplums
- Rounded yokes
- Shapelier waists
- Sleeves narrow below elbow
- Two to three rows of flowers
- Upper sleeve puffs then tightens three-quarters down [1]

Woven straw hat with pink pressed velvet flowers and leaves gracing the top, circa 1905 – 1909. $265.00 – 375.00.

Gray sheer cotton dress with white lace yoke, embroidered trim at the hem, large puffed sleeves ending in a tight lower sleeves, circa 1905. $625.00 – 825.00.

Black silk chiffon dress with sloping shoulders, Chantilly lace embellishments in a scalloped design on the wide cuffs, hem, and jacket front, circa 1905. $825.00 – 1,365.00.

1. *La Mode du Petit Journal*, April, September, October, November, December, 1905; *Delineator*, April, June 1905

Black and white silk checkered gown with stripes of inserted black lace, circa 1905.
$290.00 – 495.00.

White linen bodice, crocheted buttons, Van Dyke collar, circa 1905.
$200.00 – 495.00.

Ivory silk taffeta blouse with a V yoke of embroidered floral lace, high neck collar, circa 1905.
$145.00 – 175.00.

Pink cotton and white net dress, overskirt of inserted lace, cotton netting printed with pink roses, double puffed sleeves, small pink velvet bows, circa 1905 – 1906.
$635.00 – 950.00.

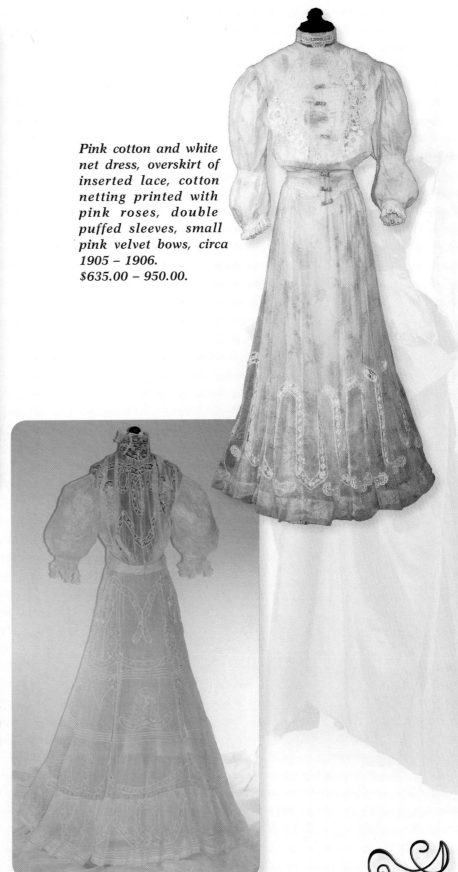

White taffeta and black Chantilly lace gown circa 1905.
$1,250.00 – 1,850.00.

White batiste gown, Valenciennes lace insertions, puffed sleeves ending in an elbow ruffle, circa 1905.
$495.00 – 785.00.

Fashion Trends for the Year 1906

(Illustrated and Non-Illustrated)

- Eton jackets
- Fichu berthas
- Panel skirts
- Pigeon breast bodices
- Puffed upper sleeves
- Ruffled elbows
- Six to eight gored skirts
- Three quarter lengths with cuffs
- Tucked shirtwaists
- Waists with shoulder straps [1]

Black silk velvet gown with lace inserts on the bodice, skirt, and sleeves, circa 1906.
$750.00 – 1,350.00.

White cotton batiste dress, wide lace collar with inserted Valenciennes lace, tiered skirt, puffed sleeves with lace ruffle at the elbow, circa 1906.
$195.00 – 245.00.

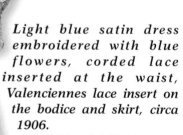

Light blue satin dress embroidered with blue flowers, corded lace inserted at the waist, Valenciennes lace insert on the bodice and skirt, circa 1906.
$825.00 – 1,450.00.

1. *Supplement to the Woman's Home Companion,* October 1906; *Le Theatre,* October 11, 1906; *Woman's Home Companion,* August 1906; *Designer,* July, August, November December 1906

Details of the lace embellishing on the skirt, as seen on the previous page.

Mustard crepe gown with hundreds of gold metal sequins strewn about the skirt, bodice, and sleeves, circa 1906.
$750.00 – 950.00.

Black lace gown over silk black under-skirt, elaborately studded with black sequins and heavy pearl beading, diagonal rows of ivory lace, netted sleeves, circa 1906.
$1,895.00 – 2,600.00.

Fashion Trends for the Year 1907

(Illustrated and Non-Illustrated)

- Bernhardt sleeves
- Drop V necklines
- Front slope hats
- Full soft skirts
- Full top sleeves
- Jumper dresses
- Jumper shirtwaist decorations
- Lingerie gowns
- Mikado (kimono style) sleeves
- Pigeon breasts
- Seven to eight gored skirts
- Sleeves full to elbow
- Top is puffed to elbow
- Waist and jumpers [1]

1. *Designer,* January – April, July, 1907

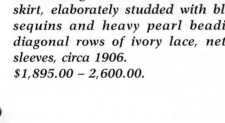

Black net lace dress over satin under-skirt, crisscross bodice, fringe and lace sleeves, circa 1907.
$1,650.00 – 1,850.00.

Ivory checkered iridescent taffeta with brown polka dots, Mikado or kimono style sleeves, brown satin cummerbund waist, and brown velvet ribbon accents on the bodice and neck, circa 1907.
$1,365.00 – 1,650.00.

This golden horsehair hat is decorated abundantly with silk roses. Provenance places this wedding hat at 1907.
$345.00 – 575.00.

Fashion Trends for the Year 1908

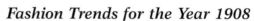

(Illustrated and Non-Illustrated)

- Ankle length dresses
- Flared skirts
- Gored skirts
- High collars
- Jumper dresses

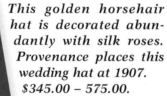

- Normal waistbands
- Pleated skirts
- Three-quarter sleeves
- Tilted hats with feathers [1]

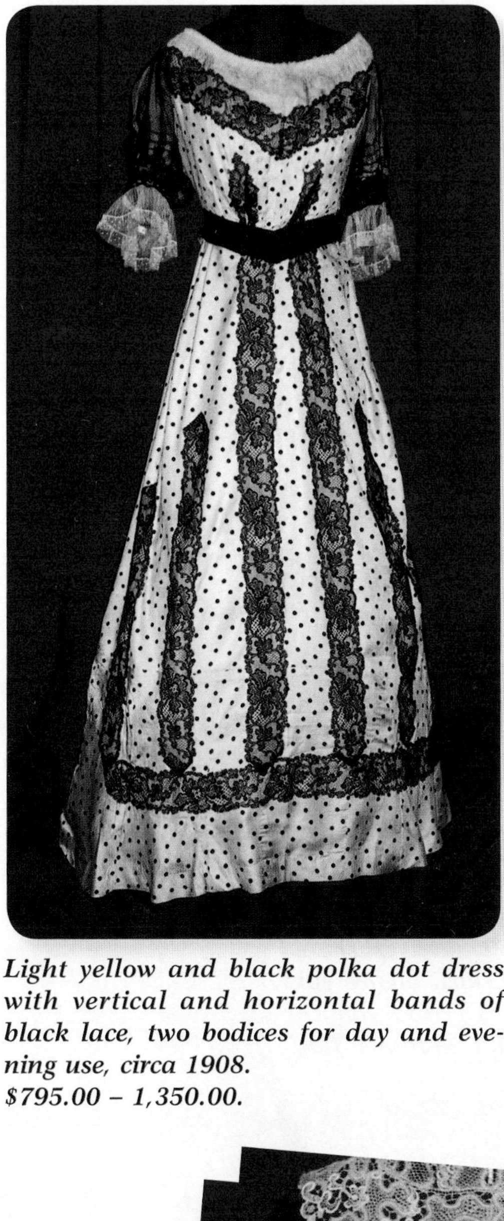

Light yellow and black polka dot dress with vertical and horizontal bands of black lace, two bodices for day and evening use, circa 1908.
$795.00 – 1,350.00.

Light olive green satin dress, sheer chiffon overlay, open collar, green satin, chiffon ruffles, and taffeta back bow, circa 1908.
$795.00 – 1,450.00.

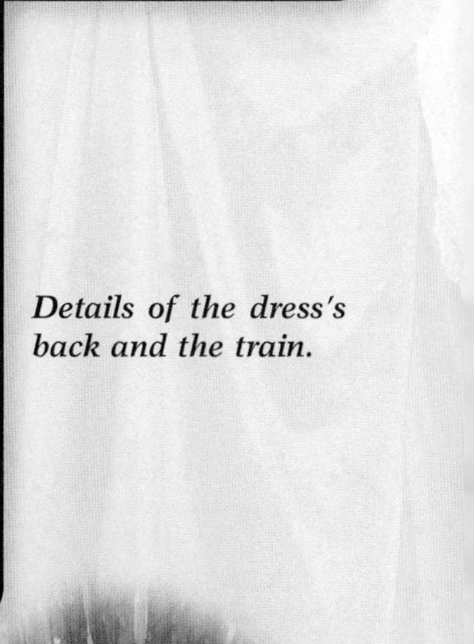

Details of the dress's back and the train.

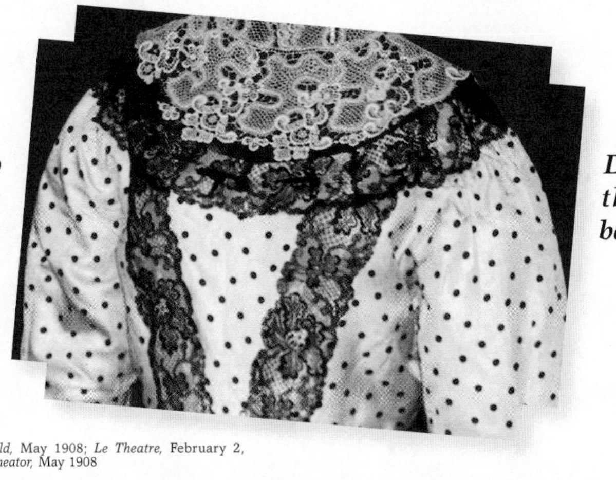

Details of day bodice allowing the wearer to transform their outfit from day to eveningwear and vice versa.

Details of the dress's back bow.

1. *Ladies World,* May 1908; *Le Theatre,* February 2, 1908; *Delineator,* May 1908

Fashion Trends for the Year 1909

(Illustrated and Non-Illustrated)

- Bands of lace
- Batiste
- Bodice sashes
- Dainty lingerie dresses
- Filet lace
- Heavily embroidered lace
- Huge hats
- Inserted lace
- Princess line dresses
- Side feathers on hats
- Tight sweeping skirts
- Tucked shirtwaists
- Yoke shirtwaists [1]

Lavender cotton dress with soutache, pleated white netting sleeves and collar, circa 1909. $300.00 – 450.00.

Black satin and crepe gown with brownish black Battenburg lace bodice and skirt inserts, circa 1909. $635.00 – 785.00.

Pink tissue silk gown with lines of embedded crocheted lace on the skirt, bodice yoke, and cuffs, silk roses on the rear bow and streamer ties, circa 1909. $1,485.00 – 1,850.00.

Details of pink tissue silk gown's back bow.

1. *Ladies World,* October 1909; *Le Theatre,* July, August, October, 1909; *Dress,* January 1909

Details of the back train, as seen on the previos page.

Blue printed brushed cotton dress, circle print, strips of lace on yoke and sleeves, circa 1909.
$250.00 – 300.00.

Polished cotton blue dress, ivory polka dots, crochet lace collar, lace appliques on the cuffs, circa 1909.
$250.00 – 300.00.

Ivory mixed lace dress, embroidered netting, circa 1909.
$825.00 – 1,365.00.

White cotton dress embroidered with flowers and bows at the skirt and bodice, circa 1909.
$675.00 – 795.00.

The 1910s ushered in an era of elegance and feminine emancipation. Women's clothing took on a sleek, more natural form. Fashionable beauties achieved their best looks through a complicated combination of layer over layer of glorious tulle, silk brocade, beaded trims and metallic laces. These magnificent wrappings covered the most elegant of society women. As women approached the coming of World War I, fashion took on a more utilitarian line with cleaner looks and less feminine frills. Women worked hard for many decades to obtain suffrage as they gained the vote in America by the end of the decade. Clothing of these times reflected the seriousness of war and the new practical role women were taking in the world outside of the home.

Fashionable changes during the decade include many fascinating and complex uses of luxury fabrics. Velvet gowns might be corded with soutache or embellished with beaded trims. Dress lines included classically inspired tunics with multi-layers. Drapery and embellishment of lace, embroidered tulle and fabric panels offered a new dimension that enveloped the feminine form. The 1910s were elegant and sophisticated. World War I gave women more activities and jobs outside of their home lives. Women needed a more tailored form and serious business-like appearance. Dresses during the war years were streamline and sensitive to sober tastes. Ladies still looked totally lovely in complicated fashions of those years. Hats begin in the early part of the decade as magnificently huge creations. Over time, they become lower, smaller and more delicate.

Black velvet gown with soutache braiding, circa 1910 – 1911.
$865.00 – 1,250.00.

Fashion Trends for the Year 1910

(Illustrated and Non-Illustrated)

- Asymmetrical bodice closures
- High tab neck inserts
- Huge feathered toques
- Princess lines
- Round plain collars
- Shirred bodices
- Straps and modesty panels
- Vertical shoulder bodices
- Waist bands
- Waistlines slightly raised
- Wide brim hats [1]

Gold beaded and embroidered collar, circa 1910 – 1912.
$50.00 – 75.00.

1. *Delineator*, October 1910; *Ladies Home Journal*, October 1910

Details of train embellishments.

Black Chantilly lace and ivory silk satin trained gown with pearl and rhinestone ornament, purple velvet and satin ribbon trims, white netting, circa 1910 – 1911.
$2,700.00 – 3,450.00.

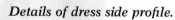

Details of dress side profile.

Black lace dress with white satin underskirt, pleated lace shoulders, brown and clear spun glass beads, circa 1910.
$865.00 – 1,250.00.

Black chiffon blouse with various types of laces under the see-through top, pearls at the cuffs and collar, circa 1910.
$150.00 – 225.00.

White cotton eyelet dress in a scrolled pattern, scallops, inserted lace bands, white embroidered flowers, circa 1910.
$200.00 – 350.00.

Navy and ivory silk print dress with ivory lace neckpiece, circa 1910.
$185.00 – 325.00.

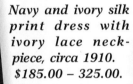

Green silk taffeta gown with ivory lace embellishments, circa 1910.
$225.00 – 285.00.

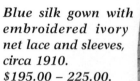

Blue silk gown with embroidered ivory net lace and sleeves, circa 1910.
$195.00 – 225.00.

Gray silk brocaded dress, asymmetrical closure, orange silk waistband, cut steel beads, orange trim, gray lace, circa 1910.
$325.00 – 485.00.

Ivory muslin dress with lace insertion, circa 1910 – 1911.
$125.00 – 150.00.

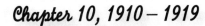

Taupe cotton and white lace dress,
circa 1910 – 1911.
$150.00 – 225.00.

Ivory silk wedding gown, overskirt
ending in a deep point, waist and
neck scarf embroidered with silver
beads, circa 1910.
$285.00 – 345.00.

White cotton voile dress
with ribbon rosettes and
lace trim on the skirt,
bodice, and cuffs, circa
1910 – 1911.
$345.00 – 425.00.

Fashion Trends for the Year 1911
(Illustrated and Non–Illustrated)

- Jumper tops
- Long close fitting skirts
- Sailor collars
- Simple capes
- Spiked aigrettes
- Straight sleeves
- Three-quarter elbow sleeves
- Two to three overlapping bands on skirts
- Upturned side brims
- Wide straw hats [1]

Musketeer style hat with a cockade of bright green and black feathers, jet ornamentation, upturned side brim, plush velvet resembling beaver, circa 1911.
$175.00 – 225.00.

Ivory silk wedding gown, fishtail train that ends in a mermaid tail point, lace sleeves and drapery over the bodice, iridescent spun glass beaded bodice ornament, circa 1911.
$1,500.00 – 3,250.00.

Picture hat musketeer style with cascading ostrich feather, jet ornamentation resembling bird feathers and plush velvet resembling beaver, circa 1911.
$175.00 – 225.00.

1. *Life Cover*, December 7, 1911; *Delineator*, January 1911; *Theatre Magazine*, April, July, September 1911; *Designer*, April 1911

Ivory crepe wedding gown, lace drapery on the bodice, hem, and cuffs, overskirt with swag and glass pearl embellishments, circa 1911. $1,200.00 – 1,900.00.

Peach satin bandeau or headpiece with silver glass beads, strands of glass ivory pearls, white ostrich feather and rhinestone hat pin, circa 1911. $175.00 – 225.00.

Ivory silk wedding gown, asymmetrical overskirt drapery, wide shirred waistband, net sleeves that end in points with beaded tassels, embroidery of light brown leaves and silver beads which have oxidized over time, circa 1911. $1,425.00 – 1,600.00.

Details of skirt embroidery and beadwork.

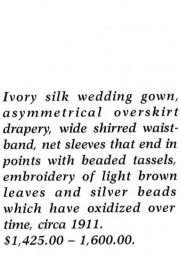

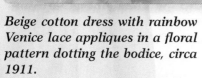

Turquoise blue silk satin gown with ivory lace cuffs and modesty insert, orange ribbon trim, sequin panels, and rhinestone trims, circa 1911.
$1,600.00 – 3,450.00.

Beige cotton dress with rainbow Venice lace appliques in a floral pattern dotting the bodice, circa 1911.
$135.00 – 225.00.

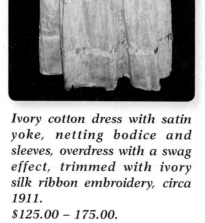

Ivory cotton dress with satin yoke, netting bodice and sleeves, overdress with a swag effect, trimmed with ivory silk ribbon embroidery, circa 1911.
$125.00 – 175.00.

Details of rhinestone trimmed lace cuff.

Details of rhine-stone and lace embellished neck-line, as seen on the previous page.

Ivory silk gown with checkerboard design, embroidery, heavy netting sleeves, glass beading, circa late 1911.
$445.00 – 565.00.

Details of sequin and beaded embroidered panel, as seen on the previous page.

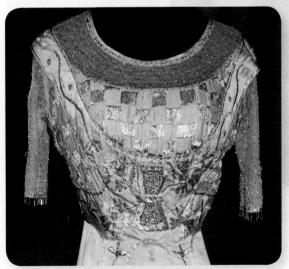

Details of checkerboard design bodice.

Ivory netting overdress with satin stitch floral and polka dot embroidery, circa 1911. $575.00 – 750.00.

Ivory silk wedding dress with detachable train, lace and netting over bodice, lace and embroidered train, circa 1911. $1,900.00 – 2,500.00.

Details of detachable train done in buttery soft silk satin with Art Nouveau style metallic embroidered flowers.

Bicorn hat of brown velvet ornamented with puffs of brown feathers, circa 1911. $175.00 – 225.00.

Fashion Trends for the Year 1912

(Illustrated and Non-Illustrated)

- Bodices look like long coats
- Necklines are open and wider
- Shawl sleeves
- Slats down skirts
- Vertical feathers on hats
- Very huge hats
- Very slim straight skirts with lines zigzagging
- Very wide hats with showers of feathers [1]

Huge black straw hat with standing cockade of rust brown colored feathers, circa 1912.
$245.00 – 375.00.

Fashion Trends for the Year 1913

(Illustrated and Non-Illustrated)

- Broken and irregular lines
- Hobble skirts
- Lower back tail to dress bodice
- Robe style bodices
- Skirts narrow at ankle
- Tiers and drapes on skirt [2]

Fashion Trends for the Year 1914

(Illustrated and Non-Illustrated)

- Braided trim
- Deep girdles
- Fan collars
- Flowing dresses
- Hats with bird wings
- Hip panels
- Long line redingotes
- Long skirts
- Looser tops
- Military looks
- Rows of flounced lace
- Ruffle at lower jumper peplum
- Scarf sash ties at the hip or waist
- Skirts that drape at the hip
- Three-quarter in length ruffled sleeves
- Tight fitting skirts
- Triple shoulder pleats
- Tunic gowns in brocaded silk
- Tunic gowns in velvet
- Two rows of side ruffles
- Vertically high hats
- Very narrow bubble skirts
- Wide hip effects
- Wide waistbands are past the hips [1]

White chiffon skirt, black lace overlay, upside down V cut trimmed with black beads, silver beads, rhinestones, circa 1913 – 1914.
$100.00 – 225.00.

1. *L'Art de la Mode,* January 1912; *Woman's Home Companion,* March, 1912; *Delineator,* January 1912; *McCall's Magazine,* November & December 1912
2. *McCall's Magazine,* December 1913; *Ladies Home Journal,* November 1913; *Delineator,* December 1913

1. *Delineator,* September 1914; *McCall's Magazine,* January, May November 1914; *Grand Luxe Parisien,* Supplement to 1914 – 1915 No. 65; *Gazette du Bon Ton,* No. 2, February 1914 Plate 16; *Journal des Dames et des Modes,* 1914 plate #82

Black hat of horsehair ruffles and vertical ostrich plumes, circa 1914.
$175.00 – 225.00.

Day robe with narrow hem, wide hips, lace cuffs with tassel trim, circa 1914.
$175.00 – 325.00.

Fashion Trends for the Year 1915

(Illustrated and Non-Illustrated)

- A-line skirts
- Ankle length dresses
- Braided trim
- Jumper looks
- Overhanging bodices
- Peplum vest looks
- Russian suits
- Side pockets
- Sleeves that cuff slightly
- Three-quarter sleeves with flared ruffle
- Uncle Sam looking coats [1]

Woven horsehair and tulle hat, transparent brim with scrolled ornamentation and scalloped horsehair, pink bunches of flowers, circa 1914.
$165.00 – 245.00.

1. *Delineator,* June & October 1915; *Woman's Home Companion,* January 1915; *McCall's,* November 1915; *L'Album Tailleur de la Femme Chic,* 1915

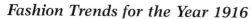

Fashion Trends for the Year 1916
(Illustrated and Non-Illustrated)

- Empire styles
- Half way down calf skirt lengths
- High fold down collars
- High small asymmetrical hats
- Loose skirts with two flying panels
- Pointed lapel collars
- Princess styles
- Rounded yoke collars
- Skirts shorter and fuller
- Tunic style dresses [1]

Black velvet hat with upturned brim, feather aigrette, and white beading, circa 1915 – 1916.
$195.00 – 225.00.

Black satin toque with braided ribbon and feather curl over short brim, circa 1916 – 1919.
$175.00 – 225.00.

Silk brocade gown, high waistband, tulle bordered square neckline and sleeves, circa 1915.
$950.00 – 1,200.00.

Ivory tulle gown with multi-layered skirt, ribbon flower embellishment, silver thread floral embroidery on the tulle, circa 1916.
$1,600.00 – 3,450.00.

1. *Delineator,* February & December 1916; *Le Costume Royale,* November 1916; *Butterick Fashions,* Summer 1916

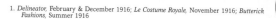

Salmon pink silk dress with ivory netting overlay, ribbon trim, metallic embroidery, circa 1916.
$595.00 – 865.00.

- Skirts between knee and ankle
- Surplice waists
- Trapeze dresses
- Underskirts flared
- Vertical bows
- Very full skirt [1]

Wide brim gold lamé crowned hat with silk flowers, transparent brim fashioned from gold metallic lace and black tulle over horsehair, circa 1917.
$165.00 – 245.00.

Fashion Trends for the Year 1917

(Illustrated and Non-Illustrated)

- Asymmetrical lines
- Exaggerated A shape
- Flat wide brim hats
- Frog closure
- High open necks
- High upturned brim hats
- Huge exaggerated hats
- Jumpers
- Military look
- Round lacy frills
- Sheer net hats

Reminiscent of the kind of headdress Cleopatra would wear, this elaborate headpiece resembles a snake made of pearls and crystal seed beads embellished with veiling made of gold metallic lace, circa 1917.
$375.00 – 525.00.

1. *Ladies Home Journal,* April 1917; *McCall's,* October 1917; *Delineator,* November 1917; *People's Home Journal,* May 1917

Black net hat, spider web shape, ornamented by ostrich feather plumes, circa 1917.
$145.00 – 275.00.

Rare gold lamé and black velvet gown, tulle bodice and sleeves, gold lamé fringe, asymmetrical panel, glass bead embellishments, circa 1917. Label: Henri Bendel.
$2,000.00 – 4,000.00.

Black satin dress with clear beaded overlay and beaded tassels on the sleeves, circa 1917.
$625.00 – 865.00.

Black Battenburg lace and netting sheer dress, circa 1917 – 1918.
$550.00 – 625.00.

Black beaded dress with beaded netting green silk velvet ribbon and black glass beaded fringe, circa 1917.
$1,175.00 – 3,450.00.

Brown silk brocade gown, wide waist band belt with vertical bow, metallic lace insert, ivory net dickey with stand up collar and wide fold down collar, lace cuffs, circa 1917.
$425.00 – 880.00.

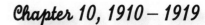

Ivory satin and lace overlay wedding dress, circa 1917. $395.00 – 485.00.

Ivory dress with black lace overlay embroidered heavily with black glass seed beads in a floral pattern, circa 1917 – 1918. $250.00 – 400.00.

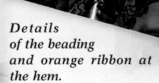

Details of the beading and orange ribbon at the hem.

White satin dress with black net overlay trimmed in orange ribbon, black beads, and sequins, circa 1917 – 1918. $1,600.00 – 1,850.00.

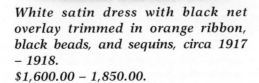

Black satin gown with black lace overlay, blue underbodice, net sleeves, and iridescent sequins in a matching shade of blue, circa 1917.
$1,100.00 – 1,600.00.

Detail of the blue sequin trim.

Gold lace and pink silk bodice with ribbon flower trim, circa 1917.
$395.00 – 520.00.

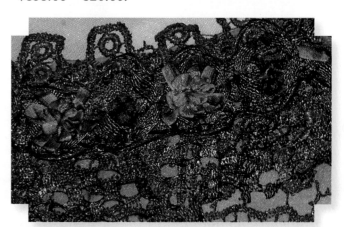

Details of the gold metallic lace with ribbon flower trim.

Fashion Trends for the Year 1918

(Illustrated and Non-Illustrated)

- Armistice collars
- Back ties
- Crisscross bodices
- Fabric folds
- Higher hats
- Jumper style dresses
- Narrow skirts and dresses
- Side panels
- Skirts inches above the ankle
- Skirts are straight but widen slightly at the hips
- Skirts with overlapping panels
- Square necklines
- Straighter lines
- Wide waistbands [1]

1. *Ladies Home Journal,* February 1918; *McCall's,* April 1918, June 1918; *Delineator,* May & November 1918

Yellow silk gown remade from a circa 1886 gown, triangular tufts of piled velvet, circa 1918.
$745.00 – 880.00.

Black lace dress with deep satin hem and waistband, circa 1918.
$550.00 – 625.00.

Fashion Trends for the Year 1919
(Non-Illustrated)

- Ankle lengths
- Jumper looks
- Low waistlines
- Semi-fitted dresses
- Severely simple collars
- Side skirts flare below the hips and tighten at the ankles
- Soutache braid
- Tie on basques
- Tie on dresses
- Vests [1]

Rust silk and velvet dress with side panels, circa 1918.
$185.00 – 275.00.

Metallic and colorfully embroidered, this tapestry purse has enameled closures, circa 1915 – 1925.
$75.00 – 150.00.

1. *B. Altman's & Co.*, Summer Apparel May 15 – June 25, Winter Suggestions 1919; *McCall's*, February 1919

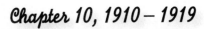

Blue cotton printed dressing gown trimmed with cotton candy pink and ruffles of ecru lace, circa 1910 – 1919. $125.00 – 175.00.

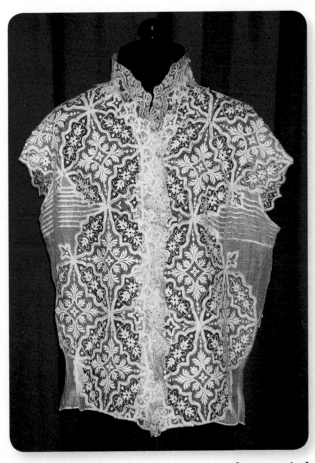

Ivory chemical lace vest, circa early twentieth century. $85.00 – 125.00.

he 1920s represented the Jazz Age and most of the Art Deco period. The decade began at the end of the Great War, bringing prosperity and peace. The decade ended with the stock market crash of 1929 signaling the next decade's Great Depression. The Roaring Twenties was a time of liberation for the feminine form. Women's clothing became more comfortable and simplistic. The simplicity did not imply a deficit of sumptuous fabrics or styles in dress or accessories.

The flapper proudly showed her liberation from feminine constraints placed on her Victorian and Edwardian grandmothers and mothers. She bobbed her hair, rolled down her stockings and shockingly danced the Charleston in a fringed beaded gown. Her bobbed hair brought about the invention of a new hat, the cloche. Cloches were helmet-shaped hats, elaborately adorned with embroidery, applique or beading. Ladies clothing adopted the severe angular lines of the Art Deco period. An interest in luxury brought a renewed interest in chiffon, which was worn twenty years earlier. Such fabrics provided the flapper with the means of achieving an ethereal, floating silhouette.

Flappers were both innocent and romantic in their dress. They visually displayed the austere lines of Art Deco fashions. A profusion of beading, metallic lace and embroidery made the simplistic and angular lines of their garments come alive. Women were breaking away from the constraining corsets and elaborately trimmed costumes of the Edwardian era. They developed a bold and saucy look that makes us reminisce fondly about the fun and wild social excesses of the Jazz Age.

Fashion Trends in the Year 1920

(Illustrated and Non-Illustrated)

- Deep U-shaped dress fronts
- Diagonal lines
- Dresses are wide at the hips
- Dresses with three-quarter length overdresses
- Five flounces
- Fur collars are tied with ribbons
- Fur girdles
- Overdresses with low waist effect
- Rounded long collars
- Separate fur collars of fur or feathers
- Seven flounces
- Side panels with embroidery

- Side pannier cascades
- Side ruffles
- Skirt hems
- Skirts end at the middle calf length
- Skirts taper at the bottom
- Skunk fur pieces with eyes
- Soutache
- Tunic tops with belts
- Two piece skirts
- Uneven tunics
- Yokes on dresses [1]

Garnet glass bead swag style purse, knitted strands of glass beads with a special silver hinge that opens up to a square shape, circa 1920s.
$225.00 – 400.00.

Rhinestone headpiece with oval center and vertical bands, circa 1920 – 1929.
$500.00 – 650.00.

1. *McCall's Magazine*, February 1920

Rhinestone headpiece with scrollwork, circa 1920 – 1929. $500.00 – 650.00.

Ivory taffeta under-skirt with rows and rows of silver metallic net embroidery covering the bodice and skirt, circa 1920 – 1924. $1,245.00 – 1,645.00.

Rhinestone headband with angular Art Deco motif, circa 1920 – 1929. $500.00 – 650.00.

Rhinestone headpiece with floral and butterfly motifs, circa 1920 – 1929. $500.00 – 650.00.

Rhinestone tiara with floral and leaf motif, circa 1920 – 1929. $650.00 – 845.00.

Rhinestone tiara with scroll motifs, circa 1920 – 1929.
$650.00 – 845.00.

Fashion Trends for the Year 1921

(Illustrated and Non-Illustrated)

- Apron tunic dresses
- Back and side bows
- Beading on dresses
- Belts at the waistline
- Child's pantalets dresses
- Circular flared cuffs
- Circular flounces
- Close to the waist fullness at the hips
- Coat dresses
- Corded panels
- Dresses embroidered in swirls
- Dresses with skirts that widen
- Embroidered abstracts
- Embroidered dashes
- Embroidered flowers
- Empire kimonos
- Fichu collars
- Flat tricorn hats
- Floppy upturned bows
- Flying dress panels
- Fuller overskirts
- Fur trim on dresses
- Gathered fabric
- Hats with feathers on the sides
- Hats with wide brims
- High square collars
- Hip adornments
- House dress and matching caps
- Kimono and bell sleeves
- Long bodied redingotes
- Loose baggy bodices
- One piece frocks full at the hips
- Pelts on coats
- Pointed panel skirts
- Short kimono sleeves with and without cuffs
- Skirt length below the knee
- Skirts at the mid-calf length
- Skirts have an extra side and ruffled flaps
- Slight fur trim
- Slightly wider skirts
- Slip-on dresses
- Smocking at the hips
- Soft tunics
- Straight pleats
- Sunbonnets
- Surplice tie on bodice
- Tied belts
- Tunic dresses
- Tunic tops
- Tunics with cascades
- Tunics with draperies on the sides [1]

Navy blue dotted Swiss dress with netted lace and bobbin lace inserts on the collars and cuffs, circa 1920 – 1922.
$145.00 – 215.00.

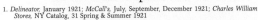

1. *Delineator,* January 1921; *McCall's,* July, September, December 1921; *Charles William Stores,* NY Catalog, 31 Spring & Summer 1921

Rear view of a bicorn of brown velvet with lace embellished insert, circa 1921.
$158.00 – 185.00.

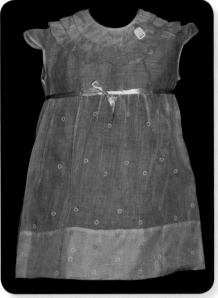

Child's powder blue starched gauze dress embroidered with polka dots, ribbon belt, three-tiered ruffled yoke collar, embroidered blue and white circles, original tag attached, circa 1921 – 1924.
$55.00 – 75.00.

Sheer white organdy dress with scalloped ruffled hem, puffed sleeves trimmed with lace and a circular bodice with rows of Valenciennes insertion lace trimming, circa 1921 – 1922.
$375.00 – 425.00.

Black crepe dress with hip shirring and ties, abstract embroidery on the cuffs and waist front panel of the bodice, circa 1921.
$258.00 – 375.00.

Fashion Trends for the Year 1922

(Illustrated and Non-Illustrated)

- Beaded embroidery
- Blouse coats
- Bouffant silhouettes
- Children's jumper dresses
- Coats with stuffed tube trim
- Colonial line shoes
- Dresses with bright braid trim and embroideries
- Dresses with collars
- Flying panels
- Front bodice panels
- Gold lace
- Gold roses
- Hats have rooster feathers
- Hip blouses
- Indian coral
- Lamé metal cloth
- Lattice trims
- Long collars
- Long tongued sandals
- Loose side panels
- Lots of side drapery
- Low belts
- Low waists
- Modesty panels
- Mousquetaire hats have turned up brims
- Russian closings
- Russian influences
- Sash aprons
- Side pleats and V necklines
- Tricorn hats
- Uneven hemlines [1]

Flapper evening gown, gold lamé fabric topped with gold lace, navy satin skirt, inserted gold lace band, teal and navy silk belt sash with hip ties, circa 1922 – 1923.
$845.00 – 1,625.00.

Ladies' navy sailor hat fashioned from wool with real fur pompoms, circa 1922 – 1923.
$75.00 – 150.00.

Child's brown velvet jumper dress, dropped waist, yellow dickey, brown and cream polka dot sailor collar, circa 1922 – 1923.
$55.00 – 85.00.

Art Deco style beaded purses with filigree frame clasps, circa 1920s.
$125.00 – 300.00 each.

1. *Delineator*, September 1922

Fashion Trends for the Year 1923

(Illustrated and Non-Illustrated)

- Arm hole slits ending in floppy points
- Arm hugging pagoda sleeves
- Back of dresses swung around lower
- Banding at the hips
- Birds on monograms
- Black and yellow on pink prints
- Blouses are sarong style
- Bloused tops
- Boat necks with no waists
- Brocade resembling the seventeenth century
- Butterflies on monograms
- Camisole tops
- Cascade draperies
- Cascade side drapery
- Checkered dresses
- Circular skirts fall in irregular ways
- Crepe dresses
- Cross stitch embroidery
- Curricular loops of ruffled ribbon
- Day wraparound dresses in prints
- Draped or circular dresses
- Drawn work running through twisted girdles
- Drawn work trim
- Drop shoulder yokes
- Embroidered wide filet lace
- Embroidery in cross stitch
- Embroidery with beads and metal threads
- Eton jackets
- Faire Isle style sweaters
- Fancy girdles at the waistline
- Fine pleats from the sides of the dress
- Fitted basques
- Flat cuffs
- Flowered or figured silk
- Fur trimmed dresses
- George Washington Ball dresses
- Girdles stuffed with tubing
- Gold lace with black and gold
- Hip and side chest bows
- Hip bands
- Hip panniers
- Hip pockets
- Hip sacks tied at the side
- Hips tied with ribbons and narrow belt
- Jabot drapery
- Jacket blouses
- Kerchief collars
- Knickerbockers for girls
- Lace hats

- Lace rosette circles on girl's dresses
- Large portrait hats
- Layered clingy skirts
- Left side draped dresses
- Long accordion pleated skirts
- Long hanging lapel collars
- Long pointed chiffon sleeves
- Long portrait collars
- Long waist draped frocks
- Long wide skirts and wide sleeves
- Loose bodices
- Metallic lace on blouses
- Metallic lace resembling cobwebs
- Monogrammed embroidery
- Open collars
- Open work yokes
- Ornament goes around dresses
- Overdresses with straight lower points and slip
- Panel drapes and ornament on dress fronts
- Paper oriental umbrellas
- Peacocks on monograms
- Pearl tassels
- Pilgrim cuffs
- Plaids
- Plaited panels
- Polka dot dresses
- Printed crepe dresses
- Ribbon flowers and bows on girls' dresses
- Sack blouses
- Sailor outfits
- Sateen evening dresses
- Side drapery
- Side panels on tunics
- Side pleats
- Silver or gold thread ornament
- Silver straight evening dresses with metal gauze
- Skirt length half way up the calf
- Skirts that narrow at the hem
- Skirts with side bows
- Skirts with side flowers
- Slip on long waist blouses
- Soft drapes at the hips
- Straight chemise dresses blouse over narrow belts
- Straight lines downward from the shoulders
- Straight tube dresses
- Stuffed tubing in girdles
- Summer brides have low waistlines and twisted girdles with a flower
- Three or four tiered skirts
- Three-quarter length flared coats

- Tie on blouses
- Tiered skirts with drapery and flouncing
- Tight pleats
- Tops have droopy collars
- Transparent bertha collars
- Two tier straight skirts
- Venetian seventeenth century style tricorns
- Waistline just below the waist
- White collars and cuffs
- Wide plain yoke collars [1]

Taupe silk blouse embroidered with abstract motifs and floral designs typical of the Arts and Crafts movement going into the Deco period, circa 1923. $98.00 – 125.00.

Girl's peach silk crepe dress, off the shoulder collar, ribbon rosettes, three tiered skirt ruffles, dropped waistline, neck tied with ribbon streamer, circa 1923. $85.00 – 158.00.

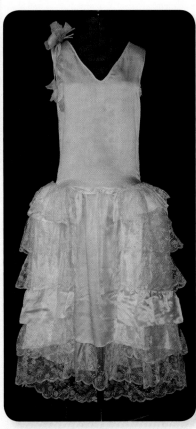

Satin wedding dress with hip panniers in the style of Lanvin of Paris, rows of ruffled lace, hip panniers with built in support at the hip to extend out the left and the right sides of the hips, flower corsage at the shoulder, circa 1923. $1,645.00 – 2,850.00.

1. *Pictorial Review,* January 1923; *Delineator,* February, March, April September, November 1923; *Butterick Quarterly,* Summer 1923; *Gimbel's Thrift Book,* Spring and Summer 1923, *McCall's Magazine,* April 1923

Brown chiffon dress with wide cape collar and full sleeves that puff at the cuff, wide crochet lace ornamentation, circa 1923. $550.00 – 625.00.

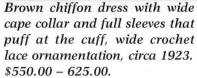

Fashion Trends for the Year 1924

(Illustrated and Non-Illustrated)

- Beading
- Box plaits
- Buttons for trims
- Chinese collars
- Convertible collar tops, double breasted
- Double flounces
- Dresses and skirts both long and straight
- Dresses gathered at the yoke
- Embroidered flower designs
- Jumpers
- Marabou trims
- Pleated frills
- Ribbed weaves
- Ribbons on dresses
- Scalloped hems
- Straight new silhouettes
- Straight pleated ruffles
- Tunic dresses
- Tunic styles [1]

Ivory chiffon dress with silver and white glass beads in floral scroll patterns. The bottom of the skirt is trimmed with rows of silver gray beads that have oxidized. The fringe is in two layers. The dress is shown with a silk lace net stole, circa 1924 – 1925.
$2,200.00 – 3,500.00.

Child's straw helmet cloche with ribbon and buckle, circa 1924.
$78.00 – 125.00.

Detail of beaded skirt fringe.

White cotton sailor style dress, triangle pockets at the waist's center, asymmetrical red trimmed collar, bows on sleeves, slightly flared skirts, circa 1924 – 1925.
$165.00 – 265.00.

1. *Designer,* December 1924

Straw slouching flapper cloche with sage satin bands, rust faux cornflower flowers and leaves, circa 1924.
$158.00 – 175.00.

Gray chiffon formal dress with gray sequins, silver beads, and rhinestones. The beadwork is in a leaf pattern throughout the straps and bodice. The skirt bottom is made of solid gray sequins, circa 1924 – 1925.
$2,850.00 – 3,500.00.

Detail of gray sequins.

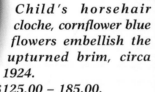

Child's horsehair cloche, cornflower blue flowers embellish the upturned brim, circa 1924.
$125.00 – 185.00.

Straw cloche with mustard velvet appliqued leaf shapes, raised band, and asymmetrical back bow, circa 1924.
$125.00 – 175.00.

Tan straw cloche with black edging, emerald green and olive green embroidery fashioned from folded feathers, faux diamond stick pin, circa 1924. $125.00 – 175.00.

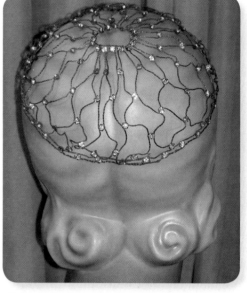

Crystal rhinestone skull cap with thread covered in gold metal, circa 1910s to 1920s. $775.00.

Ivory chiffon formal dress, white glass beaded flowers at the neck, waistline, skirt, beaded flaps, and chiffon underskirt, circa 1924 – 1925. $525.00 – 645.00.

Fashion Trends for the Year 1925

(Illustrated and Non-Illustrated)

- A-line silhouettes
- Adding side georgette panels
- Back flares
- Basque dresses
- Belts absent from dresses
- Borders for dresses
- Bouffant formals in crepes and satins
- Boyish collars
- Cascade trims
- Circular skirts
- Cloche helmet hats
- Close fitting hats
- Crochet sweaters
- Deeper pleats
- Dress bottoms are not straight
- Embroidered bands
- Embroidered outlines of flowers
- Embroidered scarves
- Empire flares in formalwear
- Eton dress
- Flared dresses
- Flared skirts
- Flowered embroidery in straight stitch
- Formal tops and straight bottoms
- Fur trims
- Harmonizing materials
- Higher waist basque waists

- Inserted godets
- Jumpers
- Kimono sleeves
- Knife pleating
- Less tubular shapes
- No huge sprawling prints
- No large designs in prints
- Overdresses
- Plaits and flares
- Poke turbans
- Printed crepes and georgette
- Roses and small flowers
- Side drapery
- Skirts with close patterns
- Slashes and contrasting undersleeves
- Slip-on blouses
- Smocking with colored threads
- Straight line coats
- Straight line dress
- Straight tops
- Swerved lace hems
- Tunics with drooping shoulders
- Turtle neck over blouses [1]

Salmon pink chiffon flapper shift dress edged in brown fur on the collar, hem, and in the hanging openwork sleeves, circa 1925 – 1926.
$200.00 – 300.00.

Micro-beaded purses, metallic colored beads, circa 1920s.
$100.00 – 200.00 each.

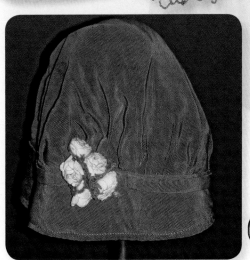

Ivory cotton dress with light blue collar, cuffs, drop waist insert decoration, and pockets, circa 1925.
$100.00 – 225.00.

Brown rayon girl's cloche with silk flowers, circa 1925 – 1926.
$85.00 – 150.00.

1. *Designer,* January, February, August, October 1925; *McCall's Magazine,* October, 1925;
The Charles William Stores Catalog, New York, Fall and Winter, 1925

Salmon pink silk bag with metallic gold cording ornamentation similar to soutache and pink beaded accents, circa 1920s.
$50.00 – 150.00.

Sheer peach and white cotton apron, ribbed fabric, peach bow appliques, appliqued pocket, embroidered flowers, leaves, and scrolls, circa 1925.
$55.00 – 85.00.

Straw cloche with silk taffeta ribbons and straw sunbursts, circa 1925.
$155.00 – 185.00.

Steel chain mail purse, Art Deco motif in blue, tan and pink, cobalt rhinestone embellishment, brass chain and closure, scalloped bottom, circa 1920s.
$100.00 – 250.00.

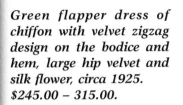

Green flapper dress of chiffon with velvet zigzag design on the bodice and hem, large hip velvet and silk flower, circa 1925. $245.00 – 315.00.

Gold metallic lamé cloche with asymmetrical upturned angular brim, gold chenille embroidery, circa 1925 – 1926. $175.00 – 185.00.

Apple green crepe dress with mustard yellow and black pointed angular collar, celluloid pin, circa 1925. $165.00 – 315.00.

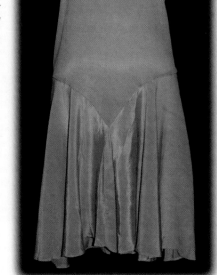

Pink crepe flapper dress, flared skirt, and sailor style collar, circa 1925. $175.00 – 250.00.

Fashion Trends for the Year 1926

(Illustrated and Non-Illustrated)

- Bishop and peasant sleeves
- Black
- Blue
- Bordered silks
- Bows and ribbons on both sides of hats
- Bows tied at the front
- Box coats
- Brims turned upward
- Bronze nail heads
- Bubble prints
- Buttons for ornament at the hip and wrist
- Capes
- Charleston hats
- Circular draperies
- Circular flounces
- Cloches with cartwheel brims
- Collars tied at the back
- Cracklehead blue (dark blue)
- Crochet collars and cuffs
- Double flannel dresses
- Draped girdles
- Dresses have no waistlines
- Drooping brims
- Ensemble hats in felt, straw, and flowers
- Flowers
- Full gathered flounces
- Fullness in dress
- Godets and kick pleats
- Gold metallic embroidery
- Green
- Hats with creased crowns
- High necks
- Irregular hemlines
- Knife pleated jabots
- Lightning bar prints
- Lipstick red
- Long sleeves
- Lovebird tan
- Low waist cut in deep points
- Overskirts gathered below belt
- Peter Pan lace collars
- Plaid girl's dresses
- Plaited sateen
- Pleated aprons
- Pleats
- Pointed tabs at the hips
- Poke hats (close fitting)
- Pumpkin
- Rayon velvet trims
- Roselea (light ash rose)
- Ruffled neck scarves
- Scalloped hems
- Scarf neck forming a high standing collar
- Sheer sleeves are long down to the wrist
- Side jabot with tassels
- Silhouette flares low at the waist
- Skirts below the knee
- Slouched cloches
- Smocking at the neck and hips
- Smocking on sleeves and waists
- Standing collars
- Straight line silhouettes
- Straight or shaped panels
- Straight skirts
- Stream ties in colors
- Streamer bows
- Streamer collars looped loosely
- Streamer collars with tied bows
- Streamer ties
- Stripes, abstract prints of flowers
- Tams with embellishments
- Three kick pleats
- Turbans
- Upturned all around brims
- Upturned brims
- Vertical stripes
- Wool knits [1]

Cornflower blue chiffon flapper dress with ecru lace inserts matching the multicolored flapper cloche below, circa 1926. $690.00 – 875.00.

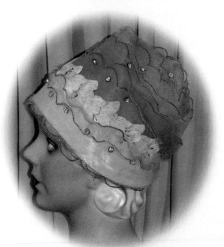

This flapper cloche of multicolored crinoline netting and silk flower pressed leaves is embedded with rhinestones. This cloche accompanies the adjacent dress, circa 1926. $175.00 – 185.00.

1. *Delineator,* January, February, April, May, June, 1926; *McCall's Magazine,* May, June, 1926; *Montgomery Wards,* Spring and Summer, 1926; *Sharood's Style Catalog,* Spring and Summer 1926; *Hamilton Garment Co. Catalog,* Spring and Summer, 1926

Fashion Trends for the Year 1927

(Illustrated and Non-Illustrated)

Black crepe gown, puffed and drooped sleeves of black netting, ivory chiffon under-blouse, embedded rhinestones in circular ornamentation on the bodice, circa 1926. $845.00 – 1,245.00.

- Basque frocks
- Boleros
- Bows on the sides of necklines and waistlines
- Boxy silhouettes
- Cloche hats
- Curved Eaton jackets
- Deep V figure lines on the bodice
- Fabric ruffled cascades
- Monograms on bodices
- Monograms on scarves
- Monograms on sleeves
- Neck ties
- Scarf collars
- Skirts below the knee
- Skirts with pointed lines and bows
- Straps at the wrist and cuffs
- Tiered ruffles slightly flare
- Waistlines at the hips
- Wing-shaped draperies [1]

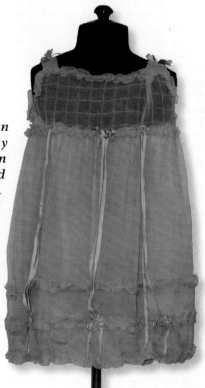

Child's emerald green chiffon dress, boxy lines, pink ribbon streamers trimmed with silk rosettes, bodice smocking, and three ruffles on the skirt, circa 1926. $198.00 – 235.00.

Burgundy velvet reticule purse with metallic ribbon flowers, circa 1920s. $25.00 –75.00.

1. *Pictorial Review,* May 1927; *Sears Catalog,* Spring and Summer, 1927

Black satin dress with wide A-line skirt, spun glass beads, satin modesty insert, scalloped open hemline, circa 1927.
$2,850.00 – 3,500.00.

Dark blue silk velvet sheath dress, long sleeves, high collar embellished with flowers made of cording covered in gold mesh metallic lace, circa 1927 – 1928.
$525.00 – 690.00.

Details of glass beading.

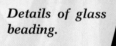

Details of the metallic gold corded flowers.

Lamé was worn by flappers as early as 1922. This metallic, gold thread lamé cloche has a turban-like appearance and dates circa 1927 – 1928. $175.00 – 185.00.

Monogrammed dress with patch first seen beginning in 1923, circa 1927 – 1928. $375.00 – 550.00.

Emerald green crepe dress with bloused collar, ivory lace modesty insert, slightly dropped waist, straight sleeves circa 1927 – 1928. $375.00 – 495.00.

Floral print woven chiffon dress, drop scalloped waistline, full skirt ruffled bottom, tied shawl chiffon collar, circa 1927 – 1928. $625.00 – 875.00.

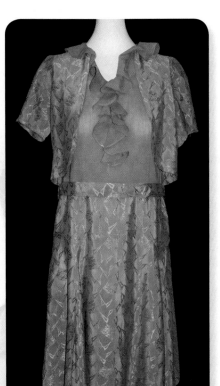

Abstract brocade patterned dress with ruffled chiffon collar, bodice, and dropped waistline flared below the hip, circa 1927 – 1929.
$375.00 – 425.00.

- Streamers
- Sunbursts of rhinestones
- Sunflowers
- Tab collars, high necklines
- Tight sprawling patterns
- Tiny decorative flowers on blouses
- Triple lines around hips
- Upward swaying evening gowns [1]

Dress with dropped waist, smocked waistband, ruffled skirt, and ecru lace collar, circa 1928.
$385.00 – 550.00.

Fashion Trends for the Year 1928
(Illustrated and Non-Illustrated)

- Collars with long skinny drooping lapels
- Cravats
- English garden prints
- Flounces suggesting underskirts
- Flowers and vines on clothing
- Girls' suspender shirts
- Higher waistlines
- Horse yoke collars
- Kimono sleeve dresses
- Large sashes with bows on the side
- Lines creeping downward
- Mannish jackets with feminine scalloped shirts
- Modernistic prints
- Pencil silhouettes
- Polka dots
- Ruffled dresses with skirt covering the knees
- Scallops from Victorian petticoats on hats
- Scallops from Victorian petticoats on jackets
- Scallops from Victorian petticoats on shirt edges
- Shirred shoulders
- Skirt ruffles similar to the Rooseveltian age

Brown velvet flapper cloche with asymmetrical ribbon tie and Deco decoration, interlocking diamonds and arrow made of felt applied to the velvet, circa 1928 – 1929.
$158.00 – 175.00.

1. *McCall's Magazine*, April, 1928

Dark green crepe dress, boxy shape, Deco style, drop waist, plain sleeves and asymmetrical knotted ascot, circa 1928.
$350.00 – 550.00.

- Long back and side panels
- Pointed sashes
- Side panniers
- Sixteenth century prints in embroidery
- Skirts dip in long points
- Skirts with deep points
- Skirts with horizontal, vertical, or slanted machine stitches
- Slender dress top with skirts flaring in triangular panels
- Straight cut dresses
- Straight skirt backs
- Surplice blouses and wrap around skirts
- Ties at the dress waists on both sides or on the back
- V necklines
- Vertical pleat skirts [1]

Brown felt hat with slightly wider upturned brim, circa 1929.
$58.00 – 75.00.

Fashion Trends for the Year 1929

(Illustrated and Non-Illustrated)

- Belts in pairs worn in opposite directions — front and back
- Belts in pairs worn in opposite directions on hips
- Cape collars
- Circular skirt fronts flare together
- Day dresses with oval openings
- Day dresses with round openings
- Day dresses with square openings
- Diagonal dress treatments
- Dipping hemlines
- Draped waistlines
- Drooped shoulders

A rt Deco stood for clean lines and geometric forms. Bias cut gowns made women sensuous objects of art. Like elegantly draped swans, women showed off their best in the decade's satin and rayon creations. The early years saw an entirely new look, the bias cut dresses and jaunty tilted brim hats that are so familiar to us. Despite the stock market's crash in 1929 and the onslaught of a long, drawn out and worldwide depression, women still managed to project images of radiant beauty.

As the decade rolled along, women became more tailored and simplistic. Some of our more modern fashions originate in the late thirties and forties. Europe fell into World War II by the late thirties. Fashion became more utilitarian and simplistic. What women could buy was limited. It was one thing to make women purchase new dresses in the Great Depression because fashion dictated longer gowns. It was another when fabric production and restrictions first in Europe and then America made it impossible to waste fabric or be frivolous in garment construction and textile use. During the late thirties into the early forties some of the most darling and innovative new hat styles of the twentieth century emerge alongside plainer clothing. Hat and millinery designs did not have the restrictions on them that fell over the garment industry. Women started the decade being glamorous and seductive icons of the Art Deco era. They would survive the deprivations of the Great Depression with spirit and elegance as seen in cinema of the Golden Age of Hollywood. They marched into World War II and lived through fashion restrictions bravely and patriotically.

Fashion Trends for the Year 1930

(Illustrated and Non-Illustrated)

- Ancient Greek style in simplistic satin gowns
- Angular hip plaits
- Bib collars
- Bows on cuffs
- Crossover dress closures
- Deep necklines
- Diagonal lines
- Draped necklines
- Draped waistlines in metallic lamé
- Draped waistlines in velvet
- Four-piece flared skirts
- Fruit prints
- High waists
- Jacket effects in dresses

- No armholes
- No belts on dresses
- No waistlines
- Pink and black
- Pointed corsages
- Princess lines
- Rickrack closings
- Short boleros
- Short ruffled elbow sleeves
- Side hip drapes
- Skirt waists below the hips
- Skirts have a V below the waist
- Skirts have two double Vs below the waist
- Skirts have an upside-down V below the waist
- Skirts have two seams that curve outward to the sides at the hips
- Slanted bolero and flared narrow sashes
- Three scallop waistlines — one full
- Three scallop waistlines — two halves on both sides of the center scallop
- Tops resemble jackets
- Two-tier skirts
- Uneven hems
- V necklines crinkled into soft bows
- V necks with no waists
- Velveteen and plaid [1]

Rust rayon hat with slight brim, ribbon embellishment, and buckle, circa 1930 – 1931.
$75.00 – 125.00.

1. *Delineator*, August, November 1930

Brown chenille cap with brim, circa 1930 – 1931. $62.00 – 85.00.

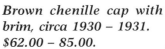

Art Deco orange rayon dress, neckline embroidered with tiny white and silver glass beads, has matching long sleeved bolero, circa 1930.
$275.00 – 315.00.

Dress with bolero tied jacket, circa 1930.

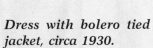

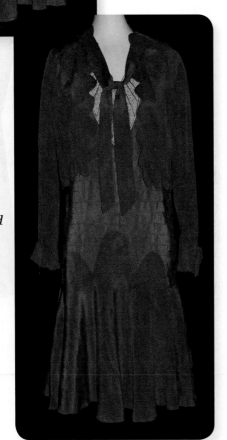

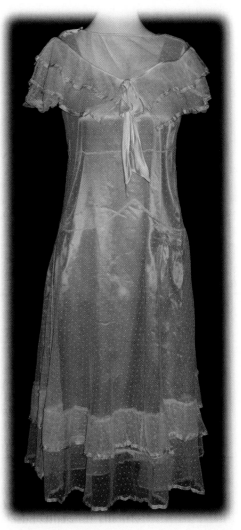

Ruffled net dress shown over a peach slip, circa 1930.
$190.00 – 275.00.

Ivory corded cloche hat with flared scalloped brim embellished with rhinestone dangles, circa 1930 – 1931. $58.00 – 78.00.

Fashion Trends for the Year 1931

(Illustrated and Non-Illustrated)

- Bow collars
- Box pleats
- Brims turned back away from faces
- Brown and green
- Chiffon dresses
- Coat dresses
- Cowl draped necklines
- Crepe dresses
- Cross stitch embroidery on dresses
- Double breasted bodice points at hips
- Droopy hats
- Fitted waists
- Flounces
- Hiplines have horizontal tucks
- Jabot collars
- Lace dresses
- Lingerie cuffs and collars
- Peasant effects
- Peplums
- Plaited frills
- Pokes
- Profile lines
- Seal coats
- Side closures
- Skirts flare at the bottom
- Skirts fall just below the knee
- Slanted lines
- Sleeves expand to the wrist
- Small buttons
- Sporty brimmed hats
- Straight sleeves cuffed at elbow or wrist
- Straighter skirts
- Transparent hats
- Tricorns
- Vestees
- Wide V droopy collars [1]

Silk satin gown with ivory lace bodice, circa 1930. $425.00 – 575.00.

1. *Wards,* Spring and Summer Catalog 1931; *McCall's,* September 1931

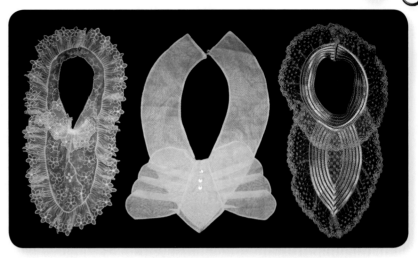

Embroidered organza bib front collars, circa 1931.
$25.00 – 45.00 each.

Gold, pink, and green lamé fabric evening bag with short strap, pink, gold, and white beading in floral and leaf pattern, circa middle to late 1930s.
$45.00 – 95.00.

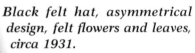

Rayon floral printed dress, puffed sleeves with contrasting piping, long skirt, asymmetrical jabot with buttons, circa 1931.
$180.00 – 250.00.

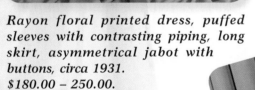

Black felt hat, asymmetrical design, felt flowers and leaves, circa 1931.
$85.00 – 145.00.

Fashion Trends for the Year 1932

(Illustrated and Non-Illustrated)

Asymmetrical woven horsehair bonnet, upturned brim on one side, silk flowers and ribbon, pattern resembling soutache, circa 1931.
$125.00 – 145.00.

Asymmetrical horsehair brim hat upturned on one side against the face, embellished with faux flowers, circa 1931.
$125.00 – 145.00.

- Belts with novelty buckles
- Black backgrounds
- Blue backgrounds
- Bolero effect dresses
- Cape sleeves
- Capelets
- Capes
- Cotton
- Cotton dresses with abstracts
- Cotton dresses with flowers
- Cotton dresses with polka dots
- Cotton foulard
- Crepe
- Diagonal pin tucks at hips
- Double flat crepes
- Embroidered collars
- Enlarged elbow sleeves
- Fitted hips
- Gored front skirts that flare
- Green backgrounds
- Hip pockets
- Lace vestees
- Long surplice fronts
- Long V necklines
- Novelty pockets
- Orange backgrounds
- Percale apron dresses
- Piped hiplines
- Piping with dainty prints
- Pleated skirts
- Polka dot florals
- Printed jackets
- Rayon
- Rayon dresses with low collars
- Red backgrounds
- Scallops
- Short sleeves flare with ruffles
- Shoulder bows
- Silk flat crepes
- Sleeves puff at the elbow then end tightly
- Sleeves puff at the elbow then stop
- Square necklines
- Ties at the collar ends
- Vest effects
- Vestees
- Wide ruffled collars [1]

1. *Wards*, 60th Anniversary sale, January & February Midwinter 1932; *Wards,* midwinter January & February 1932, *McCall's Magazine,* August 1932

Brown crepe girl's dress, pleated faux vest with puffed sleeves, slight drop waist, belt with buckle, circa 1932.
$70.00 – 155.00.

Pink rayon dress with ruffled pink yoke, high waist, lace sleeves, and lace collar effect on bodice, circa 1932.
$190.00 – 275.00.

Blue lace bias cut formal with cape collar, circa 1932.
$275.00 – 365.00.

Black straw slouch beret with large double tassel on the right side, circa 1932.
$50.00 – 85.00.

Gauze floral print dress, short sleeves with ruffles, ribbon belt and Bakelite buckle, skirt flounces of gathered ruffles, and mock buttons at the neck, circa 1932 – 1936.
$245.00 – 295.00.

Blue abstract plaid dress with flutter sleeves, belt with Bakelite buckle, circa 1932 – 1933.
$130.00 – 189.00.

Hot pink cloche, velvet leaves, flocked poppies, circa 1932.
$125.00 – 145.00.

Navy blue hat with an explosion of puffed feathers worn to one side, circa 1932.
$58.00 – 62.00.

183

Fashion Trends for the Year 1933

(Illustrated and Non-Illustrated)

- Bands of beads and sequins
- Black and white worn together
- Black gowns
- Blouses with puffs at or higher than the elbow
- Brown accessories
- Cape sleeves
- Coat dresses
- Cotton for eveningwear in hyacinth and rose
- Dress clips at dress straps
- Elbow length cape dresses
- Evening taffeta
- Gray for daywear
- Gray for eveningwear
- Gray with black
- Green
- Hyacinth
- Lace dresses in citron (a revived Edwardian color)
- Lace dresses in mauve (a revived Edwardian color)
- Lace dresses in rose (a revived Edwardian color)
- No fur on coats
- Pencil silhouettes
- Printed chiffon
- Printed sheers
- Prints in mandarin and white
- Prints in white and gray
- Prints with two lilies
- Push up sleeves
- Rose
- Scarf suits
- Split sleeves
- Swagger jackets
- Top sleeve ruffles end billowing to a loose elbow
- White [1]

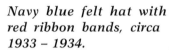

Navy blue felt hat with red ribbon bands, circa 1933 – 1934.
$58.00 – 85.00.

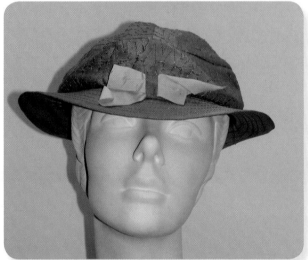

Orange taffeta hat with downward turned brim, yellow bow, circa 1933.
$58.00 – 85.00.

Black straw hat with side sweeping feathers and front nosegay of pink flowers and daisies, circa 1933 – early 1940s.
$75.00 – 85.00.

1. *Delineator*, February, March 1933

Printed floral sheer dress cut on the bias, half sleeves that tighten slightly below elbow, faux buttons, circa 1933.
$325.00 – 445.00.

Ribbed satin cap, double cockade plumes of long black feathers frame the back of the head circa 1933 – early 1940s.
$125.00 – 145.00.

Black crepe and light green velvet gown, pointed collar, sleeves open and gathered on the sides, high waist, bias cut, velvet ornamental buttons, circa 1933.
$365.00 – 450.00.

Navy straw cap with outrageous yellow bird ornament, red celluloid beak, red veil, circa 1933 – early 1940s.
$125.00 – 145.00.

Ivory lace tier gown with draped collar and pink taupe underdress, circa 1933.
$250.00 – 365.00.

- Flares below knee
- Gibson girl pleats
- High front necklines
- High sleeves flow out of low armholes
- Low backs
- Natural contour
- Neck tabs
- Neckline made from a twist of fabric
- Oversized berets
- Piping
- Pointed panels
- Princess panel contours
- Ruff neck collars
- Sailor collar
- Scarves worn around the neckline
- School girl prints
- Sleeves recede to deep cuffs
- Sleeves with points and shirring
- Swagger tunic lines
- Tweeds with swaggering lines and slit hems
- Wrap around apron dresses [1]

Detailed view of whimsical cat print.

Fashion Trends for the Year 1934

(Illustrated and Non-Illustrated)

- Assorted Hooverette day dresses
- Asymmetrical bodices
- Bateau necklines
- Bodices with surplice clip closings
- Bows
- Bright buttons
- Brown and green worn together
- Coat dresses
- Contrasting organdy with pique capelets
- Cotton prints
- Evening dress with slim silhouettes

Red cotton house dress, side wrap tie, whimsical prints of cats, circa 1934.
$130.00 – 180.00.

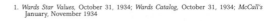

1. *Wards Star Values*, October 31, 1934; *Wards Catalog*, October 31, 1934; *McCall's* January, November 1934

Fashion Trends in the Year 1935
(Illustrated and Non-Illustrated)

House dress of blue cotton, whimsical rabbit print, and belt tie, circa 1934. $130.00 – 180.00.

Detailed view of rabbit marching.

Detailed view of rabbit pulling a cart.

- All over decorative buttons
- All shades of blue
- Basque bodices
- Berets with forward motion
- Big full sleeves
- Billowy cotton evening dresses
- Black lace sheath gowns
- Blown up sleeves
- Bodices with round yokes
- Breton sailor hats
- Cape ensembles
- Cartridge pleats
- Cellophane crowns and turbans
- Checks
- Constraining ties
- Cords and lacing on hats
- Coronet wedding headpieces
- Deep or creased crown hats with side brims
- Dolman sleeves
- Double breasted jackets
- Draped bodices
- Dresses with/without capes
- Evening gowns with high front décolletage
- Evening gowns with lower necklines
- Fashionable zippers
- Fedoras with creased crowns
- Flowered bandeau hats
- Frilly necklines
- Fringed edges
- Fullness at the tummy
- Geometrics
- Grecian princess influenced dress
- Grecian style evening gowns
- Hollywood sleeves — full at top, snug at the elbow to wrist
- Jabots
- Lacing on bodices
- Large collar and cuff sets
- Large gowns
- Large jabots
- Large neck bows
- Large puff sleeves
- Large sleeve blouses
- Lifted brims on hats
- Long short tunics
- Long straight jackets
- Matching lace
- Matellase
- Monkey fur

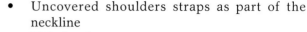

- Nautical style
- Necklines with drapery
- Necklines with jabots
- Necklines with ruffles
- Necklines with scarves
- Novelty collars
- Off the shoulder lines
- Ornamental buttons
- Oversized sleeves
- Pale colors
- Panama style hats
- Peaked berets are up in the back
- Peaked veiled turbans
- Pique
- Pleated sleeves
- Princess collars
- Printed cape suits
- Printed satin
- Prints and floral dresses
- Prints and floral suits
- Profile hats up on one side
- Quaint collars
- Quilted taffeta
- Raglan
- Ruffles, piping
- Saucer brims
- Scotch plaids
- Shirred fullness
- Shirring going down draped necklines
- Side slit skirts
- Skirts with slim lines
- Sleeved satin evening gowns with trains
- Sleeves blouse at cuff or elbow
- Sloping brims turned up in the back
- Small puffs
- Soft line fedoras
- Sport prints
- Square neckline rolls
- Square tucked crowns
- Straw berets
- Striped cottons and seersucker
- Striped seersucker
- Stripes
- Sun dresses
- Surplice collars of pleated organdy
- Swagger suits (bloused, loose, long jackets)
- Tailored suits
- Transparent picture hats
- Trouser skirts
- Turban hats with oriental influence
- Turned over collars
- Two way necklines

- Uncovered shoulders straps as part of the neckline
- Veiled turbans
- Wide hats
- Wool berets [1]

Blue striped cotton dress with ruffled pockets, collar, and sleeve edges, circa 1935.
$70.00 – 90.00.

Red striped cotton dress with ruffled pockets and collar, circa 1935.
$70.00 – 90.00.

1. *McCall's Magazine,* March, July 1935, *Montgomery Wards Catalog,* 1935 – 1936 Fall and Winter; *Sears Catalog,* July 31, 1935; *Wards,* midwinter sale, March 15, 1935; *Wards Star Value Book,* March 15, 1935; *Pictorial Review,* February 1935; *Sears Catalog,* Spring and Summer, July 31, 1935

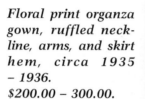

Floral print organza gown, ruffled neckline, arms, and skirt hem, circa 1935 – 1936.
$200.00 – 300.00.

Oyster colored satin wedding gown, swirls of satin piping embellish the neckline and upper portion of the cuffs, Hollywood style sleeves bloused to the elbow then end in a deep, tight cuff, circa 1935.
$2,000.00 – 2,200.00.

Bridal coronet tiara of buckram cutwork embroidered with white glass beads, circa 1935.
$85.00 – 145.00.

Spider web black lace dress, velvet neck bow and cuff trimming in fuchsia velvet, slit open neckline, diamond waist panel, belt with Deco rhinestone paste buckle, black rayon slip, circa 1935.
$345.00 – 425.00.

Brown velvet derby style hat with side chenille loops, circa 1935 – 1936.
$50.00 – 75.00.

Fashion Trends for the Year 1936

(Illustrated and Non-Illustrated)

- Blush pink worn by brides
- Boucle wool
- Button down evening dresses
- Button dress plaids
- Curved pleats down dress fronts
- Diagonal high hems
- Draped jersey gowns
- Evening dress vest tops & long skirts
- Fat shirred sleeves
- Flannels
- Floral taffeta necklines
- Flowered crepe
- Gibson girl sleeves (half leg o'mutton)
- Grape
- Halter backs with two vertical straps
- Ice blue worn by brides
- Ivory and antique ivory bridal gowns
- Jerseys
- Lamé satin cloches
- Metal cloth dresses
- New talon zipper fasteners
- Woolen dresses with puffed sleeves
- Peplums
- Plaid and velveteen
- Pointed top sleeves
- Posies on the neck
- Princess line dresses
- Puffed sleeves
- Quilted silver brocade evening dresses
- Rabbit fur
- Sheers
- Shirred rounded neckline
- Shirred three-quarter sleeves
- Short jacket tops
- Shoulder straps
- Sleeveless looks with large ruffles
- Soft jabot collars
- Soft V necks
- Striped evening dresses
- Swallow tail dresses
- Taffeta gowns
- Tweeds
- Two-piece ribbed sweater suits
- V necks and shirred yokes
- Velvet evening gowns with shoulder straps
- Velveteen
- Wraps with wing collars
- Yoke tops in circular style [1]

Dark rose and blue-gray cotton billowing floral evening gown, frilly organdy neck ruffles trimmed with red, circa 1935.
$725.00 – 950.00.

1. *Pictorial Review,* November 1936; *McCall's,* June, December 1936

Gold lamé dress with sailor style collar, circa 1936 – 1937.
$575.00 – 800.00.

Floral printed rayon taffeta gown, high pointed and puffed sleeves with horizontal folds, shirred bodice, upside down V empire waistline, circa 1936.
$745.00 – 800.00.

Black taffeta hat with large floral bow, white feather, and rhinestone embellishment, circa 1936.
$75.00 – 85.00.

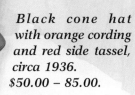

Black cone hat with orange cording and red side tassel, circa 1936.
$50.00 – 85.00.

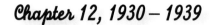

Red felt cap with shirred felt circles bordering the face, label: Saks Fifth Avenue, circa 1936 – 1946. $30.00 – 50.00.

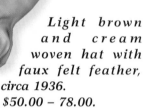

Light brown and cream woven hat with faux felt feather, circa 1936. $50.00 – 78.00.

Antique ivory liquid satin bias cut wedding gown, upside down V empire waist, folded down pointed collar, Gibson Girl or half leg o'mutton sleeves that puff at the top and narrow to the cuff, long train, circa 1936. $2,000.00 – 3,300.00.

Pink suede beret with faux side feather, circa 1936. $50.00 – 78.00.

Brown asymmetrical hat with curved side brim, circa 1936. $50.00 – 75.00.

Fashion Trends for the Year 1937

(Illustrated and Non-Illustrated)

Gray and blue striped taffeta formal, shirred bodice, high top puff sleeves, tapered sleeve ends, large back bow, upside down V empire waistline, circa 1936. $225.00 – 265.00.

- All over lace
- Alpaca light colored wool dresses
- Back yokes
- Black and gold
- Blue, brown and silver
- Boxy suits
- Corselet waistlines
- Corseted looks
- Crinkled crepe
- Crushed décolleté
- Culottes
- Decorative piping
- Deep slim V necklines
- Draped dresses
- Draped waist lamé gowns
- Fishbone shirring
- Glittering lamé
- Half puffed sleeves
- Harness straps
- Heart shaped décolleté
- High and low V necks
- High bosom dresses
- High necks
- Lace redingotes
- Long zip fasteners
- One back pleat
- Organdy shirring
- Organdy undersleeves
- Peacock blue
- Peasant dresses
- Peter Pan collars
- Pink
- Pink and navy
- Pink overskirts on formals
- Plaid suits
- Puffed sleeves
- Satin prints
- Shirred bodices and sleeves
- Shirred V collar
- Shirring between the bosoms
- Short dance dresses
- Shorter skirts
- Shoulders strap evening gowns
- Simple evening gowns with V panels
- Simple gowns with sumptuous fabrics
- Small fur trim on coats
- Strapless back evening gowns
- Striped evening dresses with flared collars
- Stripes

Red floral printed house dress with green, blue, yellow, and white in the bouquet, blue plastic buttons, small puffed sleeves, circa 1936. $99.00 – 155.00.

- Tailored velveteen
- Ties on the sleeves
- Touches of lamé
- Tubular form fitting dresses
- Two shades of red
- V shaped bodices
- Velvet and lamé dinner gowns
- Velveteen and wool
- Victorian inspirations
- White
- Winged collars
- Yellow
- Zipped up front
- Zippers down dark dress fronts [1]

Blue chiffon formal gown with empire waist, ruffle atop the bodice, silk flower adornment, thin shoulder straps, and matching ruffled bolero shown below, circa 1937. $245.00 – 315.00.

Black synthetic horsehair hat with looped flowers, circa 1937 – 1939. $75.00 – 85.00.

Chiffon bolero jacket that accompanies the formal gown.

1. *McCall's Magazine,* June – December 1937; *Pictorial Review,* January, November, 1937

Violet strapless evening gown with yellow and green sheer ribbon embroidery on the skirt and bodice, circa 1937.
$275.00 – 315.00.

Pink taffeta formal with shirred sweetheart bodice, pleated neck-line, shirred puffed sleeves, and a skirt separated into sections by piping, circa 1937.
$150.00 – 200.00.

Black taffeta formal, shirred neckline and sleeves, flowers out-lined in gold thread embroidered throughout the dress, circa 1937.
$275.00 – 315.00.

Details of blue and gold thread embroi-dery circa 1937.

Fashion Trends for the Year 1938

(Illustrated and Non-Illustrated)

- Amber
- Ascot collars
- Asymmetrical lines
- Bandaged waists
- Bengaline
- Bi-colored dresses
- Black and brown
- Black lace in the evening
- Bloused and pleated suit jackets
- Bloused jackets
- Bolero effects
- Bolero influenced dresses
- Bolero influenced overdresses
- Boleros
- Bonbon colors
- Boxy top coats
- Bright pockets and dark dresses
- Butterfly bodices
- Butterfly girdles and corsages
- Buttonholes coats
- Child dresses that widen at hem
- Clips and square necklines
- Collarless dresses
- Collarless jackets
- Cone crown hats
- Corselet effects
- Cotton lace
- Crepe floral evening gowns
- Cyclamen or fuchsia taffeta
- Dark organza
- Dark prints with borders down dress fronts
- Décolletage
- Deep purple
- Dirndls
- Dolman shorter sleeves
- Draped collars
- Draped looks on the top, shoulders and neck
- Drapery panels
- Drapery shirring on sides of bodice
- Dress clips
- Dress with shirred top and straps
- Embroidered dinner dresses
- Evening blouse wraps
- Evening dresses wrapped in crisscross fashion
- Fan folds on bodices
- Flared plaids
- Flared princess cuts
- Flared skirts
- Floral boleros over plain dresses

- Front zipper closure on dresses
- Full dirndls
- Gathered skirts
- Giant plaids
- Gibson girl gowns
- Gold
- Gray
- Guimpe dresses
- Gypsy dinner dresses
- Heart shaped décolletage
- High and low necklines
- High waists
- Honey color
- Hoop skirts with petticoats
- Horizontal shirring
- Inward turning pleats
- Jacket dresses in prints
- Jumpers
- Low waistlines
- Navy and brown
- Neck shirring
- Odd color combinations
- Petal necklines
- Pink
- Plaids with velveteen
- Plain dresses
- Princess lines
- Printed boleros with solid dresses
- Printed evening gowns
- Printed necklines
- Printed organdy
- Printed silks
- Printed tops
- Pulley strap dresses
- Pushed up shirred sleeves
- Red and green
- Rib tucks
- Rickrack
- Sheer dresses
- Shirred bodice pockets
- Shirred dresses
- Shirred fronts
- Shirred waistlines
- Shirtwaist dress blouses
- Shoulder strap evening dresses
- Silver fox
- Small hats
- Smooth shoulders
- Smooth waists
- Soutache in gold
- Square lines
- Square necklines

- Stiffened half moon sleeves that stand up
- Strapless dress off the shoulder accents
- Strapless gowns with halters
- Striped dresses with boned corsets worn outside
- Striped woolens
- Stripes
- Suspenders
- Teal
- Thin sheer bodices
- Three cornered necklines
- Tubular tunics
- Tucked shoulders
- Tuxedo lines
- Two slit necklines
- Two strings closures
- Two-way necklines, worn open or closed
- Upside down waistlines
- V line stripes
- Velvet in beige
- Velvet in rosewood
- Velvet in rust
- Velvet in stone blue
- Velvet in teal
- Velvet with bands of taffeta
- Vivid colors
- Wedding gowns that become evening gowns
- Wide shoulders
- X back straps
- Yellow
- Zip closed jackets [1]

Gray wool felt Robin Hood style hat with side tassel, circa 1938. $125.00 – 145.00.

Pink satin formal, shirred bodice pleated top, sweetheart neckline embellished with deep velvet purple flowers, attached back belt with satin buckle, circa 1938 – 1940. $185.00 – 245.00.

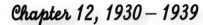

Brown velvet pixie cone hat with pearl butterfly embellishment, circa 1938. $85.00 – 125.00.

Grape satin bias cut gown with crisscross scarf neckline tied to the back of the bodice, circa 1938. $275.00 – 315.00.

Yellow taffeta formal with white and pink floral print, shirred bosom, sweetheart neckline, circa 1938 – 1940. $175.00 – 235.00.

Cornflower blue taffeta formal, flocked print covered in mica glitter, burgundy silk ribbons, silk flowers, matching head-piece of silk flowers shown right, circa 1938. Gown and headpiece: $265.00 – 315.00.

Matching silk flower headpiece that accompanies the blue formal dress, circa 1938. $25.00 – 45.00.

Pink strapless evening gown of taffeta, halter back, crisscross straps, and a fabric rose flower, circa 1938. $225.00 – 275.00.

Open crown cartwheel hat, woven black synthetic straw trimmed with red chenille dotted netting, green bows, circa 1938. $150.00 – 225.00.

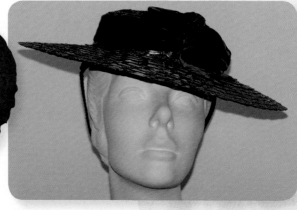

Kelly green wide brim straw hat with red velvet bow, circa 1938. $75.00 – 95.00.

Blue and pink crepe evening gown, shirred sleeves topped with pink bows, front embellished with ivory lace and faux fabric covered buttons, squared neckline that dips into a point, pleating, circa 1938. $275.00 – 365.00.

Brown felt hat with brown ribbon, wide brim, vertical and horizontal brown feathers, circa 1938. $75.00 – 85.00.

Raspberry satin dressing gown, central metal zipper closure, two waist ties resembling bows, puffed sleeves, deep V neckline, circa 1938 – 1940.
$190.00 – 275.00.

Rayon blue dress with white printed bodice top, Peter Pan Collar, bolero style jacket, circa 1938.
$90.00 – 150.00.

Ivory taffeta satin gown with Gibson Girl leg o'mutton sleeves inspired by the Victorians and Edwardians, bodice ornamented by a row of tiny buttons, matching veil (below) is an oval coronet of pleated mesh trim layered to create this Art Deco effect alongside a tiny central insert of wax flowers, circa 1938.
Gown and headpiece:
$475.00 – 575.00.

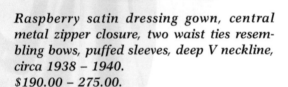

Ivory taffeta, tulle, and wax floral headpiece, accompanies the ivory gown above, circa 1938.
$25.00 – 85.00.

Fashion Trends for the Year 1939
(Illustrated and Non-Illustrated)

- 1800s revival of charming dresses
- Asymmetrical closures
- Basque bodices
- Basque bustles
- Basque evening clothing
- Basque-like jackets
- Bengaline
- Black and gold
- Blue
- Braided edged pockets
- Bright blacks
- Brown
- Bustle influences
- Buttons decorating bodices
- Chartreuse
- Checked and polka dot dresses
- Chiffon
- Cigarette silhouettes
- Circular shirring on bodices
- Collarless necks
- Cowl necks
- Culottes
- Dahlia purple
- Dark and light colors worn together
- Dark dresses with light colored coats
- Double breasted lapels
- Double spaghetti straps
- Easter egg colors
- Evening gowns with corselet waists
- Evening gowns with full shoulder straps
- Evening gowns with single straps
- Eveningwear with bustles 1880s style
- Eyelet evening gowns
- Faille taffeta
- Flares
- Flounced dresses
- Flowers and tiers
- Fluffy ruffles
- Front and back fullness
- Fuchsia
- Full skirts with flounces
- Fur coats
- Gathered back coats
- Gatherings at back
- Gingham
- Green belt-less dresses
- Gypsy skirts
- Halter top gowns with lace
- Heart shaped shirred bust

- High neck evening gowns
- High pleats
- High waist collar-less neck
- Hourglass silhouettes
- Huge crinoline bustles
- Little girl silhouettes
- Little girl style dresses
- Low bustles
- Moiré
- Moiré frocks
- Monk style dresses
- Monograms
- Moyenage silhouette
- Mustard yellow
- Navy dresses
- Off the shoulder ruffles
- Olive green
- Peplum corselet dresses
- Pinafore sundresses
- Pink prints
- Plaid gingham
- Plaids
- Pleats in flares
- Princess frocks
- Princess lines
- Puffed shoulders
- Puffed sleeves
- Rayon stripes
- Red hats
- Rippled backs
- Rippled skirts
- Robin Hood red
- Ruffles or tubing on tops
- Seersucker bayadere stripes
- Sheer dark dresses
- Sheer redingote
- Shirred and pleated lines vertical on the bosom
- Shirred dresses
- Shirring alongside bodice yokes
- Sidewise drapes of bodices
- Skirts with many gores
- Sleeves puffed at the top then tapered
- Slim fronts, full backs with hip drapery
- Slip-on coats
- Slipper satin
- Square necks
- Stiff fabrics for evening
- Stiff lamé
- Strapless or thin shoulder strap gowns
- Striped evening gowns
- Striped lamé

- Stripes running in three directions
- Suspender dirndls
- Swing skirts
- Three-quarter sleeves
- Toy hats
- Tucks and pleats on V bodices and straight on skirts
- Twin colors
- V line bodice
- V-neck high-low necklines
- Velvet
- Velvet shirred dresses
- Vestees
- Violet
- Violet accessories
- White and rust
- White frills
- White prints
- Wide waistbands
- Wider skirts
- Zigzag lines [1]

Red and black chiffon dress, bias cut silhouette, ornamental buttons, sheer sleeves, and narrow standup collar, circa 1939.
$250.00 – 275.00.

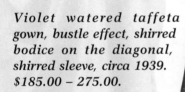

Violet watered taffeta gown, bustle effect, shirred bodice on the diagonal, shirred sleeve, circa 1939.
$185.00 – 275.00.

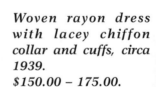

Woven rayon dress with lacey chiffon collar and cuffs, circa 1939.
$150.00 – 175.00.

1. *McCall's,* January, February, June, August – November 1939; *Fifth Avenue Modes,* Spring and Early Summer 1939

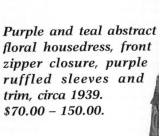

Straw tilted hat with slanted crown, back of the head strap to assure proper forward tilt position, cream straw band, circa 1939 – 1940.
$50.00 – 75.00.

Purple and teal abstract floral housedress, front zipper closure, purple ruffled sleeves and trim, circa 1939.
$70.00 – 150.00.

Straw boater with orange band and bent wooden embellishment, circa 1939.
$50.00 – 75.00.

Brown felt military inspired hat with fur trim, circa 1939 – 1940.
$60.00 – 75.00.

Fashion in the forties was sophisticated, saucy and sensible. The war years brought about shortages in fabric. Clothing became less elaborate. Styles reflected military elements and design features. Women's clothing was sleek, elegant and subtle. Women's hats, gloves and platform shoes completed the look making the plainer clothing stand out and appear glamorous. Bold colors and designs, sweetheart necklines and puffy sleeves marked new design changes. Women's clothing epitomized the spirit of the times and the way that women chose to express themselves. Even though it was difficult to maintain fashion as usual standards while the war was raging, the decade still had unique and decided fashion statement in clothing that are most remarkably appreciated by collectors today.

The forties had some of the most outrageous, lovely, and dazzling examples of millinery in fashion history. No one can deny the beauty of liquid satin gowns. The unique peplum and illusion necklines made their first appearance on fashion's stage. Women looked daring and dramatic in their shirred velvets. Sweetheart necklines graced many a party dress and bridal gown. Dramatic colors abounded in jewel tones for day and eveningwear. Sophisticated suits showed up at the workplace. The spirit of exotic places was transplanted into the fashion styles of the decade. Women of the forties made it easy to look innocent and sophisticated with wonderful charm and relish. Despite the many years of deprivation women all over the world faced during World War II, the ladies of the forties epitomized sophistication in our eyes and memories today.

Fashion Trends for the Year 1940

(Illustrated and Non-Illustrated)

- Back buttons
- Bare waistlines
- Bell silhouettes
- Bermuda shorts
- Big blowsy sleeves
- Big pockets
- Big soft pleats
- Big square pockets
- Black straw hats
- Black taffeta
- Bolero costume dresses
- Bolero ensembles
- Boleros looking like capes
- Bosom side drapery

- Bow appliques
- Bows at waistlines
- Bows at the throat
- Bracelet three-quarter sleeves
- Brocaded velveteen
- Brown shirtwaist dresses
- Burnt sugar colored dresses
- Button dresses
- Cadet style hats
- Chartreuse worn with yellow
- Checks and plaids
- Convex shaped small top hats
- Corsages in the middle of the bosom
- Corselet waist blouses
- Cotton voile formals
- Cross over dresses
- Décolletage that is daringly low
- Diamond shaped necklines
- Diamond waistlines
- Dimity formals
- Dotted Swiss formals
- Double breasted dresses
- Drapery at the hip side
- Drapery down the front
- Drapery on pockets
- Drapery over the bosom
- Drawstring waists
- Fagoting
- Fish bone drapery
- Flemish beret hats
- Formals in lawn
- Formals in muslin
- Green
- Grey chiffon prints
- Halo bridge hats
- Harem slacks
- Hats with back of head ribbon straps
- Hats with high slouched crowns and wide brims
- High girdles
- Hip drapery on the sides and horizontally
- Hooded capes
- Huge pockets
- Jacket blouses
- Jacket dresses
- Jackets and skirts don't match
- Kettle edge brim hats
- Kick pleats
- Knit slacks
- Left to right drapery
- Linen formals
- Link buttons

- Long jackets
- Long torso lines
- Long torso suits
- Loose jackets
- Low necklines
- Muted abstract prints
- Navy and black suits with white hats
- Necklace necklines
- Necklines curving up the neck
- Off the shoulder taffeta gowns
- Olive green
- Organdy formals
- Pale gray
- Party plaids
- Plaid dresses
- Plaid formals
- Plain dresses
- Plain, dark transparent dresses
- Pockets on evening dresses
- Push up bloused sleeves
- Rayon jersey
- Red dresses with white or blue
- Red gloves and hats
- Red, white and blue worn together
- Redingote frocks
- Right sided shirring
- Romper short sets
- Rounded waists
- Rows of stitching
- Ruffles on gowns
- "S" draped dinner dresses
- Sailor hats
- Sheer black lace boleros and full skirts
- Sheer black summer dresses
- Shirred bodices and bosoms
- Shirred velvet
- Shirring on the diagonal below the bust
- Shirtdresses for dinner wear
- Short V necklines
- Side drapes
- Silk suits in faille and bengaline
- Sleeved dinner dresses
- Slightly puffed short sleeves
- Slightly puffed sleeve tops
- Slim skirts
- Slim look then a godet flare
- Snoods
- Soft pleats
- Spun rayon formals
- Square necklines
- Star pointed corselet waists
- Striped dresses

- Stripes and checks
- Summer suits in tweed, gingham and sharkskin
- Sun dresses
- Sweetheart formal bodices
- Sweetheart formals with shirred bosoms
- Sweetheart neck with shoulder straps
- Three-color dresses
- Tiny straw hats with square low brims
- Tricorn hats
- Two belts on waistlines
- U necklines with yokes
- Umbrella style hats
- Vertical drapery
- Wheat colored accessories
- White gowns with red flowers
- White on black with embroidery
- Wide necks with ribbon ties
- Wool-like rayon [1]

Chartreuse and olive turban hat, 1940 – 1941.
$75.00 – 165.00.

1. *McCall's,* April, May, October 1940, *Spiegel Catalog,* Fall and Winter 1940

Tight crown hat of woven straw and ruffled halo brim of shirred taffeta, circa 1940. $75.00 – 165.00.

Ivory satin bride's hat, small brim, underside has two double rows of fine glass pearls, braided satin twist crown ornament, small bow, circa 1940. $65.00 – 85.00.

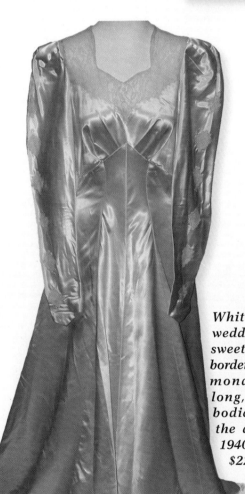

White rayon satin wedding gown with sweetheart neckline bordered in lace, diamond waistband, long, full sleeves, bodice shirred on the diagonal, circa 1940. $225.00 – 350.00.

Violet flower tilt hat with veil, circa 1940 – 1941. $130.00 – 250.00.

High crown fedora with wide brim, circa 1940. $65.00 – 85.00.

Tilt hat with a circle of curly gray lambs wool, velvet stiffened back bow, black velvet loop secures the hat on the back of the head to tilt it forward, circa 1940 – 1944.
$130.00 – 250.00.

Tilt hat with circle of black fur, back bow of velvet, black velvet loop securing the hat on the back of the head to tilt it forward, circa 1940 – 1944.
$130.00 – 250.00.

Dove gray suede snood hat, circa 1940 – 1941.
$60.00 – 85.00.

Tilted straw hat with purple and white flowers, circa 1940. $60.00 – 85.00.

White organza gown with embroidered red flowers, ruffled portrait neck, red and green ribbon bow, circa 1940. $220.00 – 265.00.

Synthetic horsehair hat with ruffled illusion brim embellished with pink roses, white flowers, and blue satin bows, circa 1940. $75.00 – 125.00.

Fashion Trends for the Year 1941

(Illustrated and Non-Illustrated)

- Black bands on wine
- Black crepe dresses
- Black rayon jersey dresses
- Bow belts
- Broomstick skirts
- Brown with blue
- Cape collars
- Capes
- Checkered taffeta shirtwaists
- Classic dirndl dresses
- Coat ensembles
- Dark sheer dresses
- Deep armholes
- Deep kangaroo (large square) pockets
- Deep throated shirt folds
- Dolman sleeves
- Double ruffle peplums
- Fan folds
- Forward looking peplums
- Four square pockets
- Fuchsia
- Full sleeves
- Gathered Mexican and South American dresses
- Green and gold evening dresses
- High rounded necklines
- Illusion marquisette gowns
- Lace redingotes
- Mexican peasant dresses dirndl style
- Navy blue with no white
- Necklace necklines
- Pinch pleats on skirts
- Point d'esprit yokes
- Red
- Red skirts
- Red, white and blue
- Saddle shoulders
- Saddle stitches
- Sheer black dresses
- Side peplums
- Sloping shoulders — padded and rounded
- Striped jackets
- Twin prints
- V necklines
- Velveteen dresses
- Very long, two piece blouses
- White collar dresses
- Woven dots [1]

Cotton dirndl dress, blue and black abstract print, back ties, circa 1941 – 1942.
$125.00 – 165.00.

1. *Mademoiselle*, July 1941; *Glamour Magazine*, August 1941, *McCall's Magazine*, May, July 1941

Rare Ceil Chapman red satin and tulle evening gown with halter strap ending in the back with four single spaghetti straps making a beautiful and unique halter effect, circa 1941.
$1,000.00 – 3,000.00.

Black and pink evening gown, black tulle skirt, double peplum trimmed with pink satin cording, pink bodice, black tulle ruffled peplum, pink cording, halter style, double spaghetti straps, circa 1941.
$245.00 – 385.00.

Fashion Trends for the Year 1942

(Illustrated and Non-Illustrated)

- Airforce blue and wine colors
- Back gathers
- Basque dirndls
- Beige
- Belt-less dresses
- Black dresses
- Black matelasse
- Bolero dresses
- Bordered materials
- Bow blouses
- Bow dresses
- Bow tie dresses
- Boxy coats
- Boxy shoulders
- Bright dirndls
- Broad shoulders
- Brown suit dresses
- Brown velveteen
- Brown worn with blue
- Callot and tie dress
- Challis prints
- Colored dickeys

- Colored yokes with shoestring ties
- Contrasting yokes
- Corduroy dresses
- Cotton and rayon
- Deep yokes
- Demi-dirndls
- Dickey dresses
- Dirndl dresses
- Dirndl jumper dresses
- Dotted dresses
- Double breasted jackets
- Drapery over busts
- Embroidered organdy
- Evening dirndls in white and yellow
- Evening frocks with slits
- Eyelet cottons
- Eyelet dickeys
- Flat pancake hats
- Floral abstract prints
- Floral print dresses
- Formals with deep sweetheart necklines
- Front gathered skirts
- Fruit prints
- Fuchsia
- Gabardine shirtfronts
- Gilet dresses
- Gingham
- Godets
- Green lamé
- Half-printed half-plain dresses
- Huge neck bows
- Jeweled buttons
- Jewelry necklines
- Linen plaid suits
- Long waist dirndls
- Matelasse
- Medals worn on black dresses
- Narrow hems
- Olive green worn with red
- Open work snoods
- Partly printed dresses
- Peg top pockets
- Peg tops
- Pink and navy
- Plaid wool with velveteen
- Polka dots
- Purple
- Red hearts on pockets
- Red prints
- Rickrack
- Rickrack dirndls
- School girl style dirndls

- Shirred bodices with rounded sides and deep V's
- Shirred side bodices
- Shoestring ties
- Short fur coats
- Silk suits
- Simple dresses
- Slanted folds on necklines
- Slim suit dresses
- Slouched front berets
- Small prints
- Soft pleats
- Soft tucks
- Square lines
- Square necklines
- Straight skirts
- Striped chambray
- Tapered yoke tucks
- Two tone-light and dark
- Umbrella skirts
- Velvet scarves
- Velveteen
- Very low V necklines with bows
- Vivid purple and fuchsia
- White prints
- Wide brim hats with scalloped brims
- Wide shirt tucks
- Wine red
- Wine velvet
- Wrap around dresses
- Yellow
- Yellow green
- Yokes with side features [1]

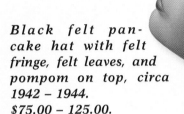

Black felt pancake hat with felt fringe, felt leaves, and pompom on top, circa 1942 – 1944.
$75.00 – 125.00.

Black velvet pancake hat with gold and silver embroidery and beads, circa 1942.
$75.00 – 125.00.

Blue felt fez hat with long navy tassel, circa 1942 – 1943.
$75.00 – 95.00.

1. *McCall's*, May, July, August, September, December 1942

Fashion Trends for the Year 1943
(Illustrated and Non-Illustrated)

- Back button dresses
- Back buttoned blouses
- Birdcage veils
- Cascaded side drapes
- Cascading headdresses
- Chartreuse
- Citron and black
- Coat dresses
- Deep U necklines
- Draped dresses
- Fan shaped veils
- Flowery pinafores
- Fuchsia
- Fur trimmed suits
- Gathered yokes
- Hat veils
- Hats with two rounded curves
- Hip drapes
- Jumpers
- Magenta
- Midriff gathers
- Pastel prints
- Purple
- Purplish red
- Rickrack on bows
- Ruffled front of dresses
- Scalloped pinafores
- Scallops on bodices
- Shawl collars
- Shirred necks
- Short evening dresses with dressy blouses
- Side button dresses
- Small peplums
- Soft bows on left side
- Square necklines
- Suits with tied waists
- Surplice closings
- Sweetheart necklines
- Tight bodices
- T-line silhouettes
- Triple bows
- Trouser pleats on blouses
- V backed sundresses with cap sleeves
- V band necklines over square necklines
- Velveteen shirtfronts
- Wide hats with narrow tops and wide brims
- Wild grape [1]

Black, pink, cream, green, and yellow synthetic straw tilt hat, veil, back ring, circa 1943. $150.00 – 385.00.

Pink floral tilt hat with rear ring and veil, circa 1943 – 1945. $125.00 – 225.00.

1. *Woman's Home Companion*, September & December 1943, *McCall's Magazine*, September, December 1943

Fashion Trends for the Year 1944
(Illustrated and Non-Illustrated)

- Apron effects
- Armed ruffled pinafores
- Back buttons
- Bare back sundresses
- Black slacks
- Blue for weddings
- Bodices fitted on the front sides
- California dirndls: wide neck and tiny sleeves
- Crepe dresses for parties
- Deep necks with tiny sleeves
- Deep rows of stitches
- Double scalloped necklines
- Evening gowns of striped taffeta and velvet
- Faint pink for weddings
- Gowns with gathers on short sleeves
- Grape juice colored dresses
- Half peplums
- Half wrap around dresses
- High necks
- High top slouch hats with pull down wide brims
- Ice blue for weddings
- Ivory for weddings
- Knee skirts
- Long sleeves with bows on cuffs
- Man tailored suits
- One-sided buttons dresses
- Open necks
- Peplum aprons
- Plaid taffetas
- Princess jumpers
- Redingotes
- Ruffled pinafore jumpers
- Shantung
- Shirred bosoms
- Shoulder straps with ruffled bodices
- Skullcaps
- Sleeveless sport frocks
- Square necklines
- Suede draped print dresses
- Tiered flares
- Tiered flounce skirts
- Two piece tunic dresses
- Wrap around dresses [1]

Cotton checkered dress, eyelet trim and square neck, circa 1944 – 1945. $45.00 – 75.00.

Bold seersucker sleeveless printed dress, back buttons, belt, one side pocket, circa 1940s to 1950s. $55.00 – 110.00.

1. *McCall's Magazine,* February, October 1944

Fashion Trends for the Year 1945

(Illustrated and Non-Illustrated)

- Airy slits and holes
- Angular wing sleeves
- Apron effect dresses
- Back fullness
- Back pleated skirts
- Beaded trim
- Black with beige and dark tan
- Black with blue and purple
- Black with fuchsia and blue
- Blue and white
- Blue lace
- Bow on side of square collar neck
- Boxy masculine shoulders
- Boxy shoulders
- Bretons
- Bright sleeves on dark dresses
- Broad shoulders
- Brown satin
- Bulky top silhouettes
- Bustle peplums
- California suits
- Calots
- Cape suits
- Capes
- Cardigan suits
- Cartwheel hats
- Chartreuse
- Checked and candy striped dresses
- Checkered coats and suits
- Collarless coats
- Collarless suits
- Color blocks
- Color contrasts
- Contrasting suits
- Curved necklines
- Curved waistlines
- Cut square and deep armhole sleeves
- Cutaway peplums
- Cutouts — small thin triangles on bodice yoke
- Dark and medium green worn with lime
- Dark sleeves on light dresses
- Darker tops
- Décolletage in heart neck lines
- Deep armholes
- Deep squares
- Diamond shaped keyhole neckline
- Dirndls for young women
- Draped sashes

- Drawstring ruffled necklines
- Dungarees
- Eyelet trimmed dresses
- Eyelets in many colors
- Fabric contrasts — crepe and satin
- Felt scalloped berets
- Fitted midriffs
- Floral corsages
- Flowered wreaths
- Flowers of felt
- Folded satin on bodice tops with thin straps
- Fuchsia
- Fuller, softer skirts
- Gold frocks
- Golden yellow
- Green
- Hats worn forward
- Hats worn to the side
- Heavy satin
- Hip side ties
- Jeep jackets
- Jumpers
- Jumpers in spun rayon
- Keyhole necklines closed with bows
- Keyhole necks
- Knee length skirts
- Lace over color
- Lace ribbon necks
- Lace touches
- Large brims with flowers and straw
- Liberation colors (red, white and blue)
- Long evening gowns
- Looser skirts
- Low bodices
- New wing sleeves
- One shoulder bare formals
- One sided looks — not wrap around
- Open and triangular keyhole neckline
- Overskirt effects
- Peasant blouses
- Peep-in necks for formals
- Pillboxes
- Profile bumpers
- Red
- Redingotes
- Reversed collars
- Rounded looks
- Ruffled horsehair
- Ruffled necklines with two thin straps
- Ruffled off the shoulder necklines
- Ruffles

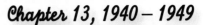

- Sailor hats
- Saw tooth necklines
- Scalloped bodice bottoms
- Scarf dress split necklines
- Shirred bodice with ruffled top
- Side buttons
- Sleeves contrast in color
- Soutache
- Split necklines
- Square necks: deep V and two lesser Vs alongside
- Square necklines with concave sides
- Square necklines with V shapes
- Square necklines
- Square necklines with rounded sides
- Stand apart collar
- Stripes
- Sulfur yellow
- Swing formal skirts
- Swing-high sleeves
- Swish peplums
- Three front pleats
- Tie wrap coats
- Tied up waistlines
- Tilted forward hats
- Triangular cut outs at the neck
- Tucked suits
- Tunics
- Turbans
- Turquoise
- Two piece dresses
- Two tone suit dresses
- V necklines
- Watered taffeta
- Wide open square necks for formals
- Wing sleeves
- Wool and crepe worn together
- Wrap around dresses
- Yellow and green
- Yoke bolero jackets [1]

Harlequin-styled wine and pink watered taffeta gown with a dramatic quartered effect on the rear and sweep train, circa 1945.
$300.00 – 400.00.

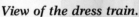

View of the dress train.

1. *Alden's Chicago Mail Order Co.*, Spring and Summer Catalog, 1945, *McCall's Magazine*, February, October, November, December 1945

Rayon dress with cut work on the bodice of net and fabric scrolls, short sleeves, curved neck, belted long skirt, and gathered waist, circa 1945. $225.00 – 265.00.

White and blue waffle textured cotton dress with blue sleeve lining and hem band, applique resembling a stenciled rose adorns the skirt, circa 1945. $180.00 – 230.00.

Straw hat with patriotic ribbon flowers and berries, known as a "Liberation Hat," circa 1945. $225.00 – 385.00.

Cornflower blue liquid satin formal gown with shirred collar, lace yoke and peplum, circa 1945. $365.00 – 425.00.

Fashion Trends for the Year 1946

(Illustrated and Non-Illustrated)

- Balloon sleeves
- Bare midriffs
- Bellhop jackets over midriff gilets
- Belted woolen dresses trimmed with sequins in all over patterns
- Belted woolen dresses trimmed with sequins in flowers
- Bolero style dresses
- Bolero suits
- Boxy shoulders
- Bumper hats
- Bumper toques
- Chartreuse
- Checkered wool
- Checks
- Corselets
- Crayon stripes on suits
- Deep cuffs worn pushed up
- Derby hats
- Draped or cowl sleeves
- Fine braiding
- Fine gingham plaid
- Flip peplums
- Forward bumper toques
- Front peplums
- Full skirts reaching to the knee
- Fur collared coats
- Gingham plaids
- Half-hats
- Halter sundresses
- High crown cloches
- Hip side bows
- Hip tucks
- Homburgs
- Hooded dinner dresses
- Jersey dirndls
- Jockey caps
- Kerchief coils
- Lantern sleeves
- Left side pleats
- Long bodices with V necklines and peplums
- Long panniers
- Long tunics
- Muskrat tuxedo coats
- Off the face berets
- Off the face bretons
- One shoulder dresses
- Panniers
- Peg pleats

- Peter Pan collars
- Pixie hats
- Pleated peplums
- Polka dots
- Pompom neck ties
- Prints with white ground
- Puckering at the waist and midriff
- Pushed up sleeves
- Rayon crepe with spangles
- Rayon velvet
- Rickrack
- Rolled brim cloches
- Ruffles at neck yokes
- Saucer brim hats
- Scalloped dirndls
- Sequin calots
- Sequins on wool dresses
- Shoulder ruffles on peasant styles
- Slim fitting waists
- Snoods
- Soutache
- Striped flannel suits
- Suede suits
- Swathed hips
- Tall cloches with small brims
- Three way stripes
- Triangle midriffs
- Triangular cutout sundresses
- Tunic shirt dresses
- Turtle neck collars
- Two way jumpers
- Two-piece shirtwaist with peplum
- Wing sleeves [1]

White tulle heart shaped halo veil with wax flowers, circa 1946.
$85.00 – 145.00.

1. *Het Rijk der Vrouw – Pris*, September 29, 1946; *McCall's*, March, June – November 1946; *Glamour*, September 1946; *Montgomery Wards*, Catalog Fall and Winter 1946 – 1947

Tulle and brocade wedding gown, shirred tulle skirt taffeta underskirt, brocaded bodice with foliage pattern, shirring at the elbows, circa 1946.
$295.00 – 325.00.

Pink wool gown with sequined berries and leaves on the shoulder and waist, circa 1946.
$289.00 – 365.00.

Black abstract printed rayon dress with illusion neckline, circa 1946.
$120.00 – 195.00.

Straw high crown hat with a mixture of flowers and ribbons, circa 1946.
$75.00 – 85.00.

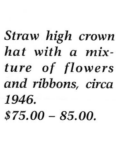

Pink gown of sheer chiffon, shirred bodice and pushup sleeves, circa 1946.
$225.00 – 295.00.

Brown felt hat with rust ostrich feathers, circa 1946 – 1947.
$200.00 – 300.00.

Pique housecoat or hostess dress, green, yellow, and red stripe print, black pointy lapels, circa 1946 – 1948.
$150.00 – 265.00.

Pink bridesmaid hat, nylon brim, open crown, and streamers (shown with a 1930s collar), circa 1946.
$75.00 – 125.00.

Halo hat with attached scarf, woven blue, red, yellow, and white netting, circa 1946. $75.00 – 85.00.

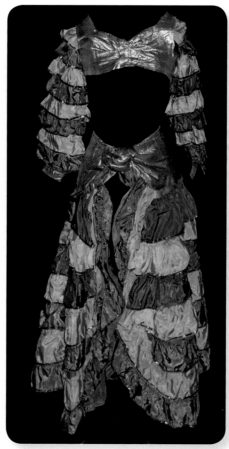

Latin inspired dance costume, ruffled overskirt and top with ruffled sleeves, circa 1946. $225.00 – 365.00.

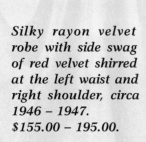

Silky rayon velvet robe with side swag of red velvet shirred at the left waist and right shoulder, circa 1946 – 1947. $155.00 – 195.00.

Fashion Trends for the Year 1947

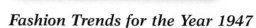

(Illustrated and Non-Illustrated)

- All over accordion pleats on the bodice and sleeves
- All over eyelet
- Ballet length formal
- Barber pole stripes
- Big pockets
- Black and white
- Blue
- Boat necklines with keyholes
- Bridal dresses with high necklines and big skirts
- Bright abstract prints
- Brocades
- Cowl draped necklines
- Dirndl dresses
- Eyelet on dark crepe
- Front flare peplums
- Geometric prints
- Green
- Gray stripes
- Guatemalan cotton play suits

- Lantern sleeves
- Long jackets
- Long torsos
- Longer skirts
- Mannish, broad, square shoulders
- Off the shoulder looks
- Peg pockets
- Peplums
- Peppermint striped ruffles on dresses
- Peruvian Indian motifs
- Pink
- Plaid topcoats
- Pointed scallop button closings
- Princess lines with flared skirt
- Redingotes
- Reversed collars
- Rounded hips
- Rounder, broader and padded shoulders
- Saw tooth square necklines
- Scarves over hips
- Seersucker stripes
- Shirred bodices
- Shirring at the sides of waists
- Sling sleeves
- Straight and narrow skirts
- Strapless gowns
- Suits with black belts
- Sundresses with bell hop jackets
- Sweetheart necklines
- Tassel fringe
- Velvet flounces
- Wrap around dresses
- Yellow
- Zip front housedresses [1]

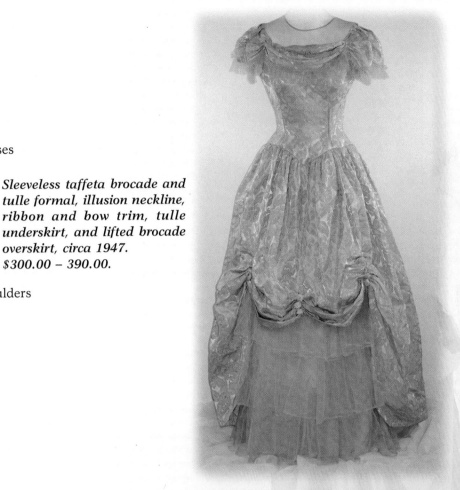

Sleeveless taffeta brocade and tulle formal, illusion neckline, ribbon and bow trim, tulle underskirt, and lifted brocade overskirt, circa 1947.
$300.00 – 390.00.

Shirred and beaded tulle halo hat, circa 1947.
$75.00 – 125.00.

Black straw toy tilt hat with veil and gigantic two white ball-ended hatpin, circa 1947.
$85.00 – 125.00.

1. *Ladies Home Journal,* October 1947; *Montgomery Ward's Catalog,* Spring & Summer 1947; *McCall's Magazine,* January – April, June – August, October 1947

Fur trimmed flat hat with rose corsage, circa 1947.
$50.00 – 65.00.

Red and white check dress, large side pockets, plastic buttons, circa 1947.
$95.00 – 125.00.

Top hat with rhinestone decorated bow and wide mesh veil, circa 1947.
$125.00 – 225.00.

Flat topped navy and burgundy satin hat, pancake style, the "New Look," circa 1947 – early 1950s.
$36.00 – 48.00.

Chartreuse pinstriped satin gown, sweetheart neckline curves towards the center, scalloped waistline, short, puffed sleeve, circa 1947. $150.00 – 245.00.

Pink taffeta formal with white and gold embroidered leaves, sleeve streamers, illusion neckline, scalloped thin peplum, circa 1947. $125.00 – 175.00.

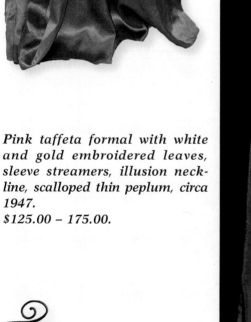

Orange-red rayon dress with sling sleeves open at the side to show a partial view of the upper arm, circa 1947. $100.00 – 185.00.

Wool suit with shirred shoulders and wrists, buttoned cuffs, circa 1947. $275.00 – 350.00.

White straw circular hat trimmed with four pink roses, circa 1947. $65.00 – 85.00.

Fashion Trends for the Year 1948

(Illustrated and Non-Illustrated)

- Backs of dresses with button-down details and peplums
- Bands of lace at the skirt waist and yokes
- Beige and black suits
- Black and blue
- Black and brown
- Bolero ensembles
- Bows on the waist backs
- Cameo necklines
- Cinched in waists
- Curved accents on collar and peplums
- Diamond necklines
- Elastic shirring on the waists and hips
- Fan drapery on the side of dresses
- Fishtail peplums
- Flared basque dresses
- Full evening skirts with molded bodices
- Hats with full birds
- Longer and slimmer dresses
- Low flared silhouettes
- Low flared skirts
- Low flounce boleros
- Moderately flared skirts with crisscross bodices
- Oversized collars
- Pantsuits
- Rickrack
- Seersucker suits
- Shirtwaist with flared skirt

Sundress with black eyelet lace and pale green backing, circa 1947. $145.00 – 185.00.

- Short jackets
- Side tier peplums
- Skirts in gathered tiers
- Soft, draped suits
- Suits with side waist bows
- Sweetheart necklines
- Tailspin peplums
- Tiered peplums
- Tiers running down the dress asymmetrically
- Topper hats

- Triangle collars
- Tunics with low flares
- Tuxedo shirts
- Two piece plaid skirts and bodices on suits
- V stripes
- Vertical feathers and wings
- Very wide skirts
- Wide cartwheel hats
- Wide rounded collars and small peplums [1]

Wide brimmed straw tilt hat, open weave, faux glass eyed parrot fashioned from feathers, red, yellow, and white flowers, label: Saks Fifth Avenue, circa 1948.
$225.00 – 385.00.

1. *Femme d'Aujourd'hui,* July 3, August 21, September 4, September 8, 1948; *McCall's Magazine,* January, February, May, July, August, October 1948

227

White linen suit, scal-
loped collar, scalloped
diagonal peplum, and
double rows of brass
buttons, circa 1948.
$275.00 – 350.00.

Black taffeta formal gown with gauntlet
gloves, pink edging on neck ruffle, skirt
ruffled ornament, circa 1948.
$350.00 – 550.00.

Red wool suit with
shirred shoulders and
wrists, buttoned cuffs,
slight peplum, circa
1948.
$275.00 – 350.00.

Cotton floral print
dress, pointed trian-
gular collar, deep
pointed cuffs, side
pockets, circa 1948
– 1949.
$89.00 – 145.00.

Fashion Trends for the Year 1949

[Non-Illustrated]

- Asymmetrical evening dresses
- Asymmetrical lines
- Bat wing or dolman sleeves
- Bengaline
- Big collars
- Blues
- Bright prints on pale ground
- Button down print dresses
- Calico and ribbon hostess & lounging coats
- Calots
- Cartwheel and helmet cloches
- Cartwheel hats
- Cascading ruffles on dress backs
- Cinched waists
- Coachman buttons
- Dark ground rayon prints
- Dimple berets
- Dog-ear pockets
- Draped turbans
- Dress Homburg hats
- Dressy pillboxes
- Empire waistlines
- Fitted midriffs
- Floating panels or stoles on evening dresses
- Floral cotton skirts
- Floral housecoats
- Floral postillions
- Formals with portrait necklines
- Frosted organdy
- Gaucho dresses
- Geometric angular dresses with slanted pockets
- Giant bows
- Giant fly-away collars
- Gingham
- Halter or V-shaped neck straps
- Hip drapery
- Hooverettes
- Hostess gowns
- House dresses with floral or striped prints
- Jersey dresses
- Long flared or slim skirts
- Look alike mother and daughter dresses
- Many buttons
- Metallic striped taffeta
- Mid-calf length
- Midriff bearing playsuits
- Off the face bonnets
- One shoulder décolleté
- One sided skirts with pockets
- Open crown bonnets
- Open crown sailor with mushroom brims
- Panama hats
- Pannier draped waists
- Peasant blouses
- Peplums with front ends and ruffled back swirls
- Petal or sweetheart necklines
- Pinafores
- Portrait necklines
- Profile berets and bretons
- Rayon shirtwaist dresses
- Rear flaring
- Reverse wrap around ties
- Rhinestones on dress bodices with nylon net
- Sailor hats
- Scoop necklines
- Shutter necklines
- Side buttons
- Small curved peplums
- Square dancing style dresses
- Square necklines
- Strapless dresses with boleros
- Swish skirt evening gowns
- Tab button pockets
- Tubular, loose flying fabric panels
- Two-tone dresses
- Waffle pique
- Windowpane checks
- Wing collars [1]

1. *Femme d'Aujourd'hui*, September 8, 1949, December 15, 1949; *Wards Sale Book*, June – July 1949; *Montgomery Ward's Catalog*, Spring and Summer 1949; *McCall's Magazine*, March, April, July – December, 1949

Chapter 14
1950 – 1959

Vibrant and lively, innocent and sophisticated, these words summed up the fashion
of the woman of the 1950s. Christian Dior's
new look appeared in 1947 making the female silhouette more dramatic with longer skirts, cinched
waists and chic flat cap hats. Clothing was more
elaborate than the previous decade. Women were
tired of the deprivation and fabric shortages of the
war years. Now the focus was on opulence. No one
can forget the diaphanous, fluffy confections women
wore to proms and formal occasions. The cocktail
dress had an unprecedented appeal. As the decade
heralded greater prosperity, women had the oppor-
tunity to express their desire for fashionable expression with new hats, more varieties of formal wear
dresses for different occasions and times of day,
and different dress design styles in color and fabric.
Whether wearing something demure or sultry, the
fifties woman successfully made her mark on fashion
history.

Fashion Trends for the Year 1950

(Illustrated and Non-Illustrated)

- Abstract prints
- Accordion pleated tops and skirts
- Angled large pockets
- Asymmetrical embroidery
- Asymmetrical lines
- Baggy sleeves
- Bib yokes
- Boleros or short jackets
- Bow collars
- Button down shirtwaists
- Checks with solids
- Cinched waists
- Circle and thin skirts
- Cone shaped crown hats
- Crisscross dresses with ties on the waists
- Curved pillboxes with side veils
- Daisy prints
- Diamond necklines
- Dolman sleeves
- Dress overlays
- Dressy shirtwaists
- Fan pleats
- Feathered hats
- Flared A-line skirts
- Flat, wide-brimmed hats
- Floral prints
- Flyaway winged collars

- Flying saucer hats
- Gauntlet gloves
- Gloves half way to the elbow
- Half turtle necks
- Hats and matching gloves
- High Johnny collars
- High necklines under the throat
- High Peter Pan collars
- Hip circling pockets
- Illusion toppers with Peter Pan collars
- Iridescent taffeta in amethyst
- Iridescent taffeta in copper
- Iridescent taffeta in gray
- Jeweled buttons
- Jumper dresses
- Kangaroo pockets
- Keyhole trapezoid neck openings
- Lapels extend to the shoulders
- Large check prints
- Large portrait hats
- Less pronounced pockets
- Mandarin or notched collars
- Midriff styles
- Monochromatic dresses
- Mother and daughter matching outfits
- Multiple rows of lace peplums
- Necklines open in dickey fashion
- Off the shoulder peasant looks
- Organdy
- Oval necklines
- Peasant styles with ruffled necklines
- Pedal pushers
- Pencil skirts flare with pleats
- Penknife prints
- Peplums and slanting collars
- Peter Pan collars
- Pocketed, rounded labels
- Polka dot prints and bows
- Portrait hats
- Portrait square necklines
- Puckered lawn and broadcloth
- Queen Anne and double folded wing collars
- Rayon gabardine
- Rayon sharkskin
- Redingotes
- Rings of flowers with veils
- Rolled collars
- Scalloped hems
- Schiffli embroidery
- Schiffli lace
- Scoop neck blouses
- Shawl collars

- Shirred cap sleeves
- Shirtwaist dresses
- Skirts below the knee
- Slit neck openings
- Slouched side berets
- Slouchy hats
- Small brimmed hats atop the head
- Square, hexagonal or straight necklines
- Strapless sundresses
- Striped or solid sundresses
- Sweaters or printed dresses in contrasting colors
- Sweetheart necklines
- Tartan plaid accents
- Thin skirts
- U-shaped necklines
- V-neck dresses
- V-neck sarong dresses
- Velvet caps
- Voile or dotted Swiss
- Wild prints
- Windowpane bodices with lattice cut work
- Winged triangular collars. [1]

Ivory velvet rounded hat with cutout felt leaves embellished with pearls and rhinestones, circa 1950.
$50.00 – 75.00.

Orange taffeta gown with V off the shoulder neckline, puffed sleeves, large portrait off the shoulder collar, circa 1950.
$125.00 – 195.00.

Black and gray ribbed suit with velvet collar, cinched peplum, rhinestone trimmed velvet cord at the throat, circa 1950.
$125.00 – 230.00.

Salmon pink crystal organza formal with velvet rose corsage, circa 1950.
$200.00 – 300.00.

1. *McCall's Magazine,* November 1950, pp. 44, 46, 66, 137, 140, 143, 144; *Montgomery Wards Catalog,* Spring and Summer Catalog 1950, 1 – 93; *McCall's Magazine,* February 1950, pp. 139, 140, 143 – 144, 146 – 148; *McCall's Magazine,* January 1950, 117 – 118, 121, 122, 125, 126; *Montgomery Wards Catalog,* Spring and Summer Catalog 1950, 1 – 93; *McCall's Magazine,* April 1950, pp. 32, 36, 50, 92, 98, 116, 126, 134, 146, 151, 156; *Montgomery Wards Catalog,* Spring and Summer Catalog 1950, 1 – 93;l; *McCall's Magazine,* October 1950, pp. 38, 120, 124, 130, 140, 143, 146, 151, 155; *Femmes d'Aujourd'hui,* July 1950, pp. 5, 6, 8, 16, 17; *McCall's Magazine,* July 1950, pp. 32, 79, 105, 110, 114, 116, 118, 120, 123, 124; *Montgomery Wards Catalog,* Spring and Summer Catalog 1950, 1 – 93

Fashion Trends for the Year 1951

(Illustrated and Non-Illustrated)

Chocolate brown taffeta dress with black stripes, diagonal stripes, angular buttoned cuffs, circa 1950.
$90.00 – 160.00.

Olive green metallic taffeta dress with rhinestone accents on the collar, circa 1950 – 1953.
$90.00 – 195.00.

- Abstract clover printed silks
- Abstract green printed silks
- Abstract lilac printed silks
- Abstract yellow printed silks
- Accordion pleats
- Asymmetrical button designs
- Brimmed bonnets
- Circle skirts
- Cloches with small brims
- Cloches with square bows
- Cloverleaf prints
- Colorful scarves
- Curved yokes in contrasting colors
- Daisies
- Double rows of buttons down the bodice and skirt
- Dresses with small ties on short sleeves
- Dyed to match Venice lace at the collars and cuffs
- Fan pleats running from the bodice down the skirt
- Fanciful buttons
- Floral prints
- Fruit and flowers in sprigs and sprays
- Geometric prints
- Gingham
- Harlequin checks
- Hexagonal necklines
- Hip pleats run vertical down skirts
- Homburgs
- Irish linen
- Jockey style hats
- Keyhole openings at necklines with bows or ties
- Large brims
- Large polka dots
- Leaves
- Lily of the valley
- Mandarin collars
- Matching mother and daughter outfits
- Narrow or flared dresses
- Navy, pastels, and dark tones
- Nylon marquisettes
- Off the shoulder sundresses
- One toned dresses with black and color accessories
- Open crown hats
- Overlapping labels
- Oversized collars muted prints, wild squares and patterns

- Pastel colors
- Peasant or Mexican style sundresses
- Peasant tops
- Periwinkle
- Pleated mermaid hemlines
- Red rusts
- Ring hats
- Rolled straw brim hats
- Roses
- Scoop necklines
- Scrunching above the bosom
- Seersucker
- Sharp bolero jackets
- Sheath dresses
- Sheer dresses of nylon and rayon
- Shelf busts
- Shell bonnets
- Shirred bodices with string ties at the throat
- Shirtwaist or knitted dresses in lime green or white
- Shrug boleros
- Shutter necklines
- Simple and straight cuffs
- Skullcaps
- Slate blues
- Small pillboxes
- Smaller toques
- Solids
- Spade collars
- Stand up collars Mandarin style
- Stripes
- Suits
- Sundresses with square necklines and big pockets
- Sundresses with sweetheart necklines
- Sweater dresses
- Sweetheart necklines
- Synthetic and natural straw and braid
- Tab collar or a bib of contrasting color with a bow
- Taffeta bows
- Tricorns
- Tunic peplums
- Wide brim hats
- Wide stripes [1]

Blue and white cotton bold checked day dress, sailor collar and buttoned band on the bodice, circa 1951. $50.00 – 90.00.

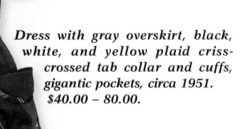

Dress with gray overskirt, black, white, and yellow plaid criss-crossed tab collar and cuffs, gigantic pockets, circa 1951. $40.00 – 80.00.

1. *McCall's Magazine*, February 1951, pp. 46, 48, 126, 131 – 132, 135, 137, 140, 142, 146, 149, 151 – 152; *McCall's Magazine*, March 1951, pp. 105, 134, 142, 146, 150, 155; *McCall's Magazine*, April 1951, pp. 134, 138, 143, 144, 146, 149, 150, 152, 154, 156; *McCall's Magazine*, May 1951; *Femmes d'Aujourd'hui*, May 1951, pp. 5 – 6, 8, 11, 16 – 17; *Montgomery Wards Catalog*, Spring and Summer 1951, pp. 1 – 89, 236 – 252

Fashion Trends for the Year 1952

(Illustrated and Non-Illustrated)

Sheer organdy dress with white tuxedo bib, high tab collar, and rhinestone buttons, circa 1951. $80.00 – 115.00.

Electric blue taffeta dress, square collar, circa 1951. $95.00 – 125.00.

- Apron effect bodices
- Bold block plaids
- Checks and stripes in black
- Checks and stripes in bright olive green
- Checks and stripes in chartreuse
- Checks and stripes in drab blue
- Checks and stripes in gray
- Checks and stripes in lavender
- Checks and stripes in rust
- Cotton broadcloth
- Crests or monogramming on diagonal skirt pockets
- Crests or monogramming on bodice pockets
- Crisscross collars
- Dolman sleeves
- Flared biased gored skirts
- Gingham dresses with puff sleeves
- Hats worn close to the crown
- Large full skirts worn with a crinoline
- Middy stripes
- Mother and daughter dresses in plaids, lace and polka dots
- Paris pockets had flaps stitched down the center
- Parisian vertical pleats
- Redingotes
- Rhinestone buttons
- Sleeveless or halter dresses
- Stand up collars
- Suits with tuxedo labels
- Toppers or short flared coats worn over dresses
- Turned up sleeves
- Two-toned dresses
- Upturned cuffs and points on the cuffs
- Waffle pique
- Winged collars and huge buttons
- Winged collars with turned up sleeves
- Wool batwing sweaters with dolman sleeves [1]

1. *Montgomery Wards,* Midsummer Sale Book 1952, pp. 2 – 17; *Florida Fashion Catalog,* Fall 1952, pp. 1 – 32; *McCall's Magazine,* Oct 1952, pp. 42, 44, 122, 138, 150, 152, 156, 160, 164, 168, 172, 176, 178

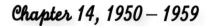

Gray wool felt elephant skirt and vest set, circa 1952 – 1954.
$125.00 – 150.00.

Slate blue sheer nylon dress with portrait collar, bow, and rhinestone buckle, white nylon pleating inside the collar, circa 1952.
$115.00 – 175.00.

Plaid airy open weave dress and portrait collar, circa 1952 – 1953.
$65.00 – 95.00.

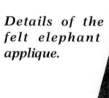

Details of the felt elephant applique.

This black wool felt poodle circle skirt has a scalloped waistband and hem. These felt poodles stand in profile amid the black foreground. Rhinestone accents are scattered about for sparkle. Poodle appliques graduate in size and are embellished with rhinestones, circa 1952 – 1954.
$118.00 – 185.00.

Grey wool felt card skirt, circa 1952 – 1954.
$100.00 – 175.00.

Fashion Trends for the Year 1953

(Illustrated and Non-Illustrated)

- Appliqued flowers on the bust and pockets
- Buttons and striping
- Cardigans
- Colorful suits
- Cotton peasant dresses
- Cotton whirly skirts
- Fiesta colors in lime green, bright blue, and cotton candy pink
- Halters with winged collars
- Nylon marquisettes
- Patio dresses
- Peasant tops
- Persian printed dresses
- Puckered nylon dresses with rhinestone accents
- Shirred and tied sleeveless tops
- Silver accessories
- Thin vertical stripes
- Three full circle skirts
- Two-tone mock halter dresses with V-necks [1]

Taffeta split front dress, Venice lace appliques, midnight blue taffeta overdress, crème taffeta and ivory tulle underdress, circa 1952.
$115.00 – 165.00.

1. *McCall's Magazine*, May 1953, pp. 42, 44, 120, 132, 136, 138, 142, 144, 146, 149, 152; *Spiegel Catalog*, 1953, pp. 1 – 70

Fashion Trends for the Winter of 1953 – Spring of 1954

(Illustrated and Non-Illustrated)

- Bicorns
- Boxy suits
- Caps worn close to the head
- Cascading trims down the sides
- Cascading trims down the skirt
- Cascading trims over the bodice
- Cascading trims over the bosom
- Dutch and shirred brim bonnets
- Feathers on hats ran in vertical directions
- Flowers at the waist
- Formal dresses with cuffed bolero jackets
- Formals in aqua
- Formals in green
- Formals in light blue
- Formals in lilac
- Formals in mauve
- Formals in pink
- Formals in powder blue
- Formals in shrimp
- Formals in white
- Hats with bows and wings
- Helmet hats
- Jewels and rhinestones as all over accents
- Jewels and rhinestones in hat bands
- Off the face cloches
- Off the face toques
- Plateau hats
- Poodle cloth
- Puritan bonnets
- Ruffled ballerina skirts with tulle and piping strips
- Small tulle off the shoulder sleeves
- Toques
- Tulle skirts cut at diagonals
- Tuxedo double breasts and rolled collars
- Two-toned nylons with scrunched bodices
- Velvet and brushed wool felt [1]

Canary yellow tulle gown with cape, Chantilly lace lattice crisscrosses, circa 1953 –1954. $235.00 – 375.00.

Pistachio green organza formal with ruffled bodice decoration and ruffled circles around the edge of the skirt, silk posy centers, circa 1953. $215.00 – 375.00.

1. *Montgomery Wards Catalog, 1953 – 1954, pp. 2 – 120*

Whimsical fifties black hat, scalloped edges, fabric covered top button, wire stem, and hanging fabric bow, label: Saks Fifth Avenue, circa early 1953 – 1954. $75.00 – 95.00.

Hot pink skullcap with silver beading and pink three-dimensional butterfly ornament, circa 1953 – 1954. $36.00 – 48.00.

Cornflower blue organza formal with pink undertones, vertical rows of shirred organza ornamenting the lower central section of the skirt, removable organza straps for transforming into a strapless gown, circa 1953 – 1954. $215.00 – 375.00.

Velvet cap with back bow, circa 1953 – 1954. $60.00 – 75.00.

Hand-painted Mexican circle skirt, rows of roses ornamented with sequins, circa 1953 – 1958. $160.00.

239

Red puckered nylon dress, portrait collar and floral lace appliques, simulated pearl buttons on the bodice, large, Paris inspired pockets, small matching belt, and lace appliques, circa 1953 – 1954. $35.00 – 70.00.

Mustard velvet winged collar halter dress, circa 1953. $125.00 – 165.00.

Blue rayon dress with soutache yoke and collar decorations, circa 1953 – 1954. $70.00 – 120.00.

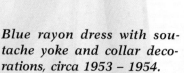

Straw slouched beret hat with side bow, circa 1953 – 1954. $50.00 – 65.00.

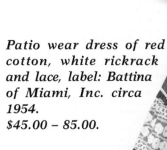

Patio wear dress of red cotton, white rickrack and lace, label: Battina of Miami, Inc. circa 1954.
$45.00 – 85.00.

Black synthetic straw cap with white roses on the brim, circa 1953 – 1954.
$25.00 – 40.00.

Fashion Trends for the Year 1954

(Illustrated and Non-Illustrated)

- Crinkled skirts with halters
- New Princess silhouette dresses
- Peasant looks and blouses
- Skirts with butterflies
- Skirts with harlequin checks
- Skirts with Mexican print designs
- Sleeveless tops [1]

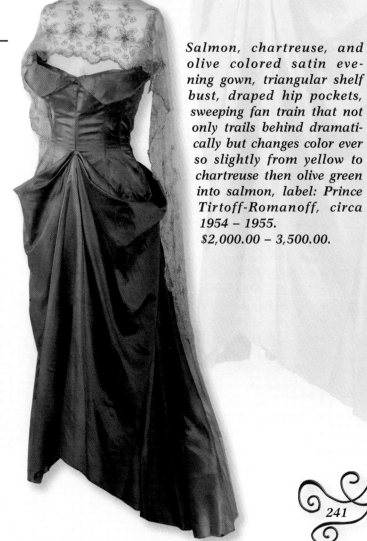

Salmon, chartreuse, and olive colored satin evening gown, triangular shelf bust, draped hip pockets, sweeping fan train that not only trails behind dramatically but changes color ever so slightly from yellow to chartreuse then olive green into salmon, label: Prince Tirtoff-Romanoff, circa 1954 – 1955.
$2,000.00 – 3,500.00.

Red and cream houndstooth checkered hat, red satin ribbons and bow, circa 1954.
$25.00 – 40.00.

1. *Montgomery Wards,* 1954 Summer Sale Catalog pp. 2 – 21.

- Sherbet colors and solids in gingham
- Skirts had many ruffles and rows
- Striped tops with boxed jackets
- Sundresses had bows at the shoulders
- Zoo characters [1]

Red pointed feather hat, circa 1955. $45.00 – 60.00.

Celery green satin formal with tulle over-skirt, matching satin shrug, green satin piping, circa 1954. $215.00 – 375.00.

Fashion Trends for the Year 1955

(Illustrated and Non-Illustrated)

- Bolero jackets
- Daisies on necklines
- Dress and sweater duos
- Egyptian prints in sundresses
- Gingham and lace sundresses
- Gingham dresses
- Halter sundresses in abstract prints
- Lace blouses
- Large polka dots
- Mambo dresses
- Musical motifs
- Parisian prints
- Permanent vertical pleats
- Princess lines and rhinestone buttons
- Printed whites with dark colored flowers
- Rhinestone studs
- Sheer coatdresses
- Sheer empire waist nylon marquisettes

Black velvet and taffeta dress with velvet ribbon appliques, circa 1955 – 1957. $125.00 – 250.00.

1. *Lana Lobell Catalog,* Summer 1955, pp. 1 – 80

Pink lace and tulle formal with shrug and netted peplum, circa 1955.
$70.00 – 130.00.

Periwinkle blue formal with taffeta underskirt, overskirt of matching tulle, bodice and peplum of tulle embroidered with gold threaded leaves and flowers, circa 1955.
$165.00 – 285.00.

Brown cotton day dress with ornamental waist buttons, circa 1955.
$80.00 – 150.00.

Red ribbed cotton sun-
dress with white seed
beaded bodice, circa
1955 – 1956.
$85.00 – 125.00.

Ivory soutache nylon sheer dress
with rhinestone embellishments,
circa 1955 – 1957.
$140.00 – 175.00.

Ice blue crystal organza gown,
circa 1955 – 1956.
$130.00 – 165.00.

Pink checkered dress, princess lines, high waist, turned down collar, cut out lace inserts, circa 1955 – 1956. $50.00 – 80.00.

Fashion Trends for the Year 1956

(Illustrated and Non-Illustrated)

- Abstract prints
- Artificial flowers
- Bouffants
- Butterflies
- Capulets
- Checks
- Cloudy sheath rayon dusters
- Cowl necklines
- Daisies
- Daisy appliques
- Decorative rickrack
- Egyptian printed sundresses
- Feathered shell hats
- Feathers horizontal across the brim
- Fez hats
- Fiesta dresses
- Flowered accents
- Formals with tiny rows of gathered tulle across the skirt
- Formals with tulle crisscrossed over the bodice
- Full circle skirts with East Indian fabric prints
- Full circle skirts with kittens
- Full circle skirts with paisley
- Full skirts
- Gingham
- Grecian key trims
- Hats had head clamps to keep the hat on the top of the head
- Jeweled fez hats
- Lilac
- Lime
- Linen looking berets
- Lower hip lines
- Nautical looks
- Necklines with rickrack
- One shoulder blouses
- One shoulder sari prints against a full skirt
- Opposite negative image print
- Pancake hats
- Peaks on the bodice and pants
- Peasant blouses
- Pedal pushers
- Pink
- Plaids
- Play clothes with rope belts
- Polka dots
- Princess lines
- Prints with book covers

Blue checked dress, empire bust, portrait collar, ornamental buttons, and scalloped collar, circa 1955 – 1956. $50.00 – 85.00.

- Prints with carnival motifs
- Prints with designs from the Casbah
- Prints with roosters
- Prints with Spanish themes
- Removable bandanas over sleeveless sundresses
- Rhinestone buttons
- Rickrack trims
- Rolled brims on cloches
- Sailor hats
- Salmon
- Sari printed cotton dresses
- Shell hats
- Side slits
- Silk organdy dresses
- Silk shantung suits with polka dots
- Taffeta and tulle confections
- Tiered ballerina skirts
- Tulle skirts striped with lace in vertical or horizontal patterns
- Turquoise
- Vertical cording
- Wide strapped sundresses
- Yellow [1]

Peacock blue and white formal, velvet bodice, horseshoe bust effect, rows of white tulle and velvet bands, circa 1956 – 1958.
$125.00 – 180.00.

Cherry red tulle formal, horseshoe bust, shirred rows of tulle, circa 1956 – 1958.
$215.00 – 375.00.

Pink organza formal and shrug, billowing organza skirt over pink tulle underskirt, clusters of pink silk flowers at the hips, skirt front, and festoons on the draped overskirt, circa 1956.
$235.00 – 375.00.

1. *Lana Lobell Catalog*, 1956, pp. 1 – 64; *Montgomery Wards*, Spring & Summer Catalog 1956, pp. 1 – 117; *Wilco Catalog*, circa 1956, pp. 1 – 42

Navy blue fancy dress, shelf bust with lace inserts, circa 1956.
$115.00 – 125.00.

Purple and chartreuse costume, circle skirt ornamented with vivid applique flowers and leaves, bordered with colored sequins, circa 1956.
$100.00 – 200.00.

Cherry red dress, shelf bodice, gold painted circles, sari style fabric, V-neck, short sleeves, circa 1956.
$90.00 – 195.00.

Cornflower blue velvet and tulle strapless gown, circa 1956.
$200.00 – 685.00.

Cotton candy pink formal, Chantilly lace overskirt, rows of ruffled tulle on the back underskirt, circa 1956.
$125.00 – 180.00.

White and gray sheer nylon party dress, rows of overlapping fabric fans adorning the bust, pink velvet ribbon belt, circa 1956.
$115.00 – 125.00.

Mint green strapless formal, shirred tulle skirt, tiny tulle ruffle topping the bodice, circa 1956.
$115.00 – 165.00.

White Chantilly lace and taffeta formal gown with rows of ruffled lace on the skirt, circa 1956 – 1957.
$215.00 – 375.00.

Royal purple velvet formal, side hip ruffle and matching velvet shrug, circa 1956.
$775.00 – 925.00.

Straw elevated pillbox hat with delicate rose, circa 1956 – 1957.
$36.00 – 48.00.

Jockey style cap, upturned brim, pink silk flowers, circa 1956.
$36.00 – 80.00.

Plum taffeta evening cocktail dress, asymmetrical ruffles, pointed wing bodice, circa 1956 – 1957. $125.00 – 165.00.

Green tulle and velvet formal, rows shirred on the skirt, dark green velvet shrug, and chevron bodice ornamentation, circa 1956 – 1957. $375.00 – 645.00.

Navy and cream hat with asymmetrical wing, circa 1956 – 1957. $25.00 – 36.00.

Fashion Trends for the Year 1957

(Illustrated and Non-Illustrated)

- Black and white
- Bodices with less waist cinching
- Bonnets
- Bows across the bust
- Capulet hats
- Cloches
- Coral and yellow
- Dainty gingham cottons
- Dome silhouettes
- Flat but high tapered brims
- Flat crowns
- Hats that are dome shaped
- Hats with artificial fruits and berries

- Hats worn off the face
- Midriff tied blouses
- Monogrammed circle skirts
- Off the shoulder blouses
- Pastel green
- Persian prints
- Plateau hats with daisy trims
- Sailor and feathered hats
- Sheath dresses and skirts had horizontal pleats
- Small dress prints
- Tambourine hats with flowers
- Velvet bows at bodice center [1]

Soft pink lace formal with rows of Chantilly lace over an organza skirt, circa 1957.
$115.00 – 180.00.

Periwinkle blue felt hat with side silk flowers and dramatic veil, circa 1957.
$50.00 – 75.00.

Green velvet and golden straw picture hat decorated with golden roses, circa 1957.
$200.00 – 300.00.

Berry bountiful skullcap of plastic currants in shades of green and red, circa 1957.
$58.00 – 120.00.

1. *Montgomery Wards,* Spring & Summer Catalog 1957, pp. 1 – 91; *Skylark Catalog,* circa 1957, pp. 1 – 33; *Montgomery Wards Catalog,* Spring Summer 1957, pp. 2 – 21

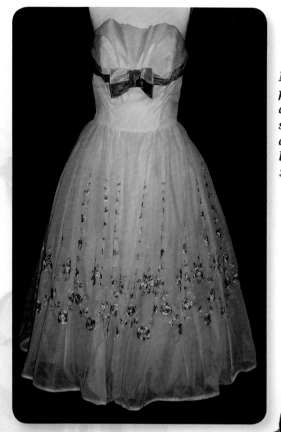

Nylon formal gown, purple and white embroidered floral decoration, satin band and bow across the center of the bodice, circa 1957. $195.00 – 235.00.

White flat topped sailor hat with large red bow and veil, circa 1957. $25.00 – 36.00.

Rose printed taffeta formal with petal bust, sheer organza cape and velvet bow, circa 1957. $150.00 – 235.00.

Salmon pink taffeta dress, rhinestone buttons, black velvet abstract floral appliques and banding, circa 1957 – 1958. $85.00 – 125.00.

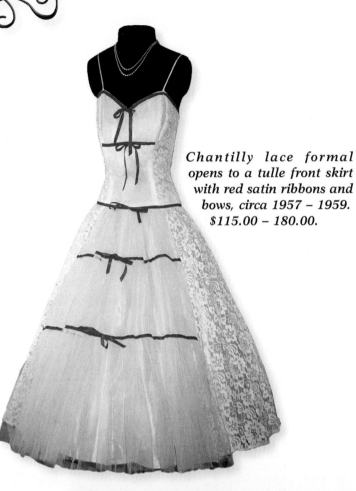

Chantilly lace formal opens to a tulle front skirt with red satin ribbons and bows, circa 1957 – 1959. $115.00 – 180.00.

Salmon pink tulle formal, attached tulle wrap, asymmetrical tulle overskirt, circa 1957 – 1958. $125.00 – 165.00.

Straw high hat with dangling black and red cherry brim ornament and a crown of leaves, circa 1957. $58.00 – 120.00.

This Valentine's Day dance formal was worn in 1957. The owner of the dress embellished this white formal with red felt hearts. $115.00 – 165.00.

White, green, and brown silk flower hat resembling
an upside down bouquet of flowers, circa 1957.
$45.00 – 55.00.

Brown, orange, white, and tan feather hat with a whimsical
crown of vertical feathers, circa 1957.
$45.00 – 55.00.

Vest and short set made
of striped cotton with
golden buttons, circa
1957 – 1958.
$45.00 – 75.00.

Fashion Trends for the Year 1958

(Illustrated and Non-Illustrated)

Light blue dress with vertical buttons and slim lines, circa 1957 to early 1960s.
$80.00 – 150.00.

- Circle skirts in abstract prints
- Circle skirts in dark checks
- Circle skirts in toast colors
- Circle skirts in turquoise colors
- Cotton prints — small dots enlarged gradually
- Cotton skirts with boat prints
- Cotton skirts with bow prints
- Cotton skirts with kitten prints
- Cotton skirts with ribbon prints
- Darker colored bouffant dresses
- Denim culotte skirts
- Floral prints
- Fringed trims
- Mother and daughter dresses in checks
- Mother and daughter dresses in stripes
- Peak-a-boo pleats
- Pedal pushers
- Pinafore gingham dresses
- Prints with graduated dots
- Prints with vertical dots
- Sherbet colored sweaters
- Slim looks [1]

Scalloped straw wide brimmed hat resembling lace and embellished with rhinestones, circa 1958.
$40.00 – 60.00.

Pink, brown, and orange floral dress with rhinestone embellishments, circa 1957 – 1958.
$85.00 – 135.00.

1. *Bellas Hess Catalog*, 1958, pp. 1 – 32; *Wards*, Mid-Summer Catalog, 1958, pp. 2 – 21

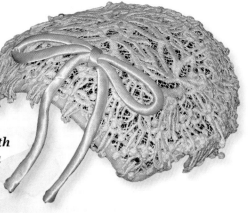

Venice lace stiffened cap with back bow, circa 1958 – 1959. $26.00 – 35.00.

Dramatic blue gathered and shirred nylon strapless gown, circa 1958 – 1959. $215.00 – 375.00.

Light pink gathered and shirred nylon strapless gown, circa 1958 – 1959. $215.00 – 375.00.

Aqua blue and gold formal, shimmering gold lamé bodice, ballerina tulle skirt, left side looped tulle ornamentation, circa 1958.
$130.00 – 180.00.

Fashion Trends for the Year 1959

(Illustrated and Non-Illustrated)

- Accordion pleats
- Banded ensembles
- Beige
- Bell crown cloches
- Berets resembling beaver fur
- Black and white checks
- Blue
- Bold silk dresses in blues
- Bold silk dresses in greens
- Bold silk dresses in oranges
- Bold silk dresses in pinks
- Bow pillboxes
- Boxy coats
- Boxy suits in blue abstract prints
- Boxy suits in bold green prints
- Boxy sweaters
- Button downed shirts
- Camel color

- Caplets
- Cartwheel hats
- Chantilly lace dresses in blue
- Chantilly lace dresses in dusty rose
- Chantilly lace dresses in white
- Chantilly lace dresses with boleros
- Checks
- Chiffon cascading down the dress's back
- Cloches
- Coral
- Cowl necklines
- Crown bonnets
- Cuffed pillboxes
- Dangled pompoms
- Draped cloches
- Earth tones
- Empire looks
- Eyelet and lace covered sheath dresses
- Feather hats
- Feathered brims
- Feathered capulets
- Feathered cloches
- Feathered toques
- Feathers worn along the crown
- Flowered caps
- Greens
- Hats with daisies
- Hats with mixed flowers
- Jeweled tones
- Large shawl collars over coats
- Mushroom collars
- Mushroom plateaus
- Mustard
- Orange
- Pagoda styles
- Petal shells
- Pillboxes
- Plateau hats
- Pleated caplets
- Pointed shells
- Rabbit fur berets
- Rayon silk dresses
- Red pepper red
- Richer and deeper jewel-toned colors
- Rose
- Rose petal hats
- Russian beaver fur hats
- Sailor hats
- Sheath dresses
- Shells
- Slender sheaths
- Smocked shoulder jackets

- Sweeping skirts
- Taller cloches
- Telescope crowns
- Tiered cloches
- Tufted bonnets
- Turbans
- Very high cloches
- Waistlines almost under the bust
- Watteau trains
- Wool felt resembling beaver [1]

White Chantilly lace strapless formal, blue appliqued three-dimensional flowers, leaves, and stems are embroidered in blue silver cord, sparkling rhinestones embellish the flowers, circa 1959.
$125.00 – 180.00.

Cotton candy pink lace formal, tulle collar in a Watteau or waterfall effect as a scarf trailing down the back of the dress, circa 1959.
$120.00 – 175.00.

Black straw large cartwheel hat trimmed with large and small white silk flowers, circa 1959.
$150.00 – 175.00.

1. *Montgomery Wards*, Spring Summer Catalog, 1959, pp. 1 – 126; *Montgomery Ward's Catalog*, Fall & Winter 1959, pp. 1 – 89, 104 – 105

Wool check suit with white collar, cuffs, and neck bow, circa 1959. $75.00 – 180.00.

Exotic blue cap of feathers in turquoise, red, and yellow, circa 1959. $36.00 – 48.00.

Caramel brown, electric blue, and green feather hat, circa 1959. $35.00 – 45.00.

Sixties fashion was all about modernization and new found feminine freedoms. Women's clothing became more streamline and refined. The feminine, demure aspect of the fifties gave way to more mature styles and colors. Women followed the fashions and the youthful eagerly adopted everything mod, floral and eventually hippie. Feminine style would be followed by feminist looks and increasingly unconventional looks. Women still had to wait for some time before they could radically change their everyday styles. They were still, after all, conventionally limited to wearing skirts and restrictive girdles. Patterns became bolder and more optical. Mod, popart and opart all reflected changing views in art and counter culture. Fashion allowed the body to be a canvas for such radical freedom of expression and rebellious change. Alongside such trends women continued to reflect stylish elegance. Lovely tailored suits, sinuous cocktail dresses, chic hats, jewel-toned shift dresses and sophisticated formal gowns were reflections of classic taste. The feminine form transformed itself once more with the introduction of the mini skirt and the outrageous micro-mini. Women adopted baby doll clothing to appear cute and innocent. No matter how it was packaged, style and glamour continued to be the trademarks of the ever-changing and increasingly emancipated sixties women.

Fashion Trends for the Year 1960

(Non-Illustrated)

- Basque jackets
- Beige with white trim
- Birdcage net on flat hair bows
- Blue floral prints
- Box tops with flutter sleeves
- Boxy suits
- Button back boleros
- Cable stripes
- Check and plaid suits
- Chignon caps
- Circle prints
- Collarless blouses with bows
- Cotton shirtwaists
- Crescent collars
- Drooped shoulders
- Flowered silks
- Flowery prints
- Frog fasteners

- Geometrics
- Gray
- Green polyester prints
- Hair kerchiefs to match dress print
- Herringbone sheaths
- High pockets
- Jamaica shorts
- Lantern puff sleeves
- Lilly of the valley
- Navy
- Neutrals
- Organdy
- Rickrack
- Saddle stitch
- Sheath dresses
- Shirt dresses
- Side wrap skirts
- Slacks in stripes and checks
- Slim midriffs with full skirts
- Slipover tops
- Spice jar prints
- Square prints
- Stripes
- Sweetheart necklines
- Three-way toned colors
- Tunic shirts
- Turbans
- Turquoise flowers
- Violet
- Wide vinyl belts
- Wing collars and puff sleeves [1]

Fashion Trends for the Year 1961

(Non-Illustrated)

- Ankle length pants
- Chevron stripes
- Clinging bodices
- Full skirts
- Jersey dresses
- Jumpers
- Mink hats
- Mink trims on dresses
- Muted abstract prints
- Muted plaids
- Soutache on bodice
- Tiny abstract prints
- V necks
- Velveteen formals [2]

1. Simplicity Pattern Book, January – March 1960
2. *Montgomery Ward's Catalog,* Fall and Winter 1961

Fashion Trends for the Year 1962

(Illustrated and Non-Illustrated)

- Acetate lace formals
- Ankle pants and slacks
- Autumn colored plaid jumpers
- Autumn colored skirts and blouses with bouffants
- Blue with green
- Boat necks
- Bow capulets
- Bow neckline dresses worn with gloves and pillboxes
- Boxy suits
- Brocade short-waist jackets over dresses
- Brocaded elegant dresses
- Capri lounge suits
- Capulets
- Cashmere coats
- Circular feather whimsies
- Cowl necks
- Crochet hats with large sequins
- Crusader hoods
- Dark blue
- Diamonds and abstracts
- Dome toques
- Double knit suits
- Floral circlets
- Flower profiles
- Fringe or twist skirts
- Greens
- High round necklines
- Italian double knits
- Jewel tone velveteen
- Knit suits
- Mink trim on hats
- Mink toques and cloches
- Nylon jersey formals
- Open crown pillboxes
- Orange
- Paisleys
- Pillbox hats
- Pinwheel helmet hat
- Pixie hats
- Pleated knit skirts
- Princess line jumpers
- Ribbed tied waist dresses
- Ruffled edge blouses
- Rust
- Schiffli embroidery
- Shirred jersey formals worn over bouffants

- Shirtwaist dresses in browns, greens, blues, purples, and prints
- Slim dresses with side bow belt ties
- Slim straight jumpers and cowl blouses
- Stand up collars
- Straight necks and full skirts
- Sweater and knit pants or skirt sets
- Tiered cloches
- Turbans
- Turtleneck shirts
- Velvet red, black, and blue formals
- Velveteen gown with empire satin waists
- Wide pleats skirts [1]

Pinwheel helmet wool knit cap with entwined iridescent spangle sequins, circa 1962.
$30.00 – 45.00.

Hot pink silk leaf cap with stamen ends that look like dewdrops, circa 1962 – 1963.
$35.00 – 45.00.

1. *Montgomery Ward's Catalog*, Fall and Winter 1962

Fashion Trends for the Year 1963

(Illustrated and Non-Illustrated)

- Capulets with bows
- Capulets with petals
- Embroidered dresses
- Embroidered sweaters
- Feathered whimsies
- Formal dresses of sheer nylon
- Huge furs
- Open crown pillbox hats
- Pillbox hats worn with straight shift dresses
- Sheer neck scarves on the rears of formal dresses
- Sheer rayon organza hats
- Spring floral hats
- Straight and flared skirts
- Turbans
- Waist high boxy bodices [1]

Outrageous and oversized, this early 1960s hat has a giant mushroom crown of stiffened green crinoline over a hat base and ornamented by an huge rose, circa 1962. $45.00 – 58.00.

Green matellase dress, heavy gold brocaded fabric, beaded buckle, rounded neckline, circa 1962. $85.00 – 190.00.

Black satin cocktail dress with tulip skirt, attached crinoline making it puff at the hips then narrow at the hem, circa 1963. $185.00 – 265.00.

1. *Montgomery Ward's Catalog*, Spring and Summer 1963

Fashion Trends for the Year 1964

(Illustrated and Non-Illustrated)

- Antique toile prints
- Blue
- Bouffant flared short skirts
- Boxy suits
- Cowl collars
- Empire skimmers
- Faux leather beanies
- Frilly bibs
- Geometric block shifts
- Granny style boots with spats
- Half hats
- Head scarves
- High crown floral hats
- High crown pillboxes
- Jockey hats
- Knee length skirts
- Lime green
- Loop boucle
- Op art shifts and matching scarves
- Open crown whimsies
- Orange
- Peter Pan or sailor collars
- Polka dots on boots, rain coats and hats
- Polyester florals and stripes in saffron yellow and orange
- Print jersey dresses
- Scoop ruffles
- Sheer pastel dress in baby doll shifts
- Streamer bows
- Stripes and flocked dots
- Synthetic straw cloches
- Tatersall checks
- Turbans
- Velour
- Vinyl raincoats and above the knee boots
- White waffle pique
- Yellow [1]

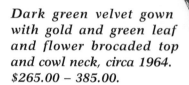

Dark green velvet gown with gold and green leaf and flower brocaded top and cowl neck, circa 1964. $265.00 – 385.00.

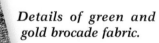

Details of green and gold brocade fabric.

1. *Montgomery Ward's Catalog,* Spring and Summer, *Montgomery Ward's Catalog,* Fall and Winter 1964

Exaggerated high hat made from synthetic white straw, brown ribbon and brown rose, circa 1964. $45.00 – 58.00.

Fluffy white marabou feather high hat, circa 1964. $55.00 – 60.00.

Fashion Trends in the Year 1965

(Illustrated and Non-Illustrated)

- A-line and slim skirts

- Abstract florals in earthtones, greens, and blues
- Accordion pleat skirts with large collars
- Acetate nylon lace dresses
- All lace dresses
- Ban-lon double knits in pastels
- Beaded knits
- Black and white
- Bows
- Boxy jackets
- Boxy waistline tops
- Brocade formals
- Brocaded high dome hats
- Bubble beret hats
- Bulky cardigans
- Burnt velvet
- Capri pants
- Chanel-inspired suits
- Checks and herringbones
- Cowl necks
- Crochet wool dresses
- Deep round collars
- Double knit dresses
- Doupponi silk formals
- Drooped shoulders
- Feather swirl hats and pillboxes
- Feathered toques
- Floral bordered prints
- Fringe bottom sweaters
- Full skirts with crinoline
- Gingham checks
- Green, blue and lime
- Half hats
- High rectangular hats
- High square turbans
- Houndstooth check dresses
- Jeweled turbans
- Jumpers
- Knit shorts
- Knit suits with short jackets
- Lace accents
- Lace and Schiffli embroidery
- Lace shifts worn to the knee
- Madras looks
- Mink and rabbit ring hats
- Mohair sweaters
- Navy and lime green
- Open crown pillboxes
- Ostrich and feather toques
- Pant sets
- Pastel crepe dresses

- Pastel knit dresses
- Pillboxes
- Pleated bodices with low collar and cuffs
- Pleated sweaters
- Poplin
- Pucci inspired prints
- Quilted jumpers
- Ribbon turbans
- Sailor dresses
- Schiffli lace
- Shift dresses
- Shimmering brocades
- Side drop profile cloches
- Sleeveless tops and boat necks
- Sleeveless polyester coat overdresses
- Slim skirts worn to the knee
- Stirrup pants
- Striped an checkered dresses
- Suit dresses done in brocades
- Sweater skirts
- Synthetic straw
- Textured linen dresses
- Textured wool dresses
- Turbans
- Velvet bows
- White rabbit off the shoulder shrugs
- Wide, round collars [1]

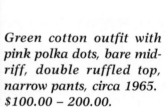

Yellow cotton outfit with white polka dots, bare midriff, ruffled top, and narrow pants, circa 1965. $100.00 – 200.00.

Navy blue cotton dress, white floral print with sailor collar, circa 1965 – 1968. $50.00 – 78.00.

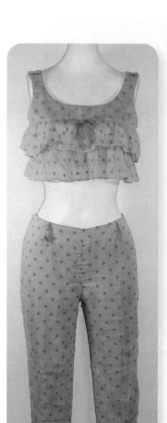

Green cotton outfit with pink polka dots, bare midriff, double ruffled top, narrow pants, circa 1965. $100.00 – 200.00.

Fashion Trends in the Year 1966

(Illustrated and Non-Illustrated)

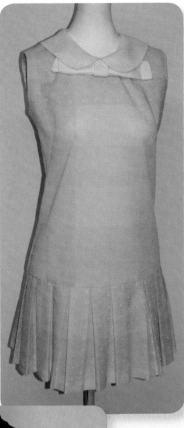

Pastel sherbet colored checked dress with dropped waist, pleated skirt, and neck bow, circa 1965 – 1966. $78.00 – 120.00.

Cocktail dress, brown lace top, accordion pleated shirred skirt, circa 1965 – 1966. $95.00 – 165.00.

- Abstract designs
- Baby doll shifts
- Below the knee hem lengths
- Black and white formals
- Block designs in shifts
- Blue
- Bows at waists
- Boxy jackets
- Dacron knits
- Daisy caps
- Double knit dresses
- Drop waist dresses with rounded collars
- Empire waists
- Fake granny boot with spats
- Fake linen dresses in orange and yellow
- Feather bands
- Floral daisy caps
- Flower pillboxes
- Full shorter skirts
- Gingham checks
- Go go style boots
- Granny boots
- Green with blue
- High crown brim hats
- Hip orange and yellow prints and stripes
- Lime green
- Linen looks
- Mod dresses
- Mustard yellow
- Nautical looks
- Navy and white
- Nostalgic formals
- Nubby knit dresses
- Off the shoulder shifts
- Old fashioned lace and bows
- One shoulder dresses
- Opart shifts
- Open crown hats
- Orange
- Pastel shifts with bib yokes
- Pinks and yellows
- Pretend boleros
- Pretend Victorian looks
- Print tops in blue, green and yellow
- Print tops in pink and orange
- Pucci-esque prints
- Ribbed cottons suits
- Rows of horizontal ribbons
- Ruffled bibs on dresses

- Ruffled eyelet boleros
- Ruffled sleeves
- Saffron
- Sailor and bowler hats
- Schiffli lace with dresses
- Shift dresses
- Shift dresses that flared
- Shifts in pastel checks
- Skimmer dresses
- Skimmers with old-fashioned style
- Skirts are above the knee
- Soft turbans
- Space age vinyl
- Square or full suits
- Synthetic straw cloches
- Synthetic straw fedoras
- Synthetic straw high pillboxes
- Synthetic straw sailors
- Tatersall checks
- Tucked empire looks
- Victorian themes
- Whimsies made of flowers [1]

White shift dress with bold circles in lime, blue, pink, and yellow bordered with navy, label: Hirshleifer's, circa 1966 – 1967.
$200.00 – 350.00.

Apricot wool two piece suit with cowl collar, asymmetrical necktie, and fake pockets, circa 1966.
$70.00 – 150.00.

Hip orange and yellow print, sheer cotton blouse, label: Vera, circa 1966 – 1968.
$80.00 – 100.00.

1. *Montgomery Ward's Catalog, Spring and Summer 1966*

Fashion Trends for the Year 1967

(Illustrated and Non-Illustrated)

- A-line dresses
- Abbreviated sleeve shifts
- Bi-color dresses
- Blue
- Bolero jackets with harem pants
- Caftan necklines
- Chartreuse
- Checks
- Coat dresses with A-line flare
- Crimped sleeves
- Diamond prints
- Double breasted capes
- Fitted box jackets
- Flare tunic dresses
- Four button shifts
- Green
- Green and orange
- Halter collars
- Jackets like over blouses
- Lime green with pink or lemon
- Lime green, chartreuse, and pink worn together
- Military jackets
- Mini length skirts
- Muted pastels
- Narrow tunic dress and slim skirt
- Neck bow collars
- Orange and pink
- Pastels in swirls
- Pastels in tiny abstracts
- Pink
- Pink, blue, and cream
- Princess lines
- Pyramid shaped coats and jackets
- Rolled and tabbed collars
- Round skullcap hats with brims
- Shirt dress with stand up collars
- Side tabs buttoned
- Silver lamé
- Swirl abstract prints
- Tent dresses
- Three tiered shift dresses
- Trapeze dresses long in length
- Turbans
- Turquoise, dark blues, and greens worn together [1]

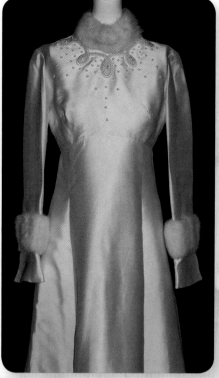

Military inspired white faux silk shantung gown, collar and wrists trimmed with white rabbit fur, bodice embroidered with pearls, circa 1967 – 1968. $265.00 – 350.00.

Psychedelic print A-line shift dress of burlap, orange, green, blue, and pink floral print, circa 1967 – 1968. $85.00 – 150.00.

1. *International Vogue Pattern Book*, Spring 1967

Fashion Trends for the Year 1968

(Illustrated and Non-Illustrated)

- A-line skimmer dresses
- Belts with wide buckles
- Bow necklines on dresses
- Boxy jackets
- Brocade evening ensembles
- Checked day dresses
- Double knit wool skirt suits
- Faux silk shantung fabric
- Large feathers, hats, pillboxes
- Linen-look skimmer dresses
- Narrow pleats
- One piece culottes — prints and bright colors
- Pant dresses
- Romantic Edwardian Guardsman coats
- Scarf headbands
- Short and cap sets
- Short and jacket sets
- Silver lamé coats and dresses
- Skinny dresses
- Square yoke dresses with full pleats
- Three-quarter sleeves
- Tunic coats and shifts
- Turquoise and orange colors
- Velvet turbans and pillboxes
- Zippered shifts [1]

Mod knit coatdress in black and white polyester, circa 1967 – 1969. $125.00 – 175.00.

Abstract print A-line shift dress, lime, olive, blue, and orange print, and pointed collar, circa 1967. $85.00 – 150.00.

Patchwork suede skirt in red, purple, blue, and tan, circa 1968. $75.00 – 140.00.

1. *Montgomery Ward's Catalog*, Spring and Summer, Fall and Winter 1968

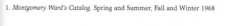

Yellow floral brocaded evening suit, Nehru or notched collar, circa 1968. $85.00 – 145.00.

Hot pink cotton sundress with triangular cutouts on the hips, circa 1968. $85.00 – 145.00.

Flower power sun suit, pink cotton with green, yellow, purple, and white floral print, bare midriff, circa 1968. $75.00 – 88.00.

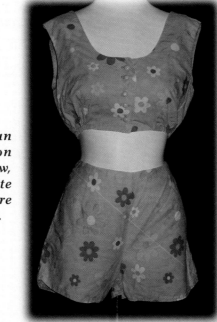

Pearl gray faux silk shantung mini dress, mandarin collar, pearls and silver bugle beads in an Indian motif, bow belt, circa 1968.
$225.00 – 385.00.

Pink floral shift dress, sleeveless, side bows at the neck and hip, small mock turtleneck stand-up collar, circa 1968.
$80.00 – 100.00.

Pink, green, yellow, and black swirl print shift dress, small turtle neck collar, circa 1968.
$85.00 – 145.00.

Fashion Trends for the Year 1969
(Illustrated and Non-Illustrated)

Black crepe and silver tinsel cocktail dress with attached scarf panels, circa 1968 – 1969.
$145.00 – 265.00.

- Asymmetrical dresses
- Below the knee boots
- Belted tweed coats
- Brocade outfits
- Capulets
- Car coats
- Chanel style blazers
- Chino separates
- Cloches of pheasant feathers
- Coat dresses
- Cowl collars
- Curved feather pieces
- Derby hats
- Dirndls
- Dots on birdcage veil
- Edwardian looks in pantsuits and skirts
- Feathered swirls
- Floating back panels of formals
- Formals with a V shaped bow under the bust
- Fur blend sweaters
- Fur collar coats of faux leopard and fox
- Gold chain belts
- Jabot blouses
- Jacket, pant and skirt sets
- Jeweled toned paisleys
- Jumper look dresses
- Jumpers worn with turtlenecks
- Knit suits
- Lace trim jabot with jumpers
- Large fox suede coats
- Leather and suede
- Long vests, skirts and jumpers
- Looped half hats
- Narrow skirts
- Open crown pillboxes
- Overblouses
- Paisley
- Plaid A-line skirts above the knee
- Ribbed knit tops and pants
- Robin Hood style hats
- Ruffled blouses
- Shift dresses
- Shirtwaist dress with narrow skirts
- Short straight waist jackets
- Silvery brocade dresses
- Square necklines
- Sweater ponchos
- Tapered pants with boot straps

Silver tinsel mini dress, circa 1968 – 1969.
$45.00 – 70.00.

- Telescope crown pillboxes
- Three-quarter sleeves
- Tunic pantsuits or jumpers
- Tunic tops with knit belts tied on the side
- Tunics with belt ties
- Tweed capes and pants
- Velvet circles
- Velvet trellis hats
- Vests and plaid pleated skirts
- Voluminous knife pleated pants
- Wide formal dancing pants
- Wool and mohair weskits and skirts [1]

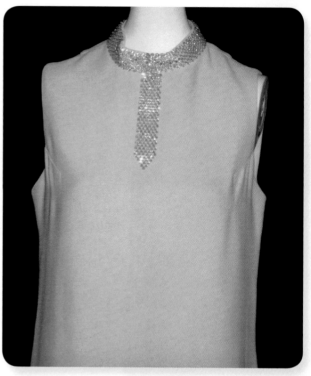

Light pink crepe mini dress with rhinestone collar, circa 1969.
$125.00 – 175.00.

Yellow polyester knit mini dress with bumblebee patches and rick-rack on cape sleeves, circa 1969.
$70.00 – 97.00.

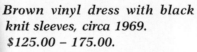

Mod orange and black military style polyester mini dress,
cable knit sleeves, circa 1969.
$125.00 – 175.00.

Brown vinyl dress with black
knit sleeves, circa 1969.
$125.00 – 175.00.

The 1970s will remain in our minds as a decade of free spirited thinking. Fashion expressed the glory of individual freedom, liberation and rebellion. It was the first decade in our history where women would begin to regularly wear pants as a sign of their daily social liberation. The seventies reflected our coming of age and of modern sensibilities. Important social changes freed women from conventional roles and traditional stereotypes. Explosive prints and psychedelic colors were trademarks of groovy style. The hippie movement and the flower child brought peasant and ethnic looks into mainstream fashion. The culture of youth and their interest in clothing made it an exciting time with many new changes. The decade was ambivalent about skirt length as it traveled to and from the mini, the maxi, and somewhere in between. Polyester freed women from the drudgeries of clothing care. "Wash and no iron" indestructible polyester made life a lot easier for women to dress in knit pants, tunics or pantsuits.

Some fashionable trends included very feminine concoctions such as peasant or prairie dresses. Long maxi gowns had decidedly Victorian and Edwardian inspired features and a romantic feel. The most important fashion fabrics that revolutionized the care and wear of clothing included polyester chiffon and knits alongside velvet, lamé and chiffon. Geometrics and flower power contrast with the earth tones of hippie clothing bringing women closer to the colors of the earth. Simultaneously the seventies showed lack of restraint when fashion trends burst forth with color, abstracts, stripes and florals. Liberation against the confines of constraining designs was about to gain a foothold. Grecian looks inspired feminine feel for gowns with classical lines and drapery. Hippies gave us long fringe vests and patchwork. Clothing was elegant, wild in style, one of a kind, reminiscent of times past and thoroughly powerful. No other decade saw such radical expression of prints and colors.

Fashion Trends for the Year 1970

(Illustrated and Non-Illustrated)

- A-line flared skirts
- Buccaneer ruffled blouses
- Button trimmed tabs
- Chain lace
- Chain link belts

- Contrasting bands
- Crinkle patent leather
- Fringed hemlines
- Fringed ponchos
- Jabot blouses
- Jumper dresses
- Jumpsuits with tunics
- Lacing on dresses
- Large fur hats
- Mini length skirts
- Navy and ginger
- Princess coat dresses
- Python prints
- Short A-line flared mini skirts
- Skinny ribbed knits
- Sweater coats
- Tweed jumpers
- V panels on dresses
- Victorian style yoke dresses [1]

White and pink formal with nylon overskirt, green crepe bow, embroidered overskirt of pink daisies, circa 1970. $75.00 – 125.00.

1. *Montgomery Ward's* Catalog, Fall and Winter 1970

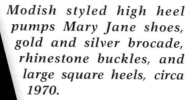

Modish styled high heel pumps Mary Jane shoes, gold and silver brocade, rhinestone buckles, and large square heels, circa 1970.
$20.00 – 50.00.

Purple polyester skimmer dress, waistband ornamented with a row of purple buttons, circa 1970.
$35.00 – 65.00.

Fashion Trends for the Year 1971

(Illustrated and Non-Illustrated)

- Bib tunics
- Body suits and jeans
- Chiffon accordion pleated pants and skirts
- Culottes

Navy mini knit dress with cream and gray striped belt, circa 1970.
$125.00 – 175.00.

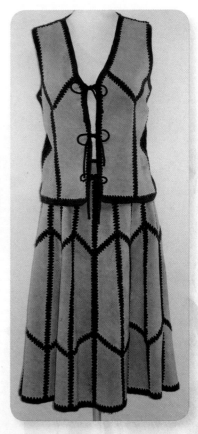

- Edwardian styles
- Flare leg jeans
- Flounced peasant outfits
- Fringe vests
- Gaucho hats
- Granny boots
- Hot pants
- Jeans with flowers, stripes, and stars
- Knicker suits
- Knickers
- Knit cape sets
- Knit pantsuits in abstracts
- Knit polyester pants
- Knit vests with culottes
- Long divided maxi skirts
- Long maxi skirts
- Long sleeve coat ensembles
- Long suede capes
- Long suede tunic and lace-up vests
- Long tunic pantsuits
- Paisley
- Pant shifts
- Peasant looks
- Plush pantsuits
- Polyester knits
- Ponchos
- Printed trench coats
- Side zip shirts
- Silver lamé
- Sleeveless vest tunic pantsuits
- Sweater capes
- Tapestry coats
- Terry tops
- Textured pant coats
- Textured polyester prints
- Wet look vinyl jackets and pants
- Wide leg jeans with stripes
- Wide leg pants in plaids and stripes
- Wrap skirts [1]

Gray suede skirt and vest set joined by blue crochet, circa 1971. $70.00 – 175.00.

Pink and wine abstract polyester print cape pantsuit, circa 1971. $25.00 – 85.00.

Brown suede hot pants with lace closure, circa 1971. $50.00 – 85.00.

Gauze floral print peasant style dress, shirred neckline, circa 1971.
$70.00 – 175.00.

Red and black plaid lamé evening maxi dress with rhinestone belt buckle, circa 1971.
$100.00 – 200.00.

Printed maxi dress, cream with saffron, orange, yellow, purple, turquoise, and chartreuse, wide fabric belt with corset lacing grommets, circa 1971.
$75.00 – 185.00.

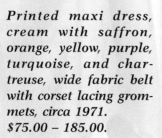

Brown, black, and white tuxedo style lamé top (part of a pants suit), circa 1971.
$75.00 – 150.00.

Fashion Trends for the Year 1972
(Illustrated and Non-Illustrated)

- Big buckles
- Black and white
- Bodysuit pant sets
- Border print dresses
- Bubble stitch jumpsuits
- Crushed velvet vests and pants with ruffled blouses
- Cut away shoulders on full length gowns
- Daisy prints
- Denim pant coats
- Djellabas
- Dresses with bolero pant sets
- Embroidered jeans
- Empire ball gowns
- Fake fur in purple
- Fake leopard furs
- Flared legs
- Flared skirts
- Fringe trims
- Fur trimmed suede
- Jacquard pant sets with front zippers
- Jerseys
- Knit pants, flared legs in abstract prints
- Knit trench coats
- Knit tunic pantsuits
- Lace empire formals
- Lace front high boots
- Laced fronts
- Lime green
- Long skirts and soft blouses
- Lounging gowns
- Maxi pleated dresses
- Mesh boots with front lacing
- Mini skirts two to three inches above the knee
- Orange
- Patchwork shirts
- Peasant girl mini dresses
- Plaid with black
- Princess lines
- Purple and gold
- Red and white
- Ruffle lace blouses
- Ruffled front and collar
- Safari looks
- Sailor jeans
- See through sleeves
- Shirred empire bodices with puffed sleeves
- Silver lamé pant sets and formal dresses

- Sleeveless vests over turtlenecks
- Stretch abstract print pants
- Suede and leather pant coats
- Tapestry pants
- Trench coats
- Tunic vests with knit pants
- Tunics in abstracts and paisleys
- Velour pant sets
- Vests, blouses, skirts, and pants in plaid
- Zippered step in dresses [1]

Blue, green, plum, and yellow print caftan, circa 1972 – 1973.
$40.00 – 75.00.

1. *Montgomery Ward's Catalog,* Spring and Summer, Fall and Winter 1972

Nylon abstract art, orange, purple, black, and white maxi skirt and matching top, circa 1972.
$90.00 – 145.00.

Mini dress, psychedelic floral print in hot pink yellow, purple, orange, and green skirt, circa 1972 – 1974.
$75.00 – 125.00.

Gold lamé body suit and matching floral print chiffon and lamé skirt, circa 1972.
$150.00 – 325.00.

Black maxi dress with quilted print skirt edged in yarn fringe, circa 1972. $125.00 – 300.00.

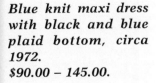

Blue knit maxi dress with black and blue plaid bottom, circa 1972. $90.00 – 145.00.

Maxi pantsuit, daisies, stripes, and polka dots in black, white, and yellow sleeveless top and wide pants, circa 1972. $75.00 – 125.00.

Fashion Trends for the Year 1973

(Illustrated and Non-Illustrated)

- Argyle look pants
- Bold plaid pants
- Djellabas
- Dress with sleeveless coats
- Junior A-line mini dresses
- Knit pantsuits and skirt sets
- Long empire waist formals
- Long A-line maxi skirts
- Lounging gowns with wide legs
- Navy checks
- Plaid bell-bottoms flaring from knee to cuff
- Ruffle top blouses
- Ruffled blouse formals with sheer sleeves
- Sling back glitter shoes
- Velvet clogs and shoulder bags
- Victorian style long dresses [1]

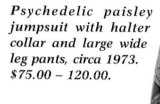

Psychedelic paisley jumpsuit with halter collar and large wide leg pants, circa 1973. $75.00 – 120.00.

Yellow and green plaid polyester knit dress with ruffled cuffs and collar, circa 1973. $25.00 – 65.00.

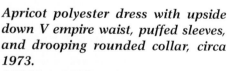

Apricot polyester dress with upside down V empire waist, puffed sleeves, and drooping rounded collar, circa 1973. $35.00 – 65.00.

Purple and lavender floral maxi dress of sheer chiffon, Renaissance inspired lower puff sleeves, circa 1973. $125.00 – 325.00.

White polyester dress with upside down V-empire waist, deep pointed collar, and bodice of tufted yarn diamonds in assorted colors, circa 1973. $35.00 – 65.00.

Knit mini skirt in cornflower blue with puffed sleeves, tapered waist, and a yoke with corded embroidery, circa 1973. $35.00 –65.00.

- Ruffled blouses
- Surplice bodices
- Sweaters and matching over vests
- Very wide pants
- Wrapped belted sweaters
- Zip front tunic pant sets [1]

Red knit polyester dress with jumper effect in gray, white, and red checked pattern, circa 1974. $35.00 – 65.00.

Sleeveless high collared maxi navy dress, checked print, bands of burgundy velvet and navy Venice lace, circa 1973. $75.00 – 125.00.

Fashion Trends for the Year 1974

(Illustrated and Non-Illustrated)

- Animal looks in fur coats
- Bright stripe skirts
- Cape coats
- Lacey knit sweaters
- Princess style dresses
- Quilted coats
- Romantic sheer Victorian dresses
- Ruffled bib dresses

Fashion Trends for the Year 1975

(Illustrated and Non-Illustrated)

- A-line mini skirts
- Acrylic knit pastel sweaters
- Bandana prints
- Big ruffles on formal dresses
- Bolero jackets with maxi skirt
- Coral
- Crisscross belts
- Cross-jackets
- Daisy halters
- Daisy lace on formals
- Double panels

1. *Montgomery Ward's Catalog, Fall and Winter 1974*

- Empire waistlines
- Evening pajamas
- Eyelet lace
- Fantasy floral prints
- Flare legs
- Floral pink and chartreuse
- Floral polyester maxi skirts worn with shirts
- Florals
- Geometric prints
- Green
- Halter sets
- Halters showing midriff
- Halters with ruffles
- Halters with spaghetti straps — maxi length
- Knit ponchos
- Large hats
- Long tail shirts
- Long vest pant sets
- Low rise jeans
- Mandarin collars
- Maxi dresses with bare midriffs
- Mock turtleneck shells
- Muslin fabrics
- Pajama formal pantsuits
- Palazzo pants
- Pant sets
- Pantsuits for evening wear
- Plaid in green and orange
- Polka dots
- Polyester boucle
- Polyester pants
- Polyester sweaters
- Prairie style dresses
- Red, white, and navy
- Rickrack
- Roses
- Ruffled necklines
- Ruffles on evening dresses
- Schiffli embroidery
- Secretary neck ties
- Shirt length style pant knits
- Short sleeve blazers and skirts
- Side tie fabric belts
- Skimmer dress with pleats and folds
- Sleeveless looks
- Smocked dress feathers
- Smocking for dresses and tops
- Smocks and checked pants
- Strawberry embroidery
- Stripes
- Suede shirt jackets

- Sweet and dainty lace bridesmaid dresses
- V necks
- Waist ties
- Wide picture brim hats
- Wildflower embroidery [1]

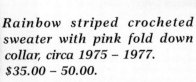

Zip front polyester jumpsuit with green and yellow diamond and square print, circa 1975.
$45.00 – 125.00.

Rainbow striped crocheted sweater with pink fold down collar, circa 1975 – 1977.
$35.00 – 50.00.

1. *Montgomery Ward's*, Spring and Summer, 1975

Brown polyester maxi dress with floral embroidery on the bodice, circa 1975.
$75.00 – 125.00.

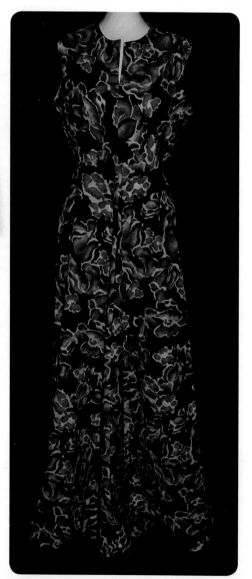

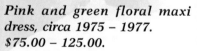

Pink and green floral maxi dress, circa 1975 – 1977.
$75.00 – 125.00.

Burgundy velvet and white lace formal, silver lace and rhinestones, circa 1975.
$125.00 – 185.00.

Blue knit maxi dress with abstract knit designed bodice, circa 1975. $75.00 – 125.00.

Goddess style evening gown with matching chiffon cape trimmed in dyed to match marabou feathers, circa 1975. $185.00 – 395.00.

Floral halter maxi dress, lace and wide flounce, circa 1975. $125.00 – 185.00.

Abstract knit maxi dress, empire top, and psychedelic florals, circa 1975.
$55.00 – 85.00.

Peach knit gown, string halter, maxi length skirt, matching bolero jacket (not shown), belted tie ending in fabric rosebuds, circa 1975.
$85.00 – 125.00.

Details of back string ties, circa 1975.

Fashion Trends for the Year 1976

(Illustrated and Non-Illustrated)

- Abstract printed T-shirts
- Big tops
- Blazer pant suits
- Boat neck tops
- Bolero jackets
- Caftan dresses
- Camisole tube tops
- Cargo pocket pants
- Crinkle cloth

- Double knits
- Draped halter bodices
- Earth cloth
- Espadrilles
- Floppy hats
- Gauze skirts
- Gauzy muslin
- Halter pantsuits with cutouts
- Halter-tops
- High cork wedges
- Jumpsuits with pleats
- Long evening dresses
- Long ruffled maxi skirts
- Melon
- Mock turtlenecks
- Muscle sleeve tops
- Navy and white stripes
- Pantsuits and platform shoes
- Patch cloth pants and vests
- Peasant floral tops
- Peasant ruffle tied dress
- Platform sandals
- Polyester knit skirts
- Polyester maxi dress pantsuits
- Printed caftans
- Renaissance looks
- Reversible skirts
- Ruffled bridal dresses
- Safari jackets
- Safari suits
- Sailor jackets
- Shirred bust
- Shirt jackets
- Short shorts
- Soft cotton voile
- Solid T-shirts
- Stretch polyester pants
- Striped V neck tops
- Tank tops
- Tunics with rope ties
- Tie dye terry
- Vests
- Western jeans
- Wrap skirts [1]

Peasant dress with orange, purple, and green ethnic embroidery on the elbows and the waist, circa 1976.
$65.00 – 85.00.

Red polyester halter outfit with black trim, keyhole openings at the navel and throat, bare midriff, circa 1976 – 1977.
$95.00 – 125.00.

1. *Montgomery Ward's Catalog,* Summer – August 30, 1976

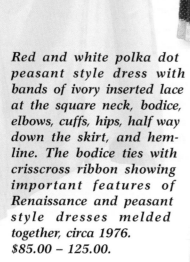

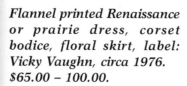

Flannel printed Renaissance or prairie dress, corset bodice, floral skirt, label: Vicky Vaughn, circa 1976. $65.00 – 100.00.

Fashion Trends for the Year 1977
(Illustrated and Non-Illustrated)

- Angel sleeves
- Aztec prints
- Blazers, vests and skirts
- Bright tops
- Checks
- Chiffon ponchos
- Coat dresses
- Cowl neck dresses
- Cowl neck knit dress
- Cross strap bags
- Crystal pleated formal jackets
- Drapery cowls
- Empire jackets
- Ethnic prints
- Feathers and beads
- Flared gauchos
- Folklore tops
- Formals with curved peplum jackets
- Gaucho outfits
- Gauchos worn with blouses and vests
- Glitter
- Halter maxi gowns
- Handkerchief sleeves
- Handkerchief tops
- High knee boots with front crisscross strings
- Hoods on zip front dresses
- Jacket and pant suits
- Jewel colors
- Jumpers with blouses
- Jumpsuits
- Keyhole necklines
- Knit dresses
- Lettuce edged sleeves
- Long skirts and short skirts
- Marabou edged chiffon cover-ups
- Maxi skirts with chiffon capes
- Metallic knits
- Mitered stripes
- Neck bandanas
- Orchid prints
- Paisleys
- Pant suits
- Pinstripe suits
- Plaid blazer sets
- Plaid skirt sets
- Plaid vest sets
- Plaids
- Pleated chiffon ponchos
- Polyester jackets and pant suits

Red and white polka dot peasant style dress with bands of ivory inserted lace at the square neck, bodice, elbows, cuffs, hips, half way down the skirt, and hemline. The bodice ties with crisscross ribbon showing important features of Renaissance and peasant style dresses melded together, circa 1976. $85.00 – 125.00.

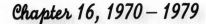

- Polyester jumpers
- Polyester pullovers
- Polyester zip up dresses
- Rhinestone trimming
- Sashes
- Serape stripes
- Shirt jackets
- Shirtwaist maxi dresses
- Sleeveless tunics
- Spaghetti or halter strap formals
- Stripes going in different directions
- Sweater vests
- Swirl prints
- Tabard outfits
- Tabards worn with gauchos
- Tabard pant sets
- Thirties style flutter sleeves
- Three piece pant suits
- T-shirt dresses
- Turtle necks
- Tweed and plaid polyester
- Tweed jumpsuits
- Tweedy sweaters with hoods
- U necklines
- Wide braided scrolls
- Zip front polyester suits [1]

Red and white bellbottom pants outfit with bolero styled top, circa 1977. $85.00 – 125.00.

Orchid printed black polyester dress, sheer sleeves, key-hole opening at the throat, long streamer ties, circa 1977. $50.00 – 85.00.

Fashion Trends for the Year 1978

(Illustrated and Non-Illustrated)

- Asymmetrical waists
- Bare shoulder knit gowns
- Blazers wrap tops
- Blouse drawstring blouses
- Blouse pullover dresses
- Boots

- Bow tie collars
- Capes
- Coat ensembles
- Corduroy skirts
- Cross bow necklines
- Cross shoulder bags
- Dickeys
- Dirndls
- Drawstring necks
- Empire dresses
- Faux suede
- Floral print below the knee dresses
- Free flowering cowl neck dresses
- Free flowering dress with no tight waists
- Front wrap blouses
- Full circle skirts
- Gaucho sets
- Grecian single shoulder drapery
- Knee skimming shorts
- Long maxi dresses
- Maxi dresses
- Men's styles for ladies (haberdashery)
- Narrower body conscious looks
- Neck ties
- Paisley
- Pared down trousers and skirts
- Peasant looks
- Peasant ties
- Pierrot blouses
- Pierrot yokes
- Quilted vests
- Round collars
- Ruffled collars
- Ruffled dresses
- Ruffled necks and wrists
- Ruffled yokes
- Shirt blouses
- Shirt dresses
- Shoulder fashion details
- Slim down skirts
- Small suede vests
- Southern belle looks
- Spilt and wrapped skirts
- Suede
- Synthetic suede
- Tiered jabots
- Tuxedo collars
- Velveteen jackets
- Vests
- Wrap jackets
- Yoked hip blouses [1]

Pink polyester draped formal gown with shirred bodice, shirred sleeves, and string ties, circa 1978 – 1979.
$35.00 – 95.00.

Fashion Trends for the Year 1979

(Illustrated and Non-Illustrated)

- Argyle vests
- Boucle knit dresses
- Clogs
- Cord tie necklines
- Corduroy suits
- Flannel suits

- Jacquard vest
- Jeans
- Jersey dresses
- Lace ties at the neck
- Long skirts with cowboy boots
- Op art small abstract prints
- Overalls
- Plaid pants
- Plaid skirts
- Polyester knit dresses
- Polyester knit pantsuits
- Quilted coats
- Ribbon neckties
- Round collar shirtdresses
- Shawl collared dresses
- Short boots
- T strap shoes
- Terry knit dress
- Textured black stockings
- Turtlenecks
- V neck pullover dress
- Western looks [1]

Classic denim jeans with heart shaped pockets. Provenance places them at 1979.
Priceless.

A-line: silhouette resembling the letter A — small on top then widens and flares on bottom.

Aigrette: cluster of upright feathers or a tufted feather plume.

Apollo knot: high, topknot hairstyle worn during the 1830s.

Asymmetrical: not symmetrical.

Bandeau: narrow headband.

Basque: a jacket style bodice that extends below the waist with a skirt or peplum.

Batiste: a fine soft plain woven cotton or linen fabric.

Bavolet: a bonnet curtain covering the back of the neck.

Bengaline: light mohair or corded silk with heavy ribbing.

Bernhardt sleeves: drooped top puff with narrow band added sometimes for elbow.

Bertha: a large, wide lace collar.

Bicorn: hat with two points on the brim.

Blonde lace: white Chantilly style lace worn in the nineteenth century.

Boat neck or bateau: a neckline that ran from one shoulder to the other.

Bolero: open jacket that lands at the waist or above the waist.

Boucle: curly or knotted knit fabric.

Breton: type of sailor hat.

Brisé fan: folding fan.

Brocade: ornate jacquard fabric with all over raised flower designs.

Bustle: a pad or support to elevate the rear end of a skirt.

Calash: eighteenth century collapsible caned bonnet to protect large hairdos.

Capote: long coat or cloak with a bonnet or hood.

Cartwheel: large, circular shaped hat.

Cellophane: shiny acetate fabric.

Challis: soft light wool or wool blend fabric.

Changeable taffeta: taffeta that appears to change color at different angles.

Chantilly lace: silk or synthetic lace, six sided mesh ground, floral or scrolled design.

Chenille: a thick silk, cotton, or worsted cord or yarn threads.

Chevron: V shaped symbol.

Chiffon: light sheer nylon, rayon, or silk fabric.

Cloche: a close fitting flapper era hat.

Coronet: woman's head decoration: a circular ornamental band worn by women.

Culottes: long skirt shorts.

Décollétage: low cut neckline or wearing a décolleté dress.

Decolleté: strapless dress or a low cut neckline.

Dirndl dress: full skirt with waistline gathering.

Dolman sleeve: wide upper shoulder sleeve that narrows as it reaches the wrist.

Drawn bonnet: shirred fabric around cane supports.

Duchesse satin: soft, shiny satin.

Empire waist: dress waistline gathered just under the bust.

Faille: fine and plain ribbed silk.

Fanchon: rounded, half-crescent bonnet resembling a cap.

Faux: fake.

Fichu: small shawl or scarf that is tied around the shoulders.

Foulard: lightweight plain — woven or twilled silk with decorative printed pattern.

Frogging: cording and knot closures.

Gaucho: long flared shorts resembling a skirt.

Georgette crepe: translucent or see through crepe.

Gigot: leg o'mutton sleeve that runs puffed shoulder to elbow then tightens towards wrist.

Gilet: sleeveless jacket.

Gimp: ornamental braid or trimming made of round cord.

Godet: inserted garment panel with a wide bottom.

Grosgrain: a heavy, woven and ribbed taffeta fabric or a type of ribbon.

Guimpe: sheer cotton waist blouse with or without sleeves.

Headdress: ornament worn on the head.

Hooverette: Depression era housedress with wrapped closure.

Horseshoe collar: fifties bust resembling a pleated horseshoe.

Jabot: fancy neck ruffle.

Jenny Lind: Swedish 19th century soprano.

Lamé: fabric woven from metallic thread.

Leg o'mutton: puffed upper sleeve that tightens towards the wrist.

Leghorn bonnet: Italian nineteenth century Tuscany straw bonnet.

Mantua: court gown with tremendous hips.

Matellase: type of brocaded fabric.

Maxi skirt: ankle to floor length skirt.

Messaline: soft silk with a twill or satin weave.

Midi skirt: calf length skirt.

Mikado sleeve: short kimono sleeve resembling Japanese robe sleeves.

Miniskirt: short skirt ending above the knee.

Moiré: watered appearance on taffeta or acetate.

Moyenage: Middle Ages.

Muslin or mousseline: gauze-like cotton fabric.

Op Art: abstract, geometric patterns oftentimes black

and white.

Organdy: a stiff, sheer cotton.

Organza: a type of silk that is similar to organdy.

Pagoda sleeve: widen to a large bell shape at the wrist.

Paletot: loose, collared cape.

Pannier: devise used to extend the hips.

Passmenterie: braiding, cording and heavily beaded trim.

Peg sleeve: thin and narrow sleeves.

Pelerine: a short shoulder cape.

Pencil skirt: hip-hugging skirt.

Peplum: bodice that flares below the waist or to the hips.

Petal bust: fifties bust decoration of three-dimensional petals.

Peter Pan collar: a small, round collar.

Pigeon breast: gathering of fabric at the chest making a puff.

Pixie: cone-like or pointed hat.

Pocketbook or Pocket Case: eighteenth – early nineteenth century case for letters or documents.

Poke or Scuttle Bonnet: a bonnet that is so large it interferes with the vision of the wearer.

Polonaise: coat worn to show an underdress.

Postillion (hat): similar to hats worn by postmen.

Princess lines: dress silhouette with no waistline.

Redingote: three-quarter length coatdress, buttoned down front opening at the center.

Revers: lapels turned over the edge of sleeves or skirts.

Rickrack: corded colorful trim in scalloped design.

Robin Hood or Tyrolean Hat: pixie hat worn in the 1930s and 1940s.

Roller print fabric: machine made printed fabric.

Satin: lustrous and thick fabric with sheen.

Sausage curls: long corkscrew curl hairstyle of the 1840s.

Schiffli: lace made from embroidery on netting.

Seersucker: striped and slightly puckered fabric of linen, cotton or rayon.

Shantung silk: plain woven fabric with uneven surface.

Sheath dress: knee length classic dress.

Shelf bust: fifties three-dimensional bust resembling a "shelf" made of fabric.

Shirred: gathered.

Shrug: short bolero style jacket.

Smocked: puckered fabric, fathered with embroidered stitches.

Snood: decorative hair net.

Soutache: ornamental braid used to trim.

Spencer: short empire waist jacket with long sleeves.

Spitafields: source of 18th century English brocade silk.

Spoon bonnet: Civil War era bonnet with a vertical oval shape.

Sweetheart neckline: heart shaped neckline.

Taffeta: synthetic or silk shiny fabric.

Tartan: plaid pattern.

Toque: round, close hat with no brim and square top.

Tricorn: hat with three points on the brim.

Tulle: netting from silk or synthetic materials.

Turban: headpiece of draped and twisted fabric.

V-neck: neckline with open yoke coming to a V.

Voided velvet: burned out velvet, velvet pike shown in fabrics.

Voile: a crisp lightweight translucent fabric made from cotton, synthetic fiber, or wool.

Waist: bodice.

Waistcoat: vest.

Watteau train: train sewn to the back top of the gown flowing downward.

Zoave jacket: bolero style Civil War era jacket imitated from an Algerian uniform.

Ackermann's Repository, January, July, 1809, Fabric Swatch Plates January 1809, May and June 1809; December, 1811, Fabric Swatch Plates March, April, August, November 1811; January 1812, Fabric Swatches March, July, April 1812; February, April, Fabric Swatches March, June 1813; October 1821; October 1823; July 1, 1824; January – December 1825; April, July – December 1826; January & May 1828; February & March 1829; Misc. Plate 26 Vol. 7.

Alden's Chicago Mail Order Co., Spring and Summer Catalog, 1945.

B Altman's & Co., Summer Apparel May 15 – June 25, Winter Suggestions 1919.

The Beau Monde, January, March, December 1832; November 1834; August 1835, Plates 2 & 3.

Bellas Hess Catalog, 1958, pp. 1 – 32.

Bell's Court, March 1, 1806; April and July 1833.

Bell's Weekly Messanger, January, June and September 1807.

Browne, Clare, ed. *Silk Designs of the Eighteenth Century from the Victoria and Albert Museum.* London: Thames & Hudson, 1996.

Butterick Fashions, Summer 1916.

Butterick Quarterly, Summer 1923.

Charles William Stores Catalog, NY Catalog 31, Spring & Summer 1921; Fall and Winter, 1925.

Columbian Magazine, February, March, May – June, August, October, December, 1844.

Corriere delle Dame, Moda di Francia, 1824, Plate no. 53.

Delineator, April no. 4, 1883; May 1886; August 1891; September 1894; February, March, June, December, 1896; January – February, April, June, October, November 1897; March, May, August, November 1898; April – August, November – December 1899; March, May, July, August, November 1900; January, 1902; April, June 1905; May 1908; October 1910; January 1911; January 1912; December 1913; September 1914; June & October 1915; February & December 1916; November 1917; May & November 1918; January 1921; September 1922; February, March, April, September, November 1923; January, February, April, May, June, 1926; August, November 1930; February, March 1933.

Demorest's Family Magazine, June 1891.

Demorest's Monthly Magazine, June & July 1876; December 1877; February & June 1878.

Der Bazar, February, March, July, September, October 1888; February – June, September – October 1889; February, April – July, August, October –

December, 1890; January, May, July – September, November – December, 1891.

Designer, July – September, December 1899; April, November, December 1900; January, April, May, June, August, November, December, 1901; October 1902; January, February, October, November, December 1903; February – April, June, September, December 1904; July, August, November December 1906; January, February, April, July, 1907; April 1911; December 1924; October 1925.

The Domestic Monthly, An Illustrated Magazine of Fashion, May 1890.

Dress, January 1909.

Edward Grossman & Co., Catalog, Fall and Winter 1901 – 1902.

Englishwoman's Domestic Monthly, August, September, October & December 1865; February, July, October, November 1866; April & June 1867; April & July 1868.

Femme d'Aujourd'hui, July 3, August 21, September 4, September 8, 1948; September 8, 1949, December 15, 1949; July 1950, pp. 5, 6, 8, 16, 17; May 1951, pp. 5 – 6, 8, 11, 16 – 17.

Fifth Avenue Modes, Spring and Early Summer 1939.

Florida Fashion Catalog, Fall 1952, pp. 1 – 32.

Fuller's Fashion Magazine, February & May 1835.

Gazette du Bon Ton, No. 2, February 1914 Plate 16.

Gimbel's Thrift Book, Spring and Summer 1923.

Glamour Magazine, August 1941, September 1946.

Godey's Lady's Book, January and March 1837; February, May – August, November, December 1838; January – December 1840; January – June, September, 1841; May 1842; January – December 1843; January, March 1844, January – December 1849; January – December 1851; January – June 1852; January, May 1853; January – December 1854; January – December 1855; January, March, June, July – December 1856; July – December 1857; January – June 1859; January – December, 1860; February, May – August, December 1861; February – August, October – December, 1862; May, June, December 1863; March, June, July, August, September, October 1864; January, March, July, August, September, 1865; Godey's Lady's Book February, March, June, July – December, 1866; January, April, June, July, August, September, 1867; January, March, May, August, November 1868; April, May, July, October – December, 1869; January, February, May, June, September 1870; January – October 1871; March – December 1872; January – March,

May – July 1873; January, April – October, December 1874; August, October – December, 1875; February – April, June – August, 1877; March 1881; January – June 1886.

Graham's American Monthly Magazine, XXXIV January – December 1849; January – December 1853.

Graham's Magazine, April, October 1841; January – December 1842; January 1846 – December 1846; January 1847; July & August 1850; January – December 1851; January – December 1852.

Grand Luxe Parisien, Supplement to 1914 – 1915 No. 65.

Hamilton Garment Co. Catalog, Spring and Summer, 1926.

Harbeson, Georgiana Brown. _American Needlework._ New York: Bonanza Books, 1938.

Harper's Bazar, Supplement December 1868, September & October 1887; January 18, 1890.

Het Rijk der Vrouw-Pris, September 29, 1946.

Holland, William. _Taste a la Mode._ 1745, February 1, 1790.

Home Magazine, January – February 1858.

Illustirte Frauenzeitung, 1884.

International Vogue Pattern Book, Spring 1967.

Journal der Luxus und der Moden, T 10, 16. 1787; 2nd anJe, 1793.

Journal des Dames et des Modes, Frankfurt 1800, Plate 18; 1801, Plate 37; 1802, Plate 366; 1803, Plates 13, 18, 19, 23; 1804, Plate 3; Supplement #26, 27, 32; 1819, Plate 24; 1822, Plate 45; 1823, Plates 2, 6, 14, 16, 22, 24, 25, 26, 32, 36, 37, 39; 1824, Plates 1, 2, 3, 6, 9, 14, 17, 19, 20, 23, 25, 26, 29, 33, 34, 42, 47; 1825, Plate 25; 1827, Plates 1, 5, 17, 19; 1830, Plates 22, 37, 39, 40 – 46, 48; 1831, Plates 1, 2, 5, 8, 9, 10, 14, 15, 17, 19, 23, 24, 26, 28, 31, 32, 34, 35, 37, 39, 40, 41, 43, 44, 45, 50, 52; 1832, Plates 2, 3, 5, 7, 8, 10 – 18, 21, 34, 35, 36, 38, 39, 40, 42, 44, 45, 46, 47, 51; 1833, Plates 4, 5, 6, 9, 10, 21, 23, 24, 26, 27, 28, 29, 32, 38, 39, 40, 41, 43, 44; 1834, Plates 27, 28, 40, 48, 52; 1835, Plate 17.

Journal des Dames et des Modes, Paris 1806, Plate 725; 1807, Plates 780, 791; 1809, Plate 609; 1814, Plate 1385; 1815, Plate 1468; 1816, Plate 1597; 1818, Plate 1778; 1819, Plate 1801; 1820, Plates 1879, 1886, 1909, 1945, 1946; 1821, Plates 1967, 1972, 1990, 2002; 1822 Plate 2037, 2107; 1823 Plates 2186, 2189, 2203; 1826, Plate 16; 1827, Plates 2474, 2482, 2496, 2552, 2502; 1824, Plate 2255; 1825, Plates 2331, 2336, 2360, 2369, 2370; 1826, Plates 2381, 2382, 2379, 2387, 2389; 1829 Plates 2689, 2714, 2727, 2720, 2721, 2722, 2725, 2726, 2737; 1830, Plates 2783, 2784, 2790, 2792, 2793, 2813, 2817, 2820, 2822, 2828, 2836, 2837, 2842, 2844, 2846; 1837, Plates 3438, 3453, 3475; Misc. Year Plate 1138; 1914 plate #82.

Journal des Demoiselles, June & August 1843; October 1880; May 1882; May 1887; July, September, November 1892; February 1899.

L'Album Tailleur de la Femme Chic, 1915.

La Belle Assemblée, July 1, 1806; January, March, April, May, August, 1808; March, April, May, November, 1809; January 1810; March, August 1811; July & December 1813; December 1815; March 1816; May, June, August 1817; April 1818; May, August, September 1819; July, October, December 1822; March & April 1824; January, February, June, August, September, October 1825; February, June, October, November 1826; No 28 April 1, 1827; No, 29 May 1, 1827; No 41 New series, May 1 & September 1828; February 1, & June 1 1829; March & May 1st, 1830; March & November 1831; May 1832; August 1838; January – December 1839; March 1840; January, March – October 1841; November 1843; January, March, May, June, July , December 1849; January – June 1851.

La Mode du Petit Journal, January, April, November 1899; September – December 1900; June 1901; February, March, August – December 1904; April, September, October, November, December, 1905.

La Mode Illustrée, 1866, Nos. 28, 44.

La Mode, Plate July 20, 1833.

Ladies Home Journal, October 1910; November 1913; April 1917; February 1918; October 1947.

Ladies Pocket Magazine, 1830.

Ladies World, May 1908; October 1909.

Lady's Cabinet, 1833; January – December 1844.

Lady's Friend, January – December 1871.

Lady's Gazette of Fashion, June – December 1845; January – June 1846; January – July 1848; January – October 1849.

The Ladies Little Messanger, #162, 1823.

Lady's Magazine, No. XXV, May 1771; April, September 1775; November 1800; July & October, 1804; April 1807; June 1815; No. 7 & 12, 1823; July 1822; No 2, August, October, November, 1824; No. 10, 1825; No. 9 No, 4, 1826; No. 8, 1827; Unknown Fashion Plate December 1827.

Lady's Monthly Museum, December 1798; December 1799.

Lana Lobell Catalog, Summer 1955, pp. 1 – 80. 1956 Catalog, pp. 1 – 64.

L'Art de la Mode, October – December 1893.

L'Art de la Mode et le Charm United, November 1901; January 1912.

Last and Newest Fashions, 1836.

Latest Fashions, 1838, 1840, 1841, 1842 and 1844.

Le Bon Ton, May 1854.

Le Bon Ton and Le Moniteur de la Mode, Monthly Report Fall 1893, October 1893.

Le Bon Ton et le Moniteur de la Mode United, August 1894, November 1895.

Le Costume Royale, November 1916.

Le Follet Courrier des Salons, 1833, Plates 289, 269, 281; 1834, Nos. 6, 17, 16, 113, 353; 1835; May 1837.

Le Mercure des Salone, Modes de Paris, 1830 No. 3, 1830 No 17.

Le Miroir des Dames, 1836 No, 89.

Le Theatre, October 11, 1906, February 2, 1908; July, August, October 1909.

Les Modes Parisiennes, 1851, February 1857.

Life Cover, December 7, 1911.

Mademoiselle, July 1941.

Magasin des Demoiselles, Journal Mensuel Museé des Familles; October & November, 1866; February, March, August, September & October, 1867; January, March, June, August, September, 1868.

McCall's, Vol. XXVI No 4, December 1899; November & December 1912; December 1913; January, May November 1914; November 1915; October 1917; April 1918, June 1918; February 1919; February 1920; July, September, December 1921; April, 1923, October, 1925; May, June, 1926; April, 1928; September, 1929; September, 1931; August, 1932; January, November 1934; March, July 1935; June, December, 1936; June – December 1937; January, March – October, December, 1938; January, February, June, August – November 1939; April, May, October 1940; May, July, 1941; May, July, August, September, December, 1942; September, December 1943; February, October 1944; February, October – December, 1945; March, June – November 1946; January – April, June – August, October 1947; January, February, May, July, August, October 1948; March, April, July – December, 1949; January, February, April, July, October, November 1950, February, March, April, May 1951; Oct 1952, May 1953.

Mirror of the World, February 1834.

Moda Firenze, Primavera, 1978.

Mode di Parigi, April, June, November 1848.

Modes de Paris Petit Courrier des Dames, March 31st, 1838.

Montgomery Ward's Catalog, Spring and Summer, 1926; *Wards Catalog,* Fall and Winter 1935 – 1936; Fall and Winter 1946 – 1947; Fall and Winter; Spring & Summer 1947; Spring and Summer 1949; Spring and Summer Catalog 1950, 1 – 93; Spring and Summer 1951, pp. 1 – 89, 236 – 252; Midsummer Sale Book 1952, pp. 2 – 17; Wards Catalog, 1953 – 1954, pp. 2 – 120; 1954 Summer Sale Catalog, pp. 2 – 21; Spring & Summer Catalog 1956, pp. 1 – 117; Spring & Summer Catalog 1957, pp. 1 – 91; Spring Summer 1957, pp. 2 – 21; Fall & Winter 1959, pp. 1 – 89, 104 – 105; Spring Summer Catalog, 1959, pp. 1 – 126; Fall and Winter 1961; Fall and Winter 1962, Spring and Summer 1963; Fall and Winter 1964, Spring and Summer, Fall and Winter 1965; Spring and Summer 1966; Spring and Summer, Fall and Winter 1968; Fall and Winter 1969, Fall and Winter 1970, Spring and Summer, Fall and Winter 1971; Spring and Summer, Fall and Winter 1972; Fall and Winter 1973, Fall and Winter 1974; Spring and Summer 1975; Summer – August 30, 1976; Fall and Winter, 1977.

Museé des Familles, September, 1859; January 1860; September 1861; No. 9, 1862; September 1863, Plate No. 12; September 1865; June 1866; October & November 1867; January & March 1868.

Myra's Journal of Dress & Fashion, October 1878; February 1, 1880.

Myra's Mid-Monthly Journal, December 15, 1879; March 15, 1882.

People's Home Journal, May 1917.

Peterson's, January – December 1856; December 1860; February 1861; March, June, October, December 1862; January – December 1863; June, August 1864, January – December 1865; January & February, December 1866; February, July, August, October, November, December 1867; May – July, September, November 1868; January – December, 1869; January, April, May, June 1870; April – July, 1871, October – November 1871; February, May – July, December 1872; January, March, August 1873; January, April, August, October 1874; February – April, June – July, September – October 1875; February, May, August, October, December 1876; April, November, December 1877; January, February, July, August, November December 1878; January, August, September 1879; February – August, October, 1880; May & October 1881; January – March, June – September, 1882; March & October 1884; January – August 1885; April – August, November – December 1886; July, October – December 1887;

January, May, June, August November, December 1888; January, April – September 1889; July, September, 1890; January 1891; January, March, June, August 1892.

Petit Courrier des Dames, 664, 666 1827; 132, Plates 856, 869, 874, 879, 900, 933; 1822; 1824, Plate 257; 1825, Plates 351, 356, 377; 1831, Plates 816, 824, 828, 849, 841; # 546, 567, July 1828; Newest Fashions, August 1831, Plate 1832; 1833, Plates 980, 997,951; October 1834; October 1835; November – December 1835; circa 1836; February 1844.

Pictorial Review, January 1923; May 1927; February 1935; November 1936; January, November 1937.

The Proprietors, October 1812.

Scheuer, Nikki. "The Elegant Art of Embroidery." *An Elegant Art: Fashion and Fantasy in the Eighteenth Century.* New York: Harry N. Abrams, Inc., 1983.

Sears Catalog, Spring and Summer 1927 and July 31, 1935, Fall and Winter 1979.

Seventeen, June 1974, July 1974.

Sharood's Style Catalog, Spring and Summer, 1926.

Simplicity Pattern Book, January – March 1960.

Skylark Catalog, circa 1957, pp. 1 – 33.

Spiegel Catalog, Fall and Winter, 1940; Spiegel Catalog, 1953, pp. 1 – 70.

Standard Delineator, September & October 1895, January – May, July, August 1896; Toilettes Publishing Co, August, September, November 1896.

Standard Designer, July, October, November 1897, June 1898.

Supplement to the Woman's Home Companion, October 1906.

Theatre Magazine, April, July, September 1911.

Townsend's Monthly Selection, March 1828, plates 220, 221; Newest Fashions for January & July 1828 James Robins & Co, January 1829, 1829, Plate 282, 1826: Plates 82, 83; 1846.

Unknown fashion plate, June 1830.

Vernor, Hood, Sharp & Poultry, May 1804, May 1806, Feb. & June 1808.

Vogue Patterns, January – February 1978.

Wards 60th Anniversary Sale, January & February Midwinter 1932.

Wards Catalog, October 31, 1934.

Wards Mid-Summer Catalog, 1958.

Wards Midwinter Catalog, January & February 1932.

Wards Midwinter Sale, March 15, 1935.

Wards Sale Book, June – July 1949.

Wards, Spring and Summer Catalog, 1931.

Wards Star Values Book, October 31, 1934, March 15, 1935.

Weiner Modenzeitung, May & August 1825; XXXV, 1829, XXIV, 1832; January 1835,1839 Nos. 30, 40, 1844, No 16 January to May 1844.

Wilco Catalog, circa 1956.

Woman's Home Companion, August 1906; March 1912; January 1915, September & December 1943.

The World of Fashion and Continental Fueilletons, 1830s Plates 433, 484, 458, 546; May 1833.

Young Ladies Journal, June 1880; March 1894; January 1896; February 1897; Young Ladies Journal, Supplement, Christmas 1887.

Index

Abstract prints
  burlap 269
  cotton 43, 121, 133, 203, 210, 268, 270, 272
  polyester ....279, 282, 287, 289 – 290
  quilted 283
  rayon 220
  silk 112, 120, 137
Apron 7, 69, 82, 168
Art Deco embroidery 168
Arts and Crafts embroidery 163
Ball gowns .... 38, 66, 77 – 80, 95, 102, 107 – 108
Bandeau... 141
Bargello.. 8
Bathing suits 89, 119
Battenberg lace 114, 150
Beaded
  bridal headpiece 189
  clothing ....44, 74, 76 – 78, 90, 99, 101 – 102
    129, 136 – 145, 149 – 151, 164 – 166, 172
  fringe 164
  hats 45, 141, 213, 223, 239
  headdress 148
  purses 18, 27, 48, 168, 180
Bell bottom pants outfit 293
Belt 97
Bendel, Henri 149
Berry hats 251, 253
Bicorn hat 144, 160
Blouse 268
Bodices
  child's 17, 20, 40, 42, 96, 115
  women's ....21, 24, 26, 30, 32, 39, 41 – 42, 44, 52
    55, 61, 69, 73 – 74, 76, 78, 82, 89,
    100, 102, 112 – 114, 117, 124,
    126, 137, 152
Bonnet veils 19, 21
Bonnets
  child's... 51, 92, 113
  cotton 34, 45, 65
  crinoline 29
  fanchon 55, 56, 59
  silk ....23, 31, 35, 45, 50 – 51, 55 – 56, 113
  straw .... 16, 18 – 19, 29 – 31, 34, 92
  velvet.. 92
Bridal headpieces 189, 200, 219
Bridal party hats 209, 221
Brocade
  polyester.. 271
  rayon 1920 – 1929 174
  rayon 1940 – 1949 .... 220, 223
  silk 18th century 8, 9, 12
  silk 1800 – 1839 ....25, 27
  silk 1840 – 1849 ....31 – 32
  silk 1850 – 1859 ....38 – 39, 43
  silk 1860 – 1869 ....47, 51
  silk 1870 – 1879 ....64, 69
  silk 1880 – 1889 ....72 – 73, 76, 78, 83, 89 – 91
  silk 1890 – 1899 .... 98 – 99, 101 – 102, 108,112
  silk 1900 – 1909 123
  silk 1910 – 1919 .... 147, 150
Buckles
  shoe 18th century 12
  19th century 117

20th century 97
Bumble bee patch 274
Butterflies 197, 239
Caftan 281
Calash bonnets 11
Cap, lace 57, 93
Cape 100, 111
Caped pantsuit 279
Cat novelty print house dress 186
Chain mail purse 1920 – 1929 168
Chantilly lace
  19th century 45, 55, 57, 59, 62, 64, 67, 84, 117
  20th century 125, 127, 136, 153, 238, 243
    248 – 249. 251, 253, 258
Chapman, Ceil 211
Checkered and checked prints
  cotton 43, 215, 234, 267
  gauze 183
  polyester 286
  silk 40, 50, 71, 126
  wool 259
Chenille
  embroidery 7, 169
  fringe and trims 87, 199
Children's dresses .... 17, 40, 49, 51, 58 – 59, 63 – 64
    78, 96, 160 – 161, 163, 182
Choker, cut steel 97
Cleopatra style headpiece 148
Cloches .... 164 – 170, 173 – 174, 183
Coat dress 270
Collars 58, 180
Coronet, bridal 189
Costume
  dance 222, 247
  fancy dress .... 100 – 101
Crepe paper flower ornament 107
Cut steel ornament 48, 97
Dance costumes 222, 247
Day cap, half mourning............................ 93
Day robe 146
Dirndl dress 210
Dresses
  18th century 13
  1800 – 1839 ....19, 20, 23, 25, 27
  1840 – 1849 ....32 – 34
  1850 – 1859 .... 40, 42 – 45
  1860 – 1869 ....48 – 59
  1870 – 1879 .... 62 – 63, 66 – 68
  1880 – 1889 .... 71 – 77, 83 – 86, 88, 90 – 91
  1890 – 1899 .... 95 – 96, 98 – 99, 100 – 112, 114, 116
  1900 – 1909 ....119 – 133
  1910 – 1919 .... 135 – 144, 147 – 155
  1920 – 1929 .... 158 – 161, 163 – 167, 169 – 175
  1930 – 1939 ....178 – 180, 182 – 183, 185 – 195
    197 – 200, 202 – 203
  1940 – 1949 .... 207, 209 – 212, 215, 217 – 218,
    220 – 226, 228
  1950 – 1959 ....232 – 253, 255 – 259
  1960 – 1969 ....263 – 264, 266 – 275
  1970 – 1979 ....277 – 278, 280, 281 – 286, 288 – 294
Dressing gowns and robes 155, 200, 222
Duster 123
Elephant felt skirt and matching vest 236

Embroidered
  clothing and fabrics ....7 – 11, 15, 66, 69, 78 – 80
                        82, 85, 97, 102, 141, 143, 160, 163, 252
  purses 1920 – 1929 168
  1930 – 1939 180
  workbag 79
Empire waistline 13, 17, 19
Enamel purse handle 154
Fanchon bonnets .... 55 – 56, 59
Fancy dress costume .... 100 – 101
Fans .... 35, 37 – 38, 82, 85, 93, 115, 117, 119
Feather-embroidered hat 166
Fez 213
Fishtail train 140
Flame stitch embroidery 8
Flocked taffeta with mica glitter 198
Floral prints
  chiffon 39, 173
  cotton 23, 41, 45, 127, 190, 193, 215, 228, 266,
                        271 – 272, 283
  flannel 292
  flocked taffeta 198
  gauze 183, 280
  organza 189
  polyester 280, 282, 288, 293
  rayon 180, 191, 195, 252, 255
  sheer 185, 277, 285, 289
  silk 21, 114
Fur trims 87, 167, 224, 269
Gibson girl revival style 192, 200
Gigot sleeves 23
Goddess style 289
Gold and silver lamé
  clothing 264
  shoes 278
Gold embroidery 195, 169, 213
Gold lamé
  clothing 149, 282
  corded flowers 172
  dresses 191, 257
  fabric 161, 222
  hats 148, 173
  purse 180
Gold metallic lace 152, 161
Half mourning cap 93
Halo hats .... 222 – 223
Halter outfit 291
Harlequin style 217
Hats
  1860 – 1869 .... 57, 58
  1870 – 1879 .... 61 – 62, 65
  1880 – 1889 ....71 – 72, 75, 85 – 86, 88
  1890 – 1899 ....96 – 98, 106, 113 – 115
  1900 – 1909 .... 120 – 121, 124 – 125, 130
  1910 – 1919 ....140 – 141, 144 – 149
  1920 – 1929 ....160 – 161, 164 – 170, 173 – 175
  1930 – 1939 ....177 – 185, 190 – 192, 194, 197
                        199, 203
  1940 – 1949...206 – 209, 213 – 214, 218 – 224, 226 – 227
  1950 – 1959 ....232, 239 – 242
  1960 – 1969 ....262 – 263, 265
  boy's 115
  girl's 58, 167

Headdresses 45, 47
Headpiece, Cleopatra style 148
Hip panniers 163
Horn fan 35
Horsehair hats ....120 – 121, 148, 181, 194, 209
Hot pants 279
Hounds tooth 241
House dresses/coats ....186 – 187, 193, 203, 215, 221
Jacket
  boy's 65
  women's 54
Jeans 295
Jenny Lind fans 35
Jet ornaments 74, 85, 124, 140
Lambs wool 208
Lamé
  clothing 148, 161, 191, 222, 257, 264, 280, 282
  hats 148, 173
  purse 180
  shoes 278
  trims 152, 161, 172
Lanvin style hip panniers 163
Lappet caps .... 49 – 50
Latin dance costume 222
Leg o'mutton sleeves .... 99 – 103, 105 – 106
                        109 – 110, 200
Letter case 8
Liberation hat.................................218
Linen purse 18
Lyons brocade silk............................. 91
Marabou feathers 265
Matellase 263
Maxi dresses .... 277, 280 – 283, 285 – 286,
                        288 – 290, 292
Maxi jumpsuits 284, 287
Mesh purse 168
Metallic
  embroidery ....41, 80, 144, 147 – 148, 154, 158
                        225, 243
  embroidery on netting................ 147 – 148, 158, 243
  embroidery on purses 154, 168
  flowers on clothing 172
  lace and trim 112, 150, 152
Mexican painted circle skirt...................239
Midriff outfits 266
Military style 52, 57, 74, 203, 269
Monogrammed patch 173
Mourning wear .... 13, 19, 21, 33 – 34, 43, 45, 51
            54, 57, 72, 74, 76, 82, 87, 92 – 93, 100, 111
                        117, 135, 137
Muffler 92
Mushroom hat 263
Muslin cap 22
Muslin clothing .... 17, 19 – 20, 22, 138
Nehru collar 271
Novelty skirts and outfits ....236 – 237, 239
Open crown hats 199, 221
Overskirt 59
Pagoda sleeves..................... 39 – 45, 48, 59
Painted clothing
  Victorian.................. 69, 78 – 79, 81, 93
  Edwardian 122
  1950 – 1959 ....239, 247

Paisley prints
  lamé 280
  polyester 281, 284
Parasol 59, 64, 88, 91, 97
Parrot hat 227
Patchwork 270
Patio dress 241
Peasant dresses .... 291 – 292
Pelerine 34
Plaid prints
  cotton 64, 73, 234, 236
  knit 283
  lamé 280
  polyester 284
  silks 33, 42, 44, 53, 56, 74
  wool 109
Playing cards felt skirt 237
Playsuit 271
Pocket case or pocketbook 8
Point de gaze lace 115
Polka dot prints
  cotton 30, 159, 266, 268, 292
  gauze 111
  organza 209
  polyester 293
  rayon 161
  silk .... 130 – 131
Poodle felt skirt 237
Prince Tirtoff-Romanoff label 241
Psychedelic prints .... 280, 282, 288 – 290
Purse
  beaded 1800 – 1839 ....18, 27
  beaded 1860 – 1869 48
  beaded 1920 – 1929 ....157, 161, 167
  embroidered metallic 1910 – 1919 154
  embroidered metallic 1920 – 1929 168
  embroidered metallic 1930 – 1939 180
  embroidered silk 1880 – 1889.............. 79
  embroidered tapestry 1910 – 1919 154
  linen beaded 18
  mesh 1920 – 1929 168
Quilting on dress 283
Rabbit novelty print house dress 187
Reticule purse
  beaded 1800 – 1839 27
  beaded 1860 – 1869 48
  embroidered silk 1880 – 1889.............. 79
  velvet with ribbon flowers 1920 – 1929 171
Rhinestone
  headpieces ....157 – 159, 166
  skull cap 166
Rhinestones
  on clothing ....166, 171, 232 – 233, 236 – 237
          255, 258, 274, 280
  on hats 170, 179, 232, 255
Ribbon embroidered flowers 112, 152, 171, 195
Robes, dressing gowns 146, 155, 200, 222
Robin Hood style hats 197
Roller printed clothing 17, 23, 30, 45
Sailor styles 161, 164, 169, 191
Saks Fifth Avenue label 192, 227, 239
Scarf 92

Scrolling cutout embellishments 120
Sequins
  on clothing ....100 – 101, 116, 129, 135 – 136,
        142 – 143, 152, 165, 220, 239, 247
  on fans 35, 117, 119
  on hats 98, 106
Shoes
  18th century 9, 12
  19th century 21, 22, 41, 48
  1960 – 1969 278
  child's 22
Shrugs .... 242 – 243, 246, 249 – 250
Silk flowers on dresses .... 194, 197 – 198, 238, 246
Skirts
  Edwardian 145
  felt elephant 236
  felt playing cards.....................................237
  felt poodle...237
  painted Mexican circle 239
  Victorian 80, 100
Sling sleeves 225
Snood 208
Soutache braiding 49, 65, 132, 135, 240, 244
Spencer jacket 15
Spitafields silk 9
Spoon bonnets... 50 – 51
Striped fabrics
  cotton ....62 – 63, 188, 221, 254
  knit 278
  silk ....11, 42, 48, 51, 54, 58, 67 – 68, 80, 95
  taffeta 233
  wool 96
Suede 270, 279
Suits.................................. 226, 232, 259, 268
Sweater 287
Tilt hats .... 207 – 209, 214, 223
Tinsel fabric and trims 104, 273
Top hats, ladies 223, 224
Tulip skirt 263
Valentine's Day dance dress 253
Velvet tufted fabric...................................... 88, 153
Vera signature blouse 268
Vest and shorts set 254
Vest, lace.. 155
Vinyl clothing 275
Voided velvet.. 78, 85 – 87
Waistcoats .... 9 – 11, 47, 65
Watered fabrics
  silk 21, 75
  rayon 202
  taffeta 2, 217
Wax floral headpieces 200, 219
Wax flowers on dress 116
Wedding gowns ....39, 68, 84, 98, 103, 105, 108 – 110
    116, 119, 123, 140 – 141, 143 – 144, 151, 163, 179
       189, 192, 200, 207, 220, 269
Wedding headpieces 200, 219
Whimsical hats 227, 239, 254
Winged features 240, 250
Workbag 79
Wrapper.. 53